SimplySeven

IE Business Publishing

IE Business Publishing and Palgrave Macmillan have launched a collection of high-quality books in the areas of Business and Management, Economics and Finance. This important series is characterized by innovative ideas and theories, entrepreneurial perspectives, academic rigor and practical approaches which will make these books invaluable to the business professional, scholar and student alike.

IE Business School is one of the world's leading institutions dedicated to educating business leaders. Palgrave Macmillan, part of Macmillan Group, has been serving the learning and professional sector for more than 160 years.

The series, put together by these eminent international partners, will enable executives, students, management scholars and professionals worldwide to have access to the most valuable information and critical new arguments and theories in the fields of Business and Management, Economics and Finance from the leading experts at IE Business School.

SimplySeven
Seven Ways to Create a Sustainable Internet Business

Erik Schlie
Professor and Associate Dean, IE Business School

Jörg Rheinboldt
Managing Director, M-10

Niko Marcel Waesche
Managing Partner, Cafelido Capital and Consulting

© Erik Schlie, Jörg Rheinboldt & Niko Marcel Waesche 2011

All rights reserved. No reproduction, copy or transmission of this publication may be made without written permission.

No portion of this publication may be reproduced, copied or transmitted save with written permission or in accordance with the provisions of the Copyright, Designs and Patents Act 1988, or under the terms of any licence permitting limited copying issued by the Copyright Licensing Agency, Saffron House, 6–10 Kirby Street, London EC1N 8TS.

Any person who does any unauthorized act in relation to this publication may be liable to criminal prosecution and civil claims for damages.

The authors have asserted their rights to be identified as the authors of this work in accordance with the Copyright, Designs and Patents Act 1988.

First published 2011 by
PALGRAVE MACMILLAN

Palgrave Macmillan in the UK is an imprint of Macmillan Publishers Limited, registered in England, company number 785998, of Houndmills, Basingstoke, Hampshire RG21 6XS.

Palgrave Macmillan in the US is a division of St Martin's Press LLC, 175 Fifth Avenue, New York, NY 10010.

Palgrave Macmillan is the global academic imprint of the above companies and has companies and representatives throughout the world.

Palgrave® and Macmillan® are registered trademarks in the United States, the United Kingdom, Europe and other countries.

ISBN 978–0–230–30817–6

This book is printed on paper suitable for recycling and made from fully managed and sustained forest sources. Logging, pulping and manufacturing processes are expected to conform to the environmental regulations of the country of origin.

A catalogue record for this book is available from the British Library.

A catalog record for this book is available from the Library of Congress.

10 9 8 7 6 5 4 3 2 1
20 19 18 17 16 15 14 13 12 11

Printed and bound in Great Britain by
CPI Antony Rowe, Chippenham and Eastbourne

Contents

List of Tables	viii
Acknowledgments	ix

1 Think outside the box, constantly experiment and evolve   **1**
   The Airbnb story   1
   "Dance like an idiot and don't sell anything"   2
   Don't think, just test   7
   The search for the perfect business model   13
   Getting started   16
   SimplySeven – that's it   19
   The making of this book   23

2 The first building block – services sales   **26**
   Plain and straightforward   26
   A business model with problems   31
   "Can I skype you?"   34

3 The second building block – subscriptions   **38**
   The heaviest weapon in the arsenal   38
   The rise and fall of AOL   40
   The "Bouncer Effect"   43
   In the "dog house"   45
   The future of clubs   46
   Getting people to subscribe   47

4 The third building block – retail   **48**
   Don't treat online like offline   48
   The million books project   50
   Early death in May 2000   51
   Being good at bricks is not enough   53
   The "Long Tail" vs. "superstar economics"   55
   Fighting the clutter   57
   The future of the shop is personal   58

Contents

5	**The fourth building block – commissions**	**61**
	Don't believe your clients are stupid	61
	The beauty of C2C	64
	Listings * ASPs * Conversion Rates = GMV	66
	Fraud	67
	The B2B trap	68
	Beware of the smart client	70
	Reports of the death of the intermediary	72
6	**The fifth building block – advertising**	**74**
	You force it, you lose it	74
	Spam and pushy banners	77
	Search revolution	78
	"The wisdom of money"	80
	The death of the newspaper	82
	The sexiness of statistics	84
	Advertising as a service	87
7	**The sixth building block – license sales**	**90**
	You will need all your friends	90
	Intellectual property 300 years after Queen Anne	91
	The indecisive history of computing platforms	94
	Distributed distribution	97
	"Stay hungry. Stay foolish." – the rebirth of Apple	98
	Platform building best practice	102
	The "Battle of Platforms" in entertainment	105
	Micro license sales – evolution continues	108
8	**The seventh building block – financial management**	**111**
	Making money with money	111
	The mysteriously slow growth of financial services online	113
	George W. Bush wrecks the party	116
	The brave and few	117
	Investment in Internet real estate	118
	Investment in Internet traffic	119
	Spread betting services	119
	Internet-based B2B, B2C, C2C and even C2B loans	119
	Substitute for the informal economy	121
	Our favorite so far: Weatherbill	121

Contents

9	**It's a freemium world**	**122**
	Paying nothing	122
	You can live on love alone	123
	Chris Anderson's 5%/95% rule	124
	A web powered by small deeds of heroism	127
	The reciprocal donation economy and innovation	128
	A fairy tale with a GNU	130
	One million lines of code	132
	Three million articles	134
	Donated power for business	137
	Competing with free	139
	The Facebook dilemma	141
	It's a freemium world	144
10	**The future of web business is personal**	**147**
	Methods and tools to guide customers	147
	Flexible payment infrastructures	148
	Payment as web services	149
	Fast-track companies taking advantage of payment web services	151
	Virtual currencies and coupons	152
	Mobile payments everywhere	155
	Guiding the customer	157
	Examples of personal businesses on the web	159
	Reputation and trust as an opportunity	160
	Back to the basics	161
Appendix	**Stress-testing the *SimplySeven***	**163**
	The selection criteria	163
	Initial results: seven confirmed and unevenly distributed	164
	Retail leads in sales	169
	Market valuations – advertising, again	172
	Margins – the beauty of aggregation	173
	Key financial indicators	174

Interviews	177
Notes	179
Index	188

List of Tables

1.1	The *SimplySeven* building blocks	20
1.2	The *SimplySeven* and founding years of leading Internet companies	22
9.1	Comparison of AT&T and Skype in 2007	140
A.1	*SimplySeven* Internet company universe	166
A.2	Total business model revenue	170
A.3	Top five revenue	170
A.4	Top five average monthly revenue/average monthly users	171
A.5	Many users and rapid growth – the advertising business model	171
A.6	Top five enterprise value/revenue	173
A.7	Top five operating income margin	174
A.8	Key financial indicators (list)	174
A.9	Key financial indicators (bubble chart)	175

Acknowledgments

This book started out with the three of us getting together on weekends to discuss Internet business models. We did not know these sessions would turn into a book someday. From the start, we used the *SimplySeven* framework in our consulting work, to discuss monetization with entrepreneurs and in the courses we have taught. It has guided us in running our own companies and as investors. During this time, we collected new ideas and continually tweaked the framework. For this reason, it is impossible to thank all that have helped with this book. But at least let us try to acknowledge some of our biggest contributors – without whom this book would surely not have existed.

A heartfelt thank you goes to Aljoscha Kaplan. Aljoscha began supporting us from the beginning as Research Assistant. Since then, he has assumed many more roles than that, helping the book along in many important ways. Julia Stauf also worked as Research Assistant, as well as Michael Heim. Michael was responsible for the financial analysis of the business models and for building our universe of representative Internet companies.

We have consulted many friends to get feedback and input about areas we were unsure about. Kenneth Neil Cukier provided insight into some of the concepts very early on. David Ko is a physicist and the founder of Kurtosis Capital Partners in London. David sharpened our thinking about financial risk. We hasten to point out that any faults with the financial chapter are entirely our own. This applies to the other chapters as well, of course. The co-founder of Europe's largest affiliate advertising network, Thomas Hessler of Zanox, explained the intricacies of affiliate advertising to us. A dear friend in Paris, Julie Kang, provided us with insight into the endurance and tenacity required running a small retail business in the real world and on the Internet.

In early 2011, we carried out interviews with leading thinkers, investors and entrepreneurs in the States and Europe. A list of the interview partners can be found at the end of this book. Each and every interview partner set aside valuable time. We know that this was a significant investment and we wish to express our deep gratitude for the time and the insight.

Acknowledgments

We also want to thank here those who helped us (and trusted us) to provide personal introductions to the interview partners: Matt Bannick, Chris Barter, Albrecht von Breitenbuch, Jason Montgomery Brown, Frédéric Court, Kenneth Neil Cukier, Steven Dietz, Kerstin Ebock, Frerk-Malte Feller, Paul Graham, Christopher Grew, Lawrence Lessig, Jessica Livingston, Roland Manger, Gabriel Graf Matuschka, Yuri Milner, Stephan Schwahlen, Reshma Sohoni and Michelangelo Volpi.

Countless improvements to the book came as suggestions from the students we taught with different versions of this material over a period of years. They were the guinea pigs for the first versions of this material. We want to thank the students of the London School of Economics and Political Science Department of Management (2011), the Leuphana University Bachelor Program (2010), the Citigroup Entrepreneurship Program in the American Academy, Potsdam (2009), Zeppelin University, Friedrichshafen (2009), the Master of Public Policy Classes of the Humboldt Viadrina School of Governance (2010 and 2011) as well as the Technical University for Design in Berlin (BTK), way back in the Winter Semester of 2006/7.

We are very thankful to IE Business School in Madrid, the academic hub where Erik works, and want to acknowledge especially the wonderful support by IE colleagues Cynthia Fernández, Oswaldo Lorenzo and Marco Trombetta. Dean Santiago Íñiguez de Ozoño has been a continuing source of encouragement throughout the project. IE is one of the leading business schools in the world; an international institution dedicated to educating business leaders through programs based on core values of global focus, entrepreneurial spirit and a humanistic approach. *SimplySeven* is one of the first books in the new IE Business Publishing Program – in association with Palgrave Macmillan. The objective of the IE Business Publishing Program is to initiate global dialogue combining academic insight and practical business experience.

We would be delighted if this book was not the end of the many exciting discussions about Internet business models we have had, but rather a new beginning with a larger community. We hope that our web site www.SimplySeven.net and the associated Facebook page /SimplySeven will become a forum for continued discussion. The web site and Facebook already contain feedback to earlier versions of some of our thinking.

Speaking of the web site, Jan Persiel created it, putting in some serious overtime. He is a master in combining communication design and web technology – drawing on countless years of experience (he doesn't want to count them). The funky illustrations on the site were created by Alexander Gellner. Alexander is a Berlin-based designer specialized in

Acknowledgments

illustrations, cartoons and motion graphics. Alexander works pro bono for The Red Cross of Germany.

We look forward to the ongoing discussion on the web. We are convinced that the most valuable insight on the topic of Internet business models will surely come from you; the book is only the beginning. Enjoy the book, please join us on the web, and take care.

CHAPTER 1

Think outside the box, constantly experiment and evolve

The Airbnb story

Like many other web start-ups, Airbnb was initially launched without a business model. The founders, Brian Chesky, Joe Gebbia and Nathan Blecharczyk, did not want payments to interfere with the attractiveness of the service. So, at first, they provided Airbnb for free. The web site connects people with space in their apartments with people looking for vacation rentals. The service has continually expanded the types of spaces offered, from private apartments to private islands. By connecting people with people, it strives to provide a positively personal experience in a foreign city – very different from an anonymous hotel room.

In Spring 2008, a few months after launching the Airbnb service, Chesky, Gebbia and Blecharczyk decided to eat their own dog food. This is the endearing Silicon Valley expression for using your own service or buying your own product. The three founders had already provided their own San Francisco living room to people. In fact, their experience from renting out their apartment space was why they launched the web site in the first place. But this time they themselves wanted an excuse to stay at an apartment they had found over Airbnb. The digital media conference SXSW in Austin was the perfect excuse. SXSW was a must visit. Everyone in digital media and the web had to be at the conference. This was the conference that made Twitter hugely popular just a year earlier.

The experience of staying in someone else's living room was wonderful – just like when they were the hosts themselves. In the morning, however, a very awkward moment came. Time to pay. Chesky felt that getting out the cash and paying for the stay somehow ruined the friendly and open relationship he had built up with his host. This was a defining moment for Airbnb. The three founders realized: this does not have to be this way.

By integrating payments into the Airbnb web site, the founders removed the awkwardness of the moment. By putting payment on the web and out of the way, they actually made their web site more compelling as a service. Gebbia, the CPO in charge of the product, puts it this way: "Facilitating easy, web-based payments is one of the most important aspects of the whole Airbnb experience, which is about a community sharing unique and exciting spaces."

The web-based payment model also made it very simple for Airbnb to add a commission on the transaction – and now the company had a business model.

The Airbnb story shows that it often takes time and experimentation to select the right business model and make it fit into the overall value proposition. In fact, the whole process of getting funded and developing the service was intensely challenging, with many setbacks along the way. Airbnb's launch was funded by selling repurposed cereal boxes with a Barack Obama cartoon at the Democratic Convention in Denver. The venture capitalist Fred Wilson from Union Square Ventures (USV) gave the investment a pass. These days, Wilson regrets this. As he explains in his blog post:

> We couldn't wrap our heads around air mattresses on the living room floors as the next hotel room and did not chase the deal. Others saw the amazing team that we saw, funded them, and the rest is history. Airbnb is well on its way to building the "eBay of spaces." I'm pretty sure it will be a billion dollar business in time.[1]

Airbnb is one example of a web site that has an engaged community and has found a sustainable business model. The history of business on the web has been a tough quest which has created many such successes but also many more disappointments. Since the beginning, entrepreneurs have looked for ways to make money on their web site in the best way possible, as a seamless, painless part of the overall web site experience.

"Dance like an idiot and don't sell anything"

SimplySeven is a guidebook designed to get entrepreneurs and executives started on finding the right Internet business model for their web site. There are certain things this book cannot do. If you are looking for a catchy book guaranteeing instant success in Internet business, go to the airport bookstore. You will find books there about striking it rich with

Web 2.0, with App development or about social media marketing and search engine optimization. It would be surprising, however, if reading these books will really help you generate sales with your web site.

Success on the Internet means creating something compelling which people love. This is the first priority and the foundation of web business. For entrepreneurs, creating a compelling service is something that has to come deep from within; it is linked to the interests and capabilities of the founding team. There are many inspirational books about entrepreneurial passion. We can recommend the books written by the former Apple evangelist, Guy Kawasaki ("Deep, Intelligent, Complete, Elegant and Emotive"),[2] by the perfectly crazy software developers, Jason Fried and David Heinemeier Hansson ("meetings are toxic," "planning is guessing," "good enough is fine"),[3] by the seed funding entrepreneur, Jessica Livingston ("nothing goes according to plan"),[4] or Yvon Chouinard, the founder of the real-world business, Patagonia ("let my people go surfing").[5]

For the founders of several successful web companies, thinking about money often was not top of mind. In fact, these entrepreneurs purposely did not want to get distracted by thinking about business models or worse, ruin their fledgling idea through half-baked monetization schemes. Ze Frank, an online games entrepreneur, offers the following memorable advice about how to become successful on the Internet: "Dance like an idiot and don't sell anything."[6]

Established, offline companies with the objective of growing their Internet revenues have an even harder time creating a truly compelling web offering – they often have to transform themselves, including their culture, their people and their processes. The music industry is a case in point. Without speaking specifically about the web, Clayton M. Christensen has explained masterfully in his books why established companies have such a hard time to change and innovate.

While writing another book about entrepreneurial passion or change management would be fun, this is not what this book is about. Instead, this book assumes you have passion if you are an entrepreneur. It assumes you can transform your existing business to take advantage of the new opportunities the Internet creates. If you are lucky, you already have a popular web site with a service people find compelling. You are moving up the famous hockey stick curve in terms of user visits.

Eventually the time will come when you have to make money. Even though it is obvious that web sites need to achieve profitable growth – some sites need this sooner than others – many entrepreneurs or executives are extremely hesitant to monetize. This hesitation does not only stem from the fact that much of the Internet is free of charge. Charging is risky. By choosing the wrong payment option, you can ruin your hard-won popularity.

People do not mind paying for things on the Internet – this is a popular misconception. But they are extremely sensitive about exactly what they are getting for their money. This is because how a business sells to its customers reveals a lot about how these businesses see their customers. A business model can only be sustainable if people feel good about how they pay.

We are not speaking about the feeling of paying too much – but about spending money the wrong way. When this happens in the real world, people are extremely angry and disappointed. There is very little that is worse in terms of customer experience than having to suddenly pay an additional fee, which had been hidden in the fine print. It was probably not the amount that was the most annoying, but instead how the charge was made.

Usually, postponing a decision is not something that is generally encouraged. The falling costs involved in launching an Internet service, however, mean that decisions about business models can be postponed. Or better yet, different business model approaches can be tested – we will discuss the importance of experimentation and measuring in the next section. Flagship Internet companies such as Google, eBay, Skype or Facebook took considerable amounts of time to make sure they had the right business model. Airbnb took the time they needed.

eBay famously began as a community service (developed on Labor Day weekend, 1995) and it was only after a while that Pierre Omidyar initiated a commissions model to be able to afford the Internet hosting costs for his popular service. The Google founders Larry Page and Sergey Brin wanted to understand the structure of the Internet better by studying "backlinks" (links referring to a given page) and stumbled upon a highly effective solution to the problem of search. They had no clue how to make money.[7]

Craigslist did everything right. In an interview with Jessica Livingston, Craigslist's Founder Craig Newmark described why he rejected banner advertising as a payment option:

> At the end of '97 we were getting about one million page views a month. At that point, Microsoft Sidewalk – or their PR people – approached me about running banner ads. I decided to not do them, because they slow the site down and are kind of dumb.[8]

It was only two years later that Newmark finally installed his "freemium" system of charging classifieds fees only for real estate and job ads, while keeping the remainder of the site free. From 1995 to 1999, Craigslist had no business model whatsoever.

That was the late 1990s. Since costs are falling continuously, it is becoming more and more affordable to focus on building a compelling web experience, which users keep coming back to – before having to think about revenues. Having a compelling site that reaches a broad base and attracts people to come back for more is the real bottleneck; this problem should be solved first.

A case in point. The New York-based venture capital fund Union Square Ventures, backers of successful next generation web companies such as Zynga, Twitter and Tumblr, looks for "large networks of engaged users" in their investments. Brad Burnham, partner at USV, emphasizes that every single element is critical for the USV Formula: "Large," "network" and "engaged." When it comes to monetization, Burnham urges its companies to look for "original and native" business models: "These are forms of monetization only your company can use, because they are unique to your specific network."[9] This is not easy and calls for some seriously creative thinking.

> ### Union Square Ventures – Large networks of engaged users
>
> Union Square Ventures has emerged as one of the leading venture capital funds of the post-New Economy era. The fund was launched in 2003 with some radical ideas about web investing. It is due largely to the success of USV that their approach has been copied by several other funds.
>
> First, USV believes that venture capital funds need to be small and nimble to adapt to the falling costs of launching web businesses. In the beginning, the fund only had two partners, Fred Wilson and Brad Burnham. Whereas during the New Economy, billion-dollar venture capital funds advertised their size on their web sites – the bigger, the better – USV was one of the first to boast about their relatively small size, $125m. This trend is evident in the numbers. In 2000, over $100bn were committed by VCs in that year alone. This number dropped to levels between $20 and $40bn in subsequent years.[10]
>
> Secondly, USV invests exclusively in what they used to call the "application layer of the web," nothing else. Recently, the target has become bolder and clearer: "Large networks of engaged users." This is a razor-sharp investment focus. Many other VCs try to diversify their portfolio and cover many different areas, from software to routers.
>
> Thirdly, USV is based in New York City. This is a big statement in itself about the global diffusion of web-investing skills and entrepreneurial experience beyond Silicon Valley.

> USV has been very successful with its radical approach. Today, it has a portfolio that makes other VCs green with envy: Twitter, Foursquare, Zynga and many, many, more great companies, including one venture we feature in this book: Heyzap.[11]

People who are not involved deeply with the Internet sometimes wonder why it is so difficult to find the right business models for a web site. On the web, completely new types of services are being launched at a rate unknown in the real world. Charging for these services is much harder because expectations are not set by decades of experience. Translating this into real-world terms, we are not talking about the challenges of opening a new hotel; we are talking about inventing a completely new way to buy a vacation. If you are offering such a completely new product or service, you need to find the right business model without any preexisting references to go by.

This can go awfully wrong, too. Take, for example, MySpace. MySpace used to be more popular than Facebook. In fact, at a certain point in time, MySpace was the rising star of the Internet. In 2005, News Corp paid $580m for it. Google wanted to sign an exclusive partnership agreement so badly that the Google founders purportedly flew to the MySpace headquarters in LA in a helicopter. Millions loved MySpace. The advertising business model probably was the right choice for the company; early on, there was an intense discussion about a subscription model instead. So far so good.

The greatest mistake of MySpace was that they betrayed their own fans by applying the advertising business model wrongly. Management plastered the site full of banner ads to meet their revenue growth targets. These banners appeared on the very pages where people proudly featured themselves to their friends. Content on a social network is created by the community, not by a media company – this makes a big difference. To top it all off, the quality of the ads was very low and featured things some people would rather not like to be directly associated with like cosmetic surgery or dietary pills. Retrospectively, it seemed obvious that advertising should not take away screen space, should not be annoying and should not invade one's privacy. MySpace was managed by smart people. They and their predecessors put a lot of love into building the service, but they disregarded the importance of getting their business model just right.

The costs for building a web business have fallen and it may be reasonable to wait and think, rather than implement the wrong business model, as we have just seen. But falling costs for web business and the abundant availability of data on the Internet provide a far better alternative to waiting and thinking: testing.

Don't think, just test

Most Internet execs and entrepreneurs measure and analyze their usage data from their web site. For example, they measure so-called drop off rates in their funnel (people that are lost while navigating through the site). This provides insight about possible problem areas, which can be improved. Far fewer web site owners use the same analytical approach to test out and improve their business model.

Very few Internet execs and entrepreneurs make systematic use of the data available to them. Sometimes we just want to scream out: "You are on the Internet, you have data, lots of data – use it." The web is a dynamically changing environment – a web site always is in constant beta. Your customers accept constant change, too. They even demand it. This expectation provides an opportunity usually not available in the offline world: the right business model can be found through testing and tweaking.

Analytics and experimentation actually go together; the ability to measure and the ability to test are a powerful combination. Obviously, even on the Internet, there are some things you cannot try out without risking your current business. But much more experimentation is possible than people realize. Three companies that have engrained analytics and experimentation into their DNA are Zynga, Idealab and Netflix.

Ken Rudin is General Manager of Analytics at the social media game company Zynga. His whole career has revolved around analytics – but this is his dream job. Imagine the possibilities to measure and test Zynga has with its more than 100 million monthly players. Rudin says about Zynga: "I've never seen a company that is so analytically driven. Sometimes I think we are an analytics company masquerading as a gaming company. Everything is run by the numbers."[12]

In a presentation he held before an association, The Data Warehousing Institute (TDWI), in August 2010, Rudin outlined three development stages of analytics: Reporting, Analysis and what Rudin calls Feedback Driven Game Design.[13] All companies report, it is necessary but usually does not lead to increased value. Analysis will result in a little more insight, but in combination with experimentation it becomes very powerful. Feedback Driven Game Design actually is the combination of analysis and experimentation. Here, we will talk about Feedback Driven Game Design as well as another form of combined analysis and experimentation, A/B

Testing. In the meantime, Rudin and Zynga have moved beyond Feedback Driven Game Design to provide personalized gaming experiences, but we will discuss this development in the concluding chapter.

Take, for example, advertising. For testing out different web page setups, for example a set of pages with advertising and one set without, A/B Testing is perfect. In the real world, it is difficult to offer advertising to one set of your customers and leave it out for the other – and then analyze the results after a month to see the impact. Even if you have the luxury of running your business in different locations and you can, say, run the advertising trial in Denver and not in Detroit, you will not come close to generating the amount of data that an Internet trial would provide you with. The length of time people spent on your web site, what they clicked at, what they avoided, what they bought.

Zynga uses "Feedback Driven Game Design." It is much more comprehensive than A/B Testing. As Rudin describes it, when Zynga comes up with an idea for a new game, they don't follow the traditional (and expensive) approach of developing a fully completed game, launching it and hoping the market likes it. Instead, they create a solid first iteration of the game (known as the Minimal Viable Product, or MVP), release it to the market, and then immediately analyze what people do in the game and what they like about the game, and then use that to drive further development and testing of new ideas. Whereas the traditional game development process was like creating a full movie, Zynga's approach is more like an ongoing television series where the story evolves over time.[14]

Feedback Driven Game Design applies to all phases of a game's life cycle, not just the initial development. It is possible to benefit from the large 100 million plus community of Zynga players to provide different players with small variations of games. This is active experimentation within a game itself. In fact, Zynga carries out hundreds of active experiments within their existing, running games to provide analytical insight into improving each game further. This is not just some experimentation, this astounding scale of testing means that a Zynga online game is a living, learning, developing organism.

Idealab – Running a business model laboratory

Bill Gross, the Founder of Idealab, is one of the few serial entrepreneurs who has proven that he cannot only found companies in succession, but in parallel. With his team, Bill Gross has incubated 75 businesses since Idealab's founding in 1996 and sold or listed 30 of these. Successes include GoTo.com (see Chapter 5), the Picasa photo service (sold to

Google in 2006) and CitySearch (which merged with TicketMaster and went public).

Bill Gross is a fervent believer in the benefits of constant measuring and experimentation in business. His interest in this approach actually predated the web. When he was 14, Gross sold plans for constructing parabolic solar collectors. This business paid for his Caltech college fees. Since he had mentioned the business in his application, it perhaps even got him into the highly regarded engineering school in the first place.

To optimize the sales of his product and his bottom line, Gross measured and improved his marketing approach continually. In order to find out which print advertisement worked best, he changed his name in the ads slightly: "B. Gross," "M. Gross," "C. Gross." Based on the initial on the incoming orders, he could track the performance of individual ads.

Bill Gross also optimized his business model, by experimenting with different approaches to selling the brochure and the plans themselves. He compared conversions when a brochure was sold for a small fee of ¢25 to conversion rates when the marketing material was provided for free. A small fee worked better than a free brochure. While less people ordered the brochure in the first place, those that did exhibited a higher rate of buying the plans.

Bill Gross founded Idealab in Pasadena, near Los Angeles, and only two miles away from his alma mater, the California Institute of Technology. Idealab is not part of the famous 50-mile radius Silicon Valley investors like to invest in, but has performed stunningly nonetheless. Sitting in a small glass office in the center of Idealab's spacious, loft-style building, Bill Gross has never been part of the established way things are done. He is, always has been, a disrupter.

Idealab itself was started as a test. Initially, €3.5m were raised to finance one years' worth of activity: 10 people and 10 ventures. Each new business was funded with $250,000 in starting capital. After the first year, the viability of Idealab was to be assessed.

It was a huge success. Seven of the ten companies were able to attract external financing. After CitiSearch, the first of these companies, was merged into TicketMaster and then listed, it became evident that Idealab could be self-funded. Idealab focuses today on two areas: Internet and energy. It only invests in companies which radically disrupt their respective markets and have the promise to achieve significant size.

A complete web site can be an MVP, too. In 1998, when Idealab's founder Bill Gross intended to launch a web site for buying automobiles, most people thought this project was doomed to failure. At this early time for web business, people were discussing if consumers would actually submit their credit card information for small purchases on the net; big-ticket items such as cars were unspeakable.

Internally within Idealab, the discussion about the viability of such a site and the correct approach raged as well. The designated project manager proposed discussions with automotive companies to achieve buy-in, running focus groups to understand consumer preferences, a sophisticated web site with menus featuring several available cars for sale as well as an initial inventory of cars. Bill Gross rejected all these proposals. Perhaps this procedure is how a large corporation would go about launching a new venture, but for Gross, it was far too slow and costly. (By the way, we don't know a single Internet entrepreneur who works with focus groups.)

Gross wanted to test the idea that cars could be sold on the Internet directly – using a minimally viable web site. The resulting web site indeed was very basic – people were asked to type their preferences into a free text-based window, and no cars were bought in advance and none were placed on stock. Instead, Bill Gross accepted a small loss on any initial cars being sold, because they would be bought directly from a dealer after the sale was made.

The first day was a huge surprise. Four cars were bought during the first hours the web site was up. Since it was proven that cars could be sold over the Internet, the site was immediately shut down and a professional version, CarsDirect.com, was developed in the subsequent six months.

Analytics can be used to evaluate test results, as Zynga and Idealab examples have shown. Business models can be refined, even proven, using experimentation. But some business models are made possible in the first place by applying analytical methods. In a farsighted book on analytics, Harvard Business School Professor Thomas Davenport describes the fascinating fact that Netflix's original business model (based on shipping DVDs to customers instead of digital downloads) would not have been viable without meticulous analytics. The high shipping costs generated by active users of the service would have eroded the company's profits. To retain their profitability, the company added a controversial "throttling" process which delayed DVD shipments for the subset of most active users.

Netflix also uses detailed analytics and algorithms to recommend films to its customers. Finally, it extracts insight derived from viewer data of similar films as a negotiation advantage vis-à-vis media rights owners.[15]

"Perpetual beta" applied to business models – that business model selection should be a process of continuous adaptation and evolution – is deeply engrained in the structure of the web itself. The fact we can test different options, and after we implement one, start to adapt and improve it immediately, is unique to web-based business. This means that the web business model design process is very different from how we design a car (or used to design a car before much of the value of the car is derived from it being closely integrated into the web). The task of designing a car takes place before a product launch.

In a guest chapter of Guy Kawasaki's book *Reality Check*, the CEO of the real estate web site Redfin, Glenn Kelman, writes on the subject of experimentation and evolution: "Everybody has to rebuild … don't get discouraged or shortsighted. Just rebuild it. This is simply how things work." In another section, he gets more descriptive and lists what is involved in the creation of a great product: "Tinkering, kvetching, nitpicking, wholesale reworking, and spasms of self-loathing."[16]

> **The Angel's Forum – Always have a business model perspective, even if it changes**
>
> Angels should have: A rich base of personal business experience combined with modesty and a true appreciation of the achievements of fellow entrepreneurs. Entrepreneurs should have: A clear business model perspective, even if it is adapted continually.
>
> Introducing Patricia Roller, member of The Angel's Forum. TAF is one of the best-known angel groups in Silicon Valley. 25 high net worth individuals are part of this association.
>
> Roller's experience is in creating iconic products people love to use. Creation is meant broadly here, including production, resources and the business aspects. Roller's task is not just to seek out and fund the most promising entrepreneurs but also to back those where her unique experience and skills can make the greatest impact. In the Internet world, this translates not just into user interfaces but into a holistic and compelling web experience.
>
> Patricia Roller co-led Frog Design, the legendary design company Steve Jobs hired to design the Apple IIc and the Macintosh. The roots of Frog Design go back to 1969. From 1982 onwards, the company operated under the name Frog Design, with Roller as Co-CEO. She negotiated the acquisition by Flextronics of an equity stake in the company in 2004, and a subsequent partnership with the private equity fund Kohlberg, Kravis, Roberts & Co. Patricia managed Frog's key accounts, HP and Motorola. Roller's achievements were recognized in 2003 by YWCA in their Tribute to Women in Silicon Valley.
>
> Roller requires from entrepreneurs a clear view of their business model at all times. Roller notes that a good indicator for business success is if there is an established market already, which is being addressed in some other less effective or compelling way.

> One of the companies that Roller is involved with is Gaga Inc. Gaga develops a platform for sports teams to communicate with their fans using social media. Leading teams such as LA Lakers or Utah Jazz use the product. Roller makes the point that while Gaga does not have a public business model yet, there is a very clear internal view what this will be. Most importantly, there is an addressable budget at large sports clubs for marketing, which is used in a mostly conventional way today.

The exciting ability to experiment on the web is not naturally given, but an aspect purposely designed into the very architecture of the Internet. As Barbara van Schewick has pointed out in her excellent book on Internet architecture and innovation, the so-called end-to-end architecture of the Internet is the reason why rapid experimentation can happen at all. In a "core centered network," innovation requires substantial systemic change on several levels. The current design of the Internet allows rampant innovation at the edges, the "ends," without requiring significant investment. In fact, van Schwick makes her point using many great examples: Innovation can happen in one's spare time (eBay, Del.icio.us, Yahoo, Facebook), can be paid for by consulting projects on the side (37signals, Blogger) or by family and friends (Amazon.com).[17]

While "end-to-end" architecture was part of the original design of the Internet, software costs have fallen considerably year over year, due to the prevalence of Open Source and ready-to-use web services. In 1997, Silicon Valley-based venture financed Internet companies still required hundreds of thousands of dollars to get started – this has been reduced to tens of thousands.[18] Y Combinator, for example, provides companies with a comfortable starting package of $150,000, courtesy of two angels, Ron Conway and Yuri Milner.[19] This would have been a small amount during the New Economy; it is ample to get going today.

Falling costs have enhanced the ability to adjust flexibly to new opportunities on the web and change business models quickly without incurring significant technology costs. There has been a "remarkable increase in the degree of entrepreneurial experimentation," according to Bill Sahlman of Harvard Business School. The same article that quotes Sahlmann also cites the Apax founder Alan Patricof and his appetite for entrepreneurs that can "pivot."[20] In the history of its existence, Skype has changed its business model several times including trying out several variants of service sales and subscriptions. Twitter is perfecting its monetization scheme based on Tweet Promotions continually as we are writing these words.

In an interview for the book, Frédéric Court, General Partner of the London-based fund Advent Venture Partners, also emphasizes the advantages of experimentation, adding that globalization of the Internet provides further possibilities: "It is becoming easier and easier to launch a product extremely fast in different markets all over the world and see where it sticks. The whole world has become a business laboratory." Court notes: "We love the globalization of opportunities via the web, especially as it enables start-ups in markets like Europe or the U.S. to remotely address high-growth emerging markets very efficiently."[21]

The costs of launching new ideas globally will fall even further. "Software as a service" (SaaS) and "cloud" offerings allow clever combinations of different services provided by different companies. Leading Internet companies such as Apple and Google have started to offer payment options as part of their platforms, essentially extending web services into the area of monetization. We will discuss this more in the concluding chapter.

As costs fall further, it will become even easier to experiment – these are exciting times. What will happen if $1,500 becomes the new $150,000?

The search for the perfect business model

Since the beginning of web business, executives and entrepreneurs have searched for the perfect business model. This quest can be segmented into three distinct phases. In the first phase, Internet entrepreneurs took their inspiration from offline business models, because this is what consumers and businesses readily understood. Offline business models provided the foundation for the seven basic business modules this book is named after.

During the first phase, several of these modules went through bubbles of popularity of their own. This is where the financial analysts and the journalists come in; they hyped certain business models as the best way to monetize Internet business. In fact, the order we use for sequencing our chapters more or less reflects the series of hype phases associated with each web business model. We do not claim, however, that the timing of these hype phases was entirely sequential. There was a lot of overlap. Our point is that each business model has gone through a period of massive investor and media interest – contributing to a boom of start-up activity surrounding the model and fallout later. The historical hype phase associated with each business model also had a positive effect, however, it was important in accelerating the evolution of each model. These hype phases we will review briefly now were distinct from what we call the three phases of development of Internet business. Let's start with the hype and return to the serious stuff in just a while.

Services were among the first Internet businesses to be hyped. The online agency iXL headed up a boom to consolidate Internet agencies which were making a living selling web development services. iXL Enterprises Inc. was founded in March 1996 but it was basically an acquisition vehicle for several agencies founded in previous years. One of the 28 acquisitions, just as an example, was Swan Interactive Media, a company founded in the summer of 1994.[22] Why on earth did people believe that building web sites was a scalable business?

Largely at the same time, perhaps a little later, investors fell in love with the subscription-based Internet business model. Subscription seemed to be the one and only way people would pay for Internet services. AOL acquired Time Warner in 2001 based on this promise. The marriage would last only until 2009. CompuServe, the subscription-based online service provider, was founded as early as the Internet itself, in 1969. One of the first Internet Service Providers (ISPs) was PSINet, launched in 1989. The ISPs challenged online service companies such as CompuServe, AOL and Apple's eWorld from mid 1990s onwards, in what was a vicious competitive battle among two different types of subscription-based business models: providers of online content and providers of Internet access only.

From subscriptions, attention shifted to another business model. Everyone became enthralled with the story of a former investment banker who analyzed all Internet businesses in detail and concluded online retail and books was perfect for him. Jeff Bezos and the Amazon team did a great job, but many others failed in other retail categories. After that phase, commissions became the perfect business model of the Internet and eBay was the darling of investors and the media. Yahoo! was a stock market darling for a while, too, but a far greater advertising business-model-based investor boom came with Google and Web 2.0. In the meantime, the New Economy crashed and Internet business recovered only slowly in the 2000s.

For a while in the first part of the 2000s, the world implicitly assumed the whole Internet would be advertising funded. Unexpectedly, in 2009, Apple shares started their ascent and made Apple the most valuable technology company in the world. But Steve Jobs did not embrace media's own advertising business model. He did a phenomenal job in reinventing Apple's business and selling media song-by-song, license-by-license for small amounts of money. Apple's online media store iTunes was not really a platform, in the sense that third parties could build up their own business on top. In 2006, however, an immensely successful App Store with a complete license sales ecosystem followed. It was the start of something new.

These hype phases distract from the fact that from the beginning, all seven basic business modules already existed. This includes financial management; for example, several online-only banks were founded during the 1990s. What is important from the perspective of this book is that during the New Economy, the offline business world was an important inspiration and the first basic online business models were tried and tested. This period is what we call the first phase of web business.

The crash of the New Economy after September 11 was a major watershed moment in the development of web business. Investments in Internet businesses and new ventures collapsed. Retrospectively, the downturn proved to be an extremely innovative time. After the collapse, more sophisticated business models appeared; the seven building blocks were cleverly combined with free services in what was termed "freemium" models. The driver behind this phase was to create the lowest possible entry barriers to participation on the web and find the most unobtrusive ways of making money. It was the Web 2.0 era and advertising was the preferred business model.

Now, in Phase Three, web-based business models have been adapted again. Executives and entrepreneurs realized that advertising could not be the only revenue pillar for a whole industry. The App Store has become a versatile payment platform for thousands of software and content developers. Innovative, new payment options are emerging every day, such as virtual currencies. Online business models are increasingly applied to the offline world.

Internet entrepreneurs and executives are developing personalized businesses that allow their customers to pay with what they want, how much they want and wherever they want. The whole spectrum of the seven building blocks is more relevant than ever to set up a personalized business, which treats its customers more like individual business partners than mass consumers. Customers don't have to adjust to business any more. And payment is not always cash; it can be anything of value: virtual currencies, data, labor, attention, sales leads and personal recommendations. And thanks to smart phones and embedded IT, online business has subsumed the offline world and follows the customer, wherever he or she may be.

Offering every person exactly what he or she wants at the right price point has always been the dream of economists. To a certain extent, personalized pricing has existed for many years, think bazaars or airline seats. But with the possibilities of the web today, we can come closer to perfect economics than ever before – in more diverse business areas. And we are not just talking about pricing, but more broadly about personalized business value and about the new possibilities that virtual currencies and mobile commerce enable.

Entrepreneurs and executives who do not strive constantly to make their business models more personal will fail. It is not easy. It is an ongoing quest. The seven building blocks are more relevant than ever and help by expanding the available options.

Getting started

Before embarking on the quest for the right business model, it is vital to understand the seven business model building blocks thoroughly, including the success factors, drawbacks and pitfalls associated with each. One of the best ways to do this is to analyze how Internet companies around you currently work with their own business model. Since business models are continually evolving, it would be hazardous not to conduct your own research. You need to be equipped with your own up-to-date analysis of what is happening on the Internet.

This book contains the necessary background for this exercise. It is divided into five parts. Chapter 1, which you are currently reading, comprises PART ONE. Then follows PART TWO, seven chapters dedicated to each of the building blocks. PART THREE is dedicated to the growing sophistication of web business models, especially the "freemium" model. The final chapter – an outlook on personal web business – makes up PART FOUR. PART FIVE is an optional Appendix containing financial data on the largest Internet companies and analysis related to the seven modules.

The five parts of the book will help you answer three different sets of questions for your web site:

(1) What are the *SimplySeven* building blocks? Should finding a business model be my priority? Why is it so important to choose the right business model? How long should I wait before choosing? How much experimentation is involved in getting one's business model right? To what extent is it an ongoing process?

(2) What are the specific lessons learned by the smartest entrepreneurs regarding each business model building block? How will web business

evolve in the future in each of these seven categories? What mistakes associated with each module should be avoided?

(3) Why is it important to provide value on my web site for free? In a "freemium" model, what should be free, what not?

(4) What is a personal business model? How can I combine business model building blocks to create individualized forms of payment? Should I take advantage of business model platforms provided by companies such as Apple, Google and Facebook? How is web business now being transferred to the real world?

(5) How are companies representing each business module represented among the top 100? What do data from the largest Internet companies tell us about the seven business modules?

Let us preview the five parts of the book briefly.

PART ONE (Chapter 1) – Think outside the box, constantly experiment and evolve

All Internet business models are composed of one or more of seven basic building blocks: services, subscriptions, retail, commissions, advertising, license sales and financial management. We will introduce these seven building blocks in Chapter 1, the chapter you are currently reading.

The seven basic building blocks represent different monetization options. The options are different answers to the question: "What exactly is being sold?" This is not trivial on the web, where new types of services also require innovative approaches to selling. Selling successfully requires a deep understanding of what exactly is sold and its value.

SimplySeven emphasizes constant experimentation in selecting and fine-tuning one's business model. It encourages thinking outside the box: business models outside the narrow range of "hyped" and fashionable candidates.

PART TWO (Chapters 2–8) – The seven building blocks and lessons learned by the smartest entrepreneurs

Most of this book consists of a chapter-by-chapter walk through each of the seven business modules. Putting these chapters together, the book becomes a navigational guide to Internet business.

There is much to learn about each business model from the leading Internet companies. Telling the story of how each of these flagship companies wrestled with their own business model helps us describe each model in a dynamic way: Why each leading Internet company used a particular model and how they have addressed the challenges of each business model over time. All seven building blocks have evolved considerably over time. It is important to point out that great companies have not always done everything right, this book is about failures as well as successes.

Finally, in each of the chapters, we will see how, occasionally, start-ups are a step ahead of the great companies and are pioneering new ways of interpreting each model. Time does not stop on the web.

While going through each business model chapter by chapter, the book draws upon and explains leading concepts that have appeared recently about the Internet such as "Wisdom of the Crowds," "Database of Intentions," "Markets are Conversations," "the Long Tail" and "Creative Commons." A lot of great insight has been developed in recent years about Internet business which we are grateful for. What we find lacking out there is a summary in one place of "the best of" of this insight. *SimplySeven*, therefore, is not only a guide to the seven business models themselves, but for the smartest thinking developed in recent years about Internet business.

If you have the chance, don't just read the chapter that applies to you. Each business model addresses different challenges associated with charging for Internet products and services. Together, the full picture emerges.

PART THREE (Chapter 9) – It's a freemium world

Chapter 9 describes when is the right time to start charging and what to charge for in the essentially free environment of the web. The Internet has been built on a foundation of free donations – this is an essential aspect of the Internet that needs to be respected. Offering value on the web for free is one of the most important ways customers are rewarded for their own nonmonetary contributions to a web site – in the form of personal data, personal recommendations or content.

> *PART FOUR (Chapter 10) – The future of web business is personal*
>
> This part describes how the seven basic business building blocks can be combined to create personalized web business. This is about providing each and every customer with the best possible payment option for him or her. Two innovations from the gaming world are leading to intense innovation in this area: virtual currencies and advanced analytics. Apple and Google are providing complete payment platforms as a web service. Personalized business is not stopping at the virtual world, however, new approaches such as credit card reading devices for small businesses are extending web business to the offline world. Whereas the seven offline basic building blocks initially were an inspiration for online, now – after a period of evolution – online is moving into the real world.

> *PART FIVE (Appendix) – Stress testing the SimplySeven*
>
> To learn more about the different business modules, we analyzed financial data from the largest Internet companies. The 2009 Nielsen list of Top 100 Internet Companies shows how frequent specific building blocks are and how rare the others are.

SimplySeven – that's it

Here are the *SimplySeven*. The list below contains the seven business modules, the flagship company associated with each as well as the most common mistake to avoid.

The term "business model" is being used by many people very differently. For most, the term "business model" is broad and refers to capabilities, market structure and many other aspects related to a company's specific way of making money.

An excellent book by Alexander Osterwalder and Yves Pigneur describes the many facets of business models and introduces a unique approach (using a so-called "canvas") to carry out what the authors call Business Model Generation.[23] The book takes a broad approach and is – we believe – a great complement to *SimplySeven*.

Table 1.1 The *SimplySeven* building blocks

Symbol (for navigating our web site)	Name	Type of purchase option	Flagship company	Most common mistake
	(1) Service Sales	Purchase of a unique, individualized product or service.	Skype	Not being able to scale.
	(2) Subscriptions	Purchase of a service contract or membership.	Blizzard Entertainment (creators of World of Warcraft)	Believing that people like to be held captive.
	(3) Retail	Purchase of a physical product.	Amazon.com	Treating online like offline.
	(4) Commissions	Fee paid for a completed sales transaction.	eBay	Thinking your clients won't deal behind your back.
	(5) Advertising	Fee paid for an opportunity to access potential customers.	Google	Invading people's space or privacy.
	(6) Digital License Sales	Purchase of a digital product.	Apple	Going solo.
	(7) Financial Management	Taking a position according to an expected financial outcome.	Emerging	Ignoring additional risks such as fraud and regulation.

Osterwalder and Pigneur's book about business model generation also uses the term "building blocks." These, however, are very different from the *SimplySeven*. There are nine of them and they essentially are generic, key aspects of any business model, such as customer segments, channels, resources and cost structures. These are important aspects of the business model of any company, "the logic of how a company intends to make money."[24]

This is where we differ. Our focus is narrow. It is the customer, not the company. We avoid a broad approach in favor of zooming in to what we believe is important for web business. To sell something, an executive or entrepreneur needs to know exactly what he or she is selling. Monetize = Productize. The *SimplySeven* are the different possible answers to the question: "What exactly is being sold?"

The product perspective makes things very simple, but not necessarily easy. Choosing a product also means knowing the customer. In fact, the better the customer is known, the easier will it be to get paid. The *SimplySeven* modules are options to match with personal customer preferences.

Why are there only seven basic modules? There are a thousand great ideas for compelling web sites, but we found that there are only seven basic ways to get paid. No more and no less – just seven. Over the past decade and a half, new companies have continually been founded within the seven categories (see Table 1.2). To have something finite and predetermined in the rapidly changing world of the Internet and the mobile web comes as a surprise to many. It certainly came as a surprise to us. In fact, we discussed this topic intensely among ourselves and with others over a number of years and have not found an eighth model.

To be fair to criticism, our approach does not cover all theoretical possibilities. We have used our SimplySeven.net web site and blog posts to discuss our ideas with the Internet community. (In fact, you can find older versions of some of the book's texts on the web site and by the time you read this, newer points of view, too.) In a lively discussion of our approach on "Hacker News" hosted by Y Combinator in January 2011, for example, one participant pointed out astutely that we had forgotten the subscription of physical goods. A subscription first and foremost is some type of long-term contract signed by a customer. Our first instinct would be to say that it does not matter if digital services or physical goods are covered by the subscription. We do make this exact distinction between retail and license sales, however. The former refers to physical goods and the latter to digital products. So why not make the difference for subscriptions, too? The participant had a point here. But, quite frankly, not too many physical good subscriptions are available on the web to make it a whole new building block.

The same applies to a further suggestion for an eighth building block by our community of discussants: cybercrime and fraud. While this would be an exciting new category, we cannot really recommend that companies purposely pick a business models related to illegal activity.

By the way, if you think you have an eighth building block, please go to our web site www.SimplySeven.net and by all means do tell us. Or if you think one of the seven is redundant. But we are – let's put it this way – mildly

Table 1.2 The *SimplySeven* and founding years of leading Internet companies

	Services	Subscription	Retail	Commission	Advertising	License Sales	Financial
Phase 1: New Economy							
1994	Swan Interactive		Amazon		Netscape		
1995	USWeb			eBay	Craigslist		
1996	iXL			eLance		Macromedia	
1997					GoTo.com		Party Gaming
1998		Celera	Boo.com	PayPal	Google	Tencent	
1999							
2000		Blizzard WOW					
2001		AOL buys Time Warner					ING Direct
Phase 2: Web 2.0							
2002					LinkedIn		
2003	Skype	Linden Lab			MySpace		
2004	New Razorfish, PatientsLikeMe		Vente Priveé	Commission Junction		Apple iTunes	
2005					Facebook, Twitter		
Phase 3: Personal Business							
2006	23andme	Weebly		Plastic Jungle, Mint.com	Scribd	Apple App Store	Weatherbill, Prosper
2007	Gazelle			Groupon, Living-Social		Zynga	
2008		Spotify		WePay, Airbnb			
2009				HayZap	Foursquare		
2010							Square Inc.
2011					Color		Bank Simple

skeptical. We know our argument based on the notion of practicality is subjective, but look at this in a whole other way: there may be a limited number of basic monetization options for a very good reason.

Despite the increasing importance of the web, our brains are still stuck in the real world. This was the case especially at the beginning of web business. From the real world, people have an understanding of different types of commercial activity – based on experience. During the New Economy, the seven modules were all adapted from the offline world. A quote by Tim Brady, Yahoo!'s first employee summarizes this nicely for advertising: "No one had any idea how big the internet was, but the model [for Yahoo!] was advertising. Advertising was well known, so it wasn't like we were making up advertising."[25] It is this realization, that there are seven models – no more – which provided the most important impetus for us to write the book in the first place.

Often, the real-world basis for our experience and understanding is not really relevant any more in a virtual world. Take, for example, the difference between subscribing to a cable movie service and buying a movie in a shop. In the real world, the subscription involved a set-top box access to a service and buying a movie involved an actual DVD and a trip to, say, Wal-Mart.

Today in our purely digital universe, if you download a movie, it is up to your provider if they want to sell their customers a long-term contract. Alternatively, they can sell a license, which allows their customers to view the film, for example, one time or over the period of one week or one month. In the digital universe, a provider can freely select one of the two business models. Is there a difference between a month-long subscription and a month-long license? Technically no. The real-world product constraints don't exist any more.

But we have to heed the constraints we carry with us from our real-world experiences. In this example, both business models still have clear advantages and disadvantages from the perspective of the provider and the customer. From the real world, we associate license with ownership and subscription with a contract and membership.

These associations and the advantages and disadvantages in terms of expectations that they create are what this book is about. Choosing the right business model matters. The options are limited by our real-world expectations. At least for our current version of brain.

The making of this book

We use the framework of seven Internet business model building blocks every day ourselves in business, investing and teaching. Each of us works with the Internet in different ways. One of us (until recently) was an executive at a global technology company, advising media clients regarding Internet business strategies and running some of their IT systems, including several web sites. Another is a successful Internet entrepreneur and an active angel investor, who co-founded a company acquired by eBay (and today contributes a significant proportion of their revenues). The third member of our group is a professor at one of the leading business schools of the world.

We admit openly that we had a lot of fun in the course of this project. This is because we enjoyed a very privileged opportunity to work together, which does not come by so often in our busy lives. For over a year, we sat down every weekend in a perfect place to think about the development of Internet business – a beautiful 19th century villa by a lake. We were joined by excellent researchers. Our work was based on courses we had held at various universities and entrepreneurship programs. We hotly debated the pros and the cons of each Internet business model. And we had additional, special responsibilities as well. One of us provided the location, another funded the researchers and the third brought the pizza.

After weeks of discussion, we noticed that the complete framework of seven building blocks was starting to fall in place like pieces of a puzzle. You will notice this, too, after seeing how the different chapters build on each other. For this reason, we do not recommend that you just read the chapter concerning a particular business model. Each chapter works by itself, but they are at their best together as an Internet business model framework – which can help guide your thinking on a daily basis. How each building block relates to the others is a very important aspect of the overall picture. Combinations are important; this is when you add aspects of one business model to compensate for the weaknesses of the other one.

We want to share with you not just our individual insights on a specific building block but also our sense of excitement about what we believe is a very fundamental way of understanding Internet business as a whole.

Before the book went into the publishing process, we used the web community to collect feedback. We posted blogs covering specific topics on the web site www.SimplySeven.net and announced these entries on Facebook as well as on specific forums. Especially valuable discussions took place on "Hacker News" hosted by Y Combinator (http://news.ycombinator.com/). These discussions improved our material.

From the very beginning, we knew what our book needed to look like: focused just on the basics, not too long. It should be possible to read the book end to end on a six-hour flight. It should be accessible to many people, not just business executives. And we tried to avoid overdosing on tech terminology, even though it can be fun.

One more point in closing. We wrote this book for ourselves and for people we know. It is the Internet entrepreneur that Jörg talks to every day. Niko has just moved out of consulting media clients and now launched a new business financing the media and marketing expenses of Internet companies. It is a book for the exciting discussions that take place all the time in business schools around the world, including IE Business School, where Erik teaches in Madrid.

There is an interesting paradox here. All three of us know many business people who would normally never work with business consultants. They simply don't need to, because they built up their own business from scratch and know every nook and cranny. They acquired all they need to know themselves. When it comes to their web site, however, these savvy business people suddenly let Internet agencies and designers make serious decisions for them. There is a huge amount of dependence on outside experts and it is often not possible to vet their level of experience and knowledge until it is too late. Many of our friends have had to change agencies and web site designers several times before finding the right partner. Their web business has suffered in the meantime.

This book will not replace an agency or designer. We also do not think it is smart to do everything yourself. There are good reasons to partner with experts. But we also think it is very important to vet your partner in advance. You need a partner who can discuss with you the business challenges posed by the web, not just technologies like Ajax or Ruby. This book will enable you to have that critical conversation – and it should be an ongoing discussion.

As we said at the start, this book is not a cookbook guaranteeing instant Internet success. Instead, you will find a framework of seven Internet business model building blocks and a detailed discussion of each. After falling in place for us like pieces of a puzzle, this framework guides our thinking on a daily basis and we believe it will also help you in the same way.

CHAPTER 2

The first building block – services sales

Plain and straightforward

This business module is straightforward. It is about buying a unique, individualized product or service on the web. Services sales have two main characteristics: they are one-off and direct. One-off means they aren't subscriptions, for example, where a contract or membership is bought over a longer period of time. Direct means that services are sold directly by the company or person providing the service. Agents help sell services indirectly; as aggregators they create marketplaces connecting providers to buyers of services. Agents make money through the advertising or commissions business models. While services sales are much more straightforward than subscriptions or agent-based models, the business model normally poses several problems: it is not recurring, it is not scalable and it does not benefit from aggregation.

A large number of services are sold over the Internet. The web sites of companies or people providing services range from basic to very sophisticated. Many services are local and cannot offer services over the web. Your hairdresser most probably has a web site. But he or she will have a hard time marketing the site on the web; the ocean is simply too large for this one fish. This is why agents such as Craigslist or Groupon provide local marketplaces for services, covering numerous major metropolitan areas globally.

It is important to understand the differences to what agents and intermediaries do. Agents help sell services; as aggregators they create marketplaces connecting providers to buyers of services. But they don't use the services sales business module themselves.

Some services can be provided partly locally, partly remotely – perhaps a single meeting or at least some phone calls are necessary. Examples are the professional services eLance is focusing on. The web business itself is filled with small to medium-sized service firms providing everything from web site design to search engine optimization. 160,000 professionals advertised their services on the eLance web site in 2010.

More and more services are provided entirely over the web. Some of these are self-help portals which provide some type of unique one-off service. One example is 23andMe, a personal genome service founded in 2006. Users all over the world can buy a service pack over the web site, which contains a tube. The customer then spits in the tube, sends it in and her DNA is analyzed by a computer. From this point on, the service is entirely web based. The data provided through the DNA can be analyzed thoroughly by the customer using sophisticated analysis tools. The customer gains information about ancestry and health traits.

EDventure Holdings – doing good through business

EDventure Holdings – That's Esther Dyson. The meeting with Esther Dyson started as scheduled on the dot at 8.30 AM in the Stanford Park Hotel in Menlo Park. This was Dyson's second meeting that morning; a group of founders had just presented their start-up pitch. And before that, she already had a swim in the hotel pool. After our meeting, she would rush off to San Francisco and then to the airport. She had just arrived from the StreamAsia conference in Phuket, Thailand, and was flying to Switzerland next.

What Esther Dyson does, is intense, not just mentally, but physically; she connects the dots between investors, founders, corporations, scientists and thinkers – and this on a global scale. She sits on a dozen boards including companies such as the global marketing group WPP and the Russian search engine Yandex.

Esther Dyson sat on the ledge in front of the hotel's large fireplace – which was blazing even early in the morning – to discuss business models. For Dyson, business models are only one aspect of a much wider picture. Dyson believes in sustainable businesses with a positive social impact. Dyson also supports non-profit initiatives such as the National Endowment for Democracy, but she writes in her bio: "Generally, I prefer to do good through profit-making enterprises, but there are things companies simply can't do."[1]

Take 23andMe. Dyson is a board member of this consumer biotechnology company. The objective of the company is to allow consumers an insight into their own genetic code. This reveals potential health areas to look out for, as well as information about a person's heritage. At first, 23andMe charged a fee for the unique, one-time service of having one's genetic data checked. Now it has added a subscription model for

$5 a month to reflect the continuously changing basis of knowledge we have about genetic information.

Dyson believes that finding the right business model is an evolutionary process. Constant adaptation and personalization of business models, however, will rarely work without a direct customer relationship. As an example, Dyson mentions American Airlines pulling out of Orbitz in December 2010 in order to strengthen its direct personal relationship with its customers. A direct relationship, including managing the loyalty program and selling adjacent services such as rentals or rooms, is crucial for the future of American Airlines in an increasingly online-dominated travel industry.

Direct relationships and loyalty points can be used in a wide range of industries. The same scheme can be used to incentivize people to improve their health and, for example, carry out regular fitness. In her blogpost for Project Syndicate, Dyson mentions three companies which run different types of services allowing people to collect health points or challenge one another to carry out healthy activities: HealthRally, Contagion Health and MedRewards.[2] These types of schemes represent real value to health insurance companies, it is imaginable that such types of health points someday join a growing set of valuable virtual currencies (like flyer miles).

Users and customer value are always the first concerns Dyson has when assessing a company. One of her Tweets: "Bad sign in angel pitch: 'Due to [blah blah], we feel this is an opportunity investors will enthusiastically support.' What about users??"[3]

Another example is tax return services. Offshore tax return services were the most thought provoking case cited in Thomas Friedman's 2005 bestseller *The World is Flat* – a wonderfully readable collection of anecdotal evidence and personal stories about what Friedman calls "Globalization 3.0." Globalization and Internet-based workflow solutions together mean that services can now be offered worldwide, taking advantage of lower offshore cost rates. Tax return services are great for offshoring, because the services consist entirely of data. Many Americans may not know it, Friedman writes, but their accountants may be living across the globe in India. In his book, Friedman described the specific service provided by Indian entrepreneur Jaithirth (Jerry) Rao. Rao's business was acquired by EDS in June 2006 after Friedman's book came out, and it is now part of HP By the way, if you are looking for Rao's service on the web for your own tax returns, you will not find it, because the front end still is an American C.P.A., and she, in turn, administers the service over a web site.[4]

Most pure play Internet services which can be sold and delivered entirely over the Internet and work with personal data are free. This lowers the threshold for people to participate. The web sites don't sell their services directly; they make their money through advertising. An example is RealAge.com, a service for uploading personal fitness data. The data is analyzed over the web and the real age of the customer is established, along with fitness advice. Alternatively, web-based services can make money by selling customer data in anonymous form, which is a license or intellectual property (IP) sale. For example, PatientsLikeMe, a community web site for people with life-changing diseases, sells its IP to the pharmaceutical industry. It is entirely possible that tax returns will someday be done for free if the data is regarded as valuable and can be resold.

There is no doubt that the Internet has revolutionized the sale and delivery of many different types of services. Take airlines, for example, which fits into our model because it sells one-off services directly. Airlines have not only cut costs by selling tickets online, they use the Internet to develop much deeper client relationships than they ever had before. Airline miles, which are akin to a virtual currency managed by consumers over the Internet, deepen the relationship further. The Internet probably is the most important sales and customer relationship channel for airlines, period. Throw in globalization, and you have two forces that together have a massive influence on the services part of the economy, which in several countries, including the U.S., represents more than 70% of GDP.

Cutting-edge design agencies like San Francisco-based Ideo and its CEO, Tim Brown are reinventing consulting by focusing on improving services (instead of products). Ideo has pioneered "design thinking." This approach champions the obvious but often ignored idea that the perspective of the customer should be the starting point for service improvements. Ideo is not embarking on this mission alone, others are also supporting the cause. SAP's Hasso Plattner funded the "D-School" at Stanford to study and teach services innovation and design thinking. Other leading academic institutions such as Berkeley and the Rotman School of Management are doing the same. These new programs are to a large part all about making services work in the era of the Internet and mobile web.[5]

We like services-based businesses because with their often-low investment costs, they are an opportunity for small, local businesses and entrepreneurs in emerging economies. We recognize the fresh new thinking being carried out on the topic of services. What we have a problem with is the strength of the service sales building block compared to the other six in this book. Services sales is not normally a scalable business model. Many services are labor-based, and there are only so many hours a person, or even a hundred people, can work. Labor is expensive in developed countries, especially educated labor. This is an obvious problem if you are the direct provider of services. In addition, customer acquisition costs are high in a one-off world. Since each sale is unique, there rarely is the opportunity to spread the cost among many customers. If you are an agent, the scalability problem is not yours but that of your clients'.

Services sales only makes sense if one or more of these criteria apply: (1) It is scalable, (2) customer acquisition costs are low or (3) customers are somehow "locked in" and keep coming back. Air travel, for example, is a business with relatively high entry barriers, including high capital and fixed costs and regulation. This has been changing over the past years, with low-cost entrants attacking margins, raising customer acquisition costs for the providers and reducing "lock in" on specific routes. Airline miles are a way to address some of these challenges and the popularity of such programs has probably saved more than one incumbent carrier from oblivion. My local hairdresser does not have a points program yet, but probably will introduce one soon. We will look at these criteria one by one in this chapter to understand how services firms have met the challenges intrinsic to one-off, direct sales.

By the way, many companies using the services sales model are not pure play Internet companies – like airlines. The Internet is growing in importance as a sales and delivery channel for services for these companies, especially if the emerging mobile web is included. In time, real and online economies will be connected to each other seamlessly.

One important provider of services on the Internet does not qualify as a case for this book because it is not a business – government. Many governments around the world are expanding into the Internet and trying to run as much of their administrative business digitally as possible: license plate registrations, submitting tax returns or voting. E-Government has huge advantages in terms of cost savings as well as practicality for citizens.

Yes, airlines and government are services that increasingly use the Internet, but in this chapter we will focus on one pure play internet services company that has successfully made the services sales model work: Skype. The impact of Skype on the telecommunications industry cannot be overstated. Skype has over 500m user accounts. 13% of all long distance phone calls in 2009 were made with Skype, a whopping 54bn minutes, according to the telecommunications analysis company TeleGeography. This makes Skype the largest long distance phone carrier in the world, by far.[6]

While Internet communication is free, Skype charges for calls to mobiles or fixed lines. There is a subscription, too, but Skype made most of its $551m in 2008 revenue through pre-paid phone credits.[7] Paying for each call made qualifies for the services sales module. Skype is an exceptional company in many regards. It has some particular advantages, which reduce customer acquisition costs and increase "stickiness." But even Skype is seeking to expand into other business models, for example, offering by subscription services to enterprises.

A business model with problems

Service sales is a business model building block which usually has a couple of severe problems: it is not recurring, it is not scalable, it does not benefit from aggregation and it does not participate in future value creation like some financial models do. All the other business model building blocks in this book are generally better – unless you have managed to set up an exceptional services business, such as Skype.

Service sales does not automatically drive recurring revenues like subscriptions do. For this reason, successful services concepts usually try to convert their customers over time into subscribers. Skype, for example, makes most of its money with top-up phone credits, which is a services model, but tries to pursue its customers to join the subscription service through significantly cheaper call tariffs. The personal genetics service 23andMe offers subscriptions now, too. Most companies offering services don't even go down this path, however. They offer a limited version of their service for free and then go directly into a subscription model. Many multiplayer online games work this way, such as Blizzard Entertainment's World of Warcraft.

The problem with the one-off nature of buying a service is that the service has to be resold to the client over and over again. Customer acquisition is costly. Skype and mobile phone carriers, which use top-up cards, have the advantage of network effects. People don't like to lose the list of Skype contacts they built up over time as well as their Skype identity. For many of the same reasons, people don't like to change their mobile phone number (even though regulation in some countries mandates that numbers should be transferable to other carriers). These factors make the services sales model work in these exceptional circumstances. Other services companies don't have this advantage. They try to work with loyalty points programs. Airlines do this, but so do many others. My hairdresser has not figured this out yet because he figures I need to come back to get my hair cut regularly.

But my coffee shop does provide points for each espresso I drink and every sixth is on the house. In the future, both my hairdresser and my favorite coffee shop will use mobile payment technologies, such as Square, Inc., to track my purchases and to offer loyalty schemes.

Service sales usually are not scalable, either, in the way that product sales are. This is because most services are labor-based. Many services are also local; they cannot be offered remotely. What companies often forget in times of growth is that scalability also means the ability to scale down. This may be much more important than the ability to scale up. To survive an economic cycle, companies need to be able to "breathe."

Several web services companies expanded in the New Economy of the late 1990s, adding local offices and people at a rapid pace. They were able to scale up very rapidly. Take a look at the history of iXL, one of the top web design companies of the New Economy. iXL was actually founded as a financial vehicle to acquire agencies and through mergers create a unique, worldwide agency network.

- iXL was founded in Atlanta in 1996, grew with venture capital and through an IPO. It acquired more than 28 agencies and had 20 offices worldwide with a total of over 1,000 employees.
- Some of the acquired agencies were founded before iXL was, such as Swan Interactive Media, established in 1994.
- The crash came. iXL merged into Scient in 2001 after heavy restructuring and delisting from NASDAQ.
- Salt Lake City-based SBI acted as consolidator and purchased assets from Scient/iXL, Lante, MarchFirst (formerly USWeb & CKS Group) and Excelerate; many of these companies' employees still are together today as part Avenue A | Razorfish.
- In 2004, aQuantive, Inc. (NASDAQ: AQNT) bought SBI.Razorfish (500 employees) from SBI Group.
- SBI Enteris, the technology arm of SBI Group, was sold to Enterpulse in 2006.
- And so on.

Quick summary: During a recession, a large service-based organization is not a fun business to be in.

Sure, growth is expensive for Amazon.com, because it has to build up its logistics and warehouses. But the retail business model is based on product sales and these simply scale better. Even more attractive is being in the business of license sales. Apple sells music, videos and apps in its online Apple stores. The fact that all these products are digital means that it makes very little difference in terms of cost to Apple if it sells 10,000 or 100,000 items in its store. Scaling down is just as simple. Skype, of course, has the advantage that it is an entirely digital service that can scale very well. Its peer-to-peer technology is specifically made to scale massively using distributed computing power.

Many agents help sell services, but they are not in the services sale business themselves. Several, such as Craigslist or Groupon, have local web sites which reflect the local character for the services they help to sell. Craigslist can scale easily because advertisers add themselves to the web site by themselves without requiring human support. Craigslist offers most of its listings for local services for free and makes money on only a few categories such as real estate sales and rentals. Groupon has an innovative group-buying concept where local services offer discounts when a set number of potential clients sign up. Both Craigslist and Groupon are growing fast by adding new cities in the States and internationally. Groupon probably was the fastest growing Internet company ever in terms of revenues in its first three years of existence, a powerful demonstration of how much marketing need exists for local services. Aggregators can scale easily because growing the number of services on their platform means very little additional cost.

eLance is an agent focusing on professional services which can to a large extent be delivered remotely. eLance was founded in 1998 and initially financed during the New Economy. It invested US$60m to become the "eBay for outsourcing." After the crash in 2001, it almost did not survive but then recuperated through a sale of software assets and the revival in Internet business. Internet-based professional services are key to the success of eLance because they can be delivered – at least in part – remotely. A search for "web design" on eLance in the summer of 2010 resulted in over 52,000 listings; of the first 25 results, 14 were Indian web design companies, 6 were from Pakistan, one each from Ukraine, Uzbekistan, Romania and Argentina. And one company from Kansas. These 25 are the web design companies with the highest reputation scores on eLance, based on credentials such as number of jobs completed, feedback received and certifications. Many are very small companies, with only a handful of practitioners.

Mostly, services are paid for on delivery. This means that service providers often do not benefit from the future value their services create. If a web design company, for example, helps create a web site that leads to huge success it will still only receive its fee for these services. To put forward a more extreme example, Skype does not charge by the success of the phone call it transmits, even if it is a business call. The reason this is not done is because the impact of services is hard to measure. Even if it were possible to see if a web site was successful in terms of the number of visitors to the site or transactions, what was the percentage contribution of the web designer to this success? If results in services were more directly measurable, one would expect many more companies using business models with financial risk positions.

With so many drawbacks, why actually get into the service sales business model in the first place? What service sales are is simple and straightforward. Customers feel much more in control and not locked in like in a subscription model. Most importantly, services business often have low barriers to entry and are a welcome starting point for small businesses and entrepreneurs in emerging economies. And everybody needs services. When certain aspects are in play, service sales can be a great business model. Take a look at Skype.

"Can I skype you?"

Skype was founded with a clear vision: "We are launching Skype as the telecoms company of the future. . . . We hope that one day, instead of saying 'I'll call you', people will say 'I'll skype you.'"[8] The ambition of the two Scandinavian Skype founders, Niklas Zennström and Janus Friis, was nothing less than becoming a global telecommunications leader.

Very few venture capitalists believed this vision; in fact, Skype took more than a year to get any funding. 20 different venture capital funds refused to invest in 2003. It did not help that the founding team was notorious for having founded Kazaa, a music file sharing service which media companies believed was operating on the borders of legality. At the time, there were several U.S. lawsuits against the Skype founders because of Kazaa. When Skype was pitched, it did not have its service ready yet either. And it did not have the final concept for a business model; voice services were supposed to be paid for by advertising.[9]

In the end, it was a small crew of brave investors that went ahead, including Luxembourg-based Mangrove, a European VC headed by an American, Mark Tluszcz. Before Mangrove entered, private founding investor Howard Hartenbaum supported the company. Hartenbaum and then Tluszcz saw what others didn't. Voice over Internet telephony itself was not new. But the fact that Skype proposed to use peer-to-peer technologies meant that it could scale massively without adding much technology of its own. In fact, Skype proved later that it could add 150,000 new users each day without spending anything on new hardware or connectivity.[10]

This meant that Skype had a very low break-even point. And it could be a massive threat to the telecommunications industry if it got the technology right. That Zennström and Friis could do peer-to-peer was obvious, they were the guys responsible for Kazaa. And behind them stood the original technology team which developed Kazaa – based in Estonia, a tiny Baltic state known for cutting-edge IT and security technologies.

> **August Capital – investing in the really big play**
>
> Before he joined August Capital, Howard Hartenbaum was the founding investor in Skype. He invested in Skype at a time when no other investors would touch it. It was a tiny company founded by entrepreneurs who were facing lawsuits from the music industry because of their previous company, Kazaa. Hartenbaum was not distracted by this. What fascinated him was one aspect only: the ability to massively scale at incredibly low cost.
>
> As a peer-to-peer technology, Skype is effectively using an underutilized resource, the computing power on everybody's desktop. Through this technology, Skype is able to replicate what long distance telecommunications companies are providing at hundreds of times higher costs. Just for comparison, in 2007, AT&T had 309,000 employees and Skype 700. According to the research publication TeleGeography, Skype is the largest long distance phone carrier in the world, by far ("International Phone Traffic Growth Slows, while Skype Accelerates," TeleGeography Press Release, January 19, 2010). Yet, investing in Skype at the time it was just two smart technology guys with an idea (and facing a lawsuit) takes a huge amount of vision and courage.
>
> Today, Hartenbaum looks for companies with a Skype-type potential. He is partner at August Capital, one of the most distinguished investment partnerships on Menlo Park's Sand Hill Road. August Capital's portfolio lists companies that its partners invested in previously as well as those that the fund is currently financing. That list is impressive. It contains not just Skype but also tech titans such as Microsoft, Seagate, Sun, Atheros and Intuit, the web payments company WePay (featured in this book) and new technologies such as the Bubbli we-can't-really-give-it-a-label-yet-it-is-too-innovative "360° experience smart phone photography."
>
> August Capital recently invested in a company, RelayRides, which leverages another underutilized resource: cars parked on a street. The company provides a system to lend out those cars to people for a specific time period; to people who need a car temporarily, but don't want to own one. One can imagine the potential of this play, not only in industrialized

> countries but also in emerging economies. The company is a further example of newer web ventures enabling users to access a resource in a personalized way exactly when they need it and how they need it.
>
> Hartenbaum makes it clear that the companies that August Capital invests in do not need a business model from the beginning. He very much accepts, even welcomes that many companies seek to build a base for experimenting with different business models before arriving at something that works. Initially, Skype had no business model at all. Later, Skype adjusted its model several times, including fixed line connect service fees and subscriptions. But what the company does need is the potential to be big, very big.

Eighteen months later in 2006, following several rounds of additional funding with other VCs including U.S. investment legend Tim Draper (who supposedly performed a dance in front of analysts to celebrate his investment), eBay bought the company for $2.6bn in cash and shares. This returned $180m on a total $1.9m investment by Mangrove.[11] In the year that eBay bought Skype, Eric Schmidt, CEO of Google said: "Skype . . . is as disruptive to the economics of the telecommunications industry as China has been to the global manufacturing sector."[12]

eBay has since sold Skype again to a group of private investors, not because it was not profitable or growing but because it did not fit into the core strategy of eBay. And being part of eBay perhaps even obstructed Skype's growth.

Advertising was not the right business model for Skype. This is not because advertising itself is a bad business model, far from it – some of the biggest Internet players such as Google search are powered by advertising. Many of these services, however, offer information or entertainment of some kind. As part of a service in which people only want to talk to one another and not carry out any information-related activities, advertising can be perceived of as more than annoying.

However, people were willing to pay for certain specific services provided by Skype, namely to dial into telecommunication lines ("SkypeOut"), to receive calls from regular phones ("SkypeIn") or voice mail. This is because these services cost money anyway and Skype was cheaper by far. "We want to make as little money as possible per user," Zennstrom was quoted in *The Economist*, "[because] we don't have any cost per user, but we want a lot of them."[13]

Next to almost unlimited scalability, Skype had a further advantage that other services companies can only dream of. It is a concept that is naturally viral. This means that Skype users directly benefit from recruiting further Skype users. With each additional user, the network on Skype expands for free calls, since Skype-to-Skype is free. And Skype is "sticky," too, because users don't like to change services and leave their contacts behind. Therefore, Skype solved all three challenges usually associated with services sales businesses: limited scalability, high customer acquisition costs and the threat of switching to another service.

Skype has already changed the telecommunications landscape forever. This does not mean that the company does not have to stay alert on its heels, however. It is looking for ways to expand its subscription revenues, because recurring income makes every CFO happy. The way it is doing this is by offering a new service to enterprise users. It can do this much more freely than before, when it was still part of eBay. Skype management is also wrestling with licensing issues for its peer-to-peer technology because its new investors have come into conflict with the original founders. Furthermore, there are several new contenders out there trying to eat Skype's lunch, for example start-ups like Gizmo5 and giants such as Google and Apple.[14] But the world would be boring without competition.

These advantages mean that Skype is the picture-book company for the services sales model. Services sales should not automatically be disregarded by entrepreneurs; if set up correctly even the weakest model of the seven can be just perfect. Microsoft acquired Skype not only for its scalable technology or its millions of customers but also because of its great business model prowess – as a successful services sales-based company.

CHAPTER 3

The second building block – subscriptions

The heaviest weapon in the arsenal

This business model is the heaviest weapon in the *SimplySeven* arsenal. Selling subscriptions is like asking people if they like to be chained to a wall. Some of you may have actually tried to sell subscriptions yourself; then you know what it is like. If customers don't like them and sales people try to stay away, then why are they used at all?

There normally is only one person who really likes subscriptions: the CFO. In contrast to other business models, subscription creates a constant and predictable revenue stream for the company. But a business model is of no use without customers. There are some tough prerequisites for subscriptions to be the right model for an Internet business.

Normally, a client will always prefer other business models where they have more control over payments, even if they are slightly more expensive. Subscription models exist which run out over a certain set period of time without automatic extensions. An example is a rail pass. While these types of subscriptions are more customer friendly, they still don't do away completely with the feeling of being chained up.

To succeed, a subscription contract or membership needs to be really, really convincing. Potential subscribers actually think quite deeply about the aspect of predictability. A simple sanity check is made by most people before signing up: with what certainty will I use the service how many times during the subscription period to justify the price? The sanity check also is used to reconsider existing subscriptions. In times of economic hardship, this check is made more frequently and with greater rigor. One of our favorite buttons on a web site is the "unsubscribe" button.

The sanity check will result in a green light in favor of subscribing for only one of two reasons. The first is necessity. The customer needs the service regularly and has no alternative. The customer looked for cheaper or better services, but they don't exist. Bad luck for the customer – he or she has to subscribe. Utilities, mobile phone services or Internet access fit into this category. If the service can be avoided then it will, for example, by taking a bicycle in summer instead of the rail service.

The second is unmatched attractiveness. Mind you, we are not speaking of a service just being nice to have. The service has to be so compelling and one-of-a-kind that your customers will do anything for it, even sign up for a subscription. Some financial information services like Bloomberg or Thomson Reuters fit the bill. Or Blizzard Entertainment's online game World of Warcraft. If you happen to offer such a service as a company, then you have lucked out. Not only can you actually offer premium prices, you may actually want to charge more just to underline your status as an exclusive service.

One would think it is easy to classify services into either the category "utility" or "compelling." It is not. Take the example of an annual membership to an exclusive golf club. An exclusive golf club must be really compelling and unique. Being a member of a golf club is obviously not a necessity. Or is it? For some, it may be just that. When the iPhone was launched in January 2007, many felt the need to own one. They even switched mobile provider subscriptions to get one. Interestingly, we like to think of some subscription services which we find compelled to subscribe to because they are attractive as being necessities. This is a trick we play with our own minds to justify subscription, and it is something worth exploring in this chapter.

Being perceived of as being both attractive and necessary is the lucky draw. Very few services can pull this off, it is a Steve Jobs-type coup d'état. There are far more services, we mentioned utilities or mobile phone services, that are necessary, but not one-of-a-kind. Some of these are regulated by government; in this case, profits are not set by the market. Otherwise, the lack of unique differentiating characteristics combines with tough competition to create an environment of cut-throat pricing. Welcome to the harsh world of commodity services.

It is not uncommon for a service to start off in a premium position and later fall into the commodity box. A lucky draw of attractiveness and necessity is great for the profit margin but generates envy. The competition will hunt the premium provider down relentlessly, eventually forcing it into commodity pricing. This is what happened to AOL; it was thrown into the commodity shark pool with hundreds of other Internet service providers.

But let's be realistic. Chances are that your specific service is neither necessary nor compelling. Then you should stay away from the subscription business model.

The rise and fall of AOL

The rise and fall of AOL is not just a dramatic story, it is instructive because it highlights the dangers of self-delusion. In 2001, shareholders, bankers and journalists thought AOL was a premium brand – so much so that they supported Time Warner's acquisition by AOL – even though the long decline into being a commodity provider had actually begun already in 1996.

Let us zoom back into the first half of the 1990s. For most people who did not have the privilege of being a university student or researching in a lab, online services were the only game in town. Two of these were the most prominent: CompuServe and AOL. And, yes, from 1994 to 1996 there was an unsuccessful online service provided by Apple, too, called eWorld. But this was the period during which Steve Jobs was not at Apple.

These online subscription services offered many of the things available on the Internet today, but they were provided by a single company as a proprietary offering. First and foremost was email. Then came various discussion forums, where people exchanged views on topics like printer compatibility, health programs and cooking recipes. CompuServe had more of a background in business and IT, whereas AOL was focused on topics that interested the typical American household. Finally, online services also offered content themselves such as news, sports, entertainment and weather.

Please note the order of the different services listed. What was really powering the online services were the cooking recipes and the sports forums, but not the sports news themselves. Not many executives got this. Especially not media executives, who like to think content is king. Sure, there is some really exclusive content that does not exist anywhere else. The Superbowl or World Cup Soccer. Or a Harry Potter movie. This content really is king; but kings are rare.

What was really fascinating for the subscribers of the online services in the early days was ability to interact among themselves. Email was a novel way of communicating in the early 1990s; these were the days of the fax machine. Just as cool as email were forum discussions. People could exchange views on a wide variety of topics and draw upon their own expertise forums for "dog lovers" and "new age spirituality" became really popular. This content would later be called "user generated." It still powers the Internet and social networks today.

Several important things happened around 1994 which caused this closed world to open up. The Internet, previously only available for the US military, in academic environments and for research institutions, was now accessible to the public through Internet Service Providers (ISPs). The first of these, PSINet, was launched in 1989. Some ISPs actually had cult status, the most famous probably being the Whole Earth Lectronic Link (The WELL) in Northern California. The WELL was launched as a bulletin board system in the mid 1980s, becoming an ISP in the early 1990s. In 1994, Marc Andreessen made the Netscape browser available for download – an easy navigation tool for content on the World Wide Web. The www itself had been created a few years earlier by Tim Berners-Lee in an European research lab. People were excited by these developments because, in contrast to the online services CompuServe and AOL, content provided by the ISPs on the www was open to all.

Next to their proprietary content and their closed forums, CompuServe and AOL also offered access to the Internet and the www for their subscribers. In the mid 1990s, they were still growing their subscriber base fast. The success of the web initially accelerated the growth of the online services by making them even more attractive. A host of exciting, new content was made available through Internet access. But when did the service reach a type of negative tipping point? From what point in time did subscribers join not because of the content and forums exclusive to the online service but simply because they wanted to access the Internet? It was the beginning of the end for AOL and CompuServe.

The tipping point must have been around 1996. Astute observers in the media industry would have noticed a particularly instructive event that took place in Europe that year. It was the launch of Europe Online, or rather, how it was launched. Witnessing the success of CompuServe and AOL, one of the largest media companies in Europe, the German publisher Burda, had just completed preparations for its own proprietary online service called Europe Online. The investment was significant and the preparations had taken months. The service was to be launched in several European countries at the same time and was based in Luxembourg. Just before the launch, however, Burda switched strategies. Instead of using proprietary software engineered by AT&T, they launched Europe Online as an ISP based on the Netscape browser and the www.

In the meantime, on the other side of the Atlantic, the online services initiated a cut-throat price battle among themselves. CompuServe was in the leading position with three million subscribers. It was the premium provider, charging a staggering $10 an hour in the late 1980s and early 1990s. After starting with a per hour rate as well, AOL was enticing subscribers to switch to its service by charging a flat monthly fee. To compensate, the subscription models became more complicated. Basic fees were lowered but the providers charged for additional, on-top services.

This is exactly what cable company providers or telcos do with the packages they offer. One example of an AOL premium service was the award-winning online role-playing adventure game, Neverwinter Nights, which was available from 1991 to 1997. AOL even offered some of its content for free to lure potential subscribers. In this way, a fairly sophisticated subscription pricing model developed in the second half of the 1990s.

Falling subscription prices were the best indication that online services entered the competitive, commodity space. Imagine a graph with four quadrants which illustrates this shift. The four quadrants represent the four possible combinations of high/low uniqueness and high/low necessity. The quadrant that online services moved into was low uniqueness/high necessity. (One quadrant actually is blotted out: high uniqueness/low necessity. The blotted out quadrant refers to the fact that people tend to perceive services that they find uniquely attractive as necessary as well.)

Today, Internet access has become a commodity to such an extent that it is given away in combination with cable or a phone line. Or, seeing it differently, the telephone line is being provided for free as a value add for Internet access. More and more has to be packaged into the bundle so that it can be sold. Unless you have massive scale, this is not a great business to be in. But at least providers of necessary commodity services are not in the so-called dog house quadrant on the bottom left. The most unattractive place to be is if you are neither necessary nor one-of-a-kind.

Not being in the "dog house" meant that CompuServe and AOL at least survived – for a while. The boom of the New Economy at the end of the 1990s even meant they were able to survive surprisingly well. Financial analysts liked the subscription business model of the online services because of the recurring revenues. Shareholders went for AOL stock. In the end of the 1990s, AOL had acquired CompuServe and became the gorilla of online services. Media companies looked at AOL with envy; for them at the time, online services seemed to represent the future of media. This delusion peaked in 2001 with the acquisition of Time Warner by AOL for the massive sum of $105 billion in stock. The shareholders of one of the largest media companies in the world actually allowed themselves to be bought by an online services company, which was already heavily slipping into a commodity space. Time Warner was and still is one of the top four entertainment companies globally next to Disney, News Corp and Viacom.

A few months later, September 11 initiated the crash of the New Economy. Time Warner woke up to a nightmare come alive. AOL shares plummeted, the number of subscribers stagnated and the online service had to keep lowering its prices to retain its members. AOL Time Warner had to conduct a goodwill write-off resulting in a 2002 loss of $99bn. Finally, in 2009, AOL was disentangled from Time Warner, ending an almost decade-long experiment with online subscription services gone awry. The new, independent AOL is now switching business models and trying out advertising – combining it with content production and deep use of analytics technology. It recently acquired two successful online-only, advertising funded media businesses, Huffington Post and TechCrunch.

AOL is a great example of a premium provider of subscriptions services, which thought for a moment too long that they were infallible and that their customers would not walk out the door. Suddenly, they found themselves in the same quadrant as a host of commodity ISPs. Not the services themselves had changed, but the world around them had. There was a world out there which was far more exciting and cool than AOL.

The "Bouncer Effect"

The managers of luxury brands know a thing or two about selling at a premium price. It has very little to do with the quality of the clothes themselves. It is not about what you sell, but how you sell it, how you package it and, most importantly, whom you sell to. If you get the right people to wear your clothes, success will follow. It is much the same with premium subscription services. The secret sauce of premium services very rarely is the content of the service itself. As we mentioned before, there is very little content out there that actually is exclusive and unique. The secret sauce is the very people who use your service – your subscribers.

Let us zoom into the trading floor of a big bank. We see a massive, open space filled with screens. In fact, most traders have multiple screens. They don't just use Reuters, they also have Bloomberg and perhaps some others, too. The content offered by these services is largely the same. If a broker just wanted a service to follow the development of the market, she would just need one of these services, or none at all, since much of this information actually is freely available on the Internet. It is not the content – at least not just the content. The traders are staring at multiple screens because their competitors on their trading floor and in other banks are staring at the same multiple screens. All the people relevant to the market are checking out the same screens. Not one of them can afford to miss anything the others could potentially see. Even if it is only a fraction of a minute earlier on one service compared to the other. This is enough justification. It is so compelling, in fact, that the traders would say that their financial information service subscriptions are a necessity.

The same secret sauce applies to Blizzard Entertainment's World of Warcraft game. WoW was not the first, so-called Massively Multiplayer Online Role-Playing Game (MMORPG); we already mentioned AOL's Neverwinter Nights. And WoW is not the only MMORPG on the market today – there probably are thousands such games. But the success of WoW is utterly amazing. More than ten million subscribers pay about $10 a month to play the game. The subscription expires by itself; there are options to purchase one, two, three or six months in advance. However, longer-term prepaid periods are discounted only in a very limited way. For many members, the fee represents a significant amount of money. They join because all the other gamers who count are in the club, too.

We call this secret sauce the "Bouncer Effect." It is not about what the club offers. Golf clubs are pretty much the same everywhere (a golfer would disagree with us). It is about how the club presents itself, it is about the packaging, but mostly, it is about the other members. To be more precise, it is about the type of other members. It is not just simply about everyone being there. It is about the right people being there.

A vast amount of literature exists about "Network Effects." Bob Metcalfe, a brilliant thinker who also invented Ethernet, an important networking technology, famously said that the value of the network equals the square of the members on the network. "Metcalfe's Law" explains why certain services and software take up significant market shares and the second and third in line often lose out.[1] "Network Effects" are general, referring to all scenarios in which the value of being a member in the network increases when others join. When this happens, members often persuade others to join, too, creating a "viral" marketing effect. "Bouncer Effects" implies that a single company controls the door. "Network Effects" and "Viral Marketing" usually apply as well in these situations. These companies can charge a premium. And they can launch subscription services successfully. Apple iPhones are so attractive that they allow mobile operators to charge premium subscriptions. WoW enjoys a similarly lucky position today.

Sustaining a position in the top quadrant is extremely difficult, however. WoW growth is slowing. There are worrying developments taking place in the lucrative segment of financial information services. Another information service, Thomson, acquired Reuters in 2008 and Thomson Reuters is offering basic services for a low price of $25 to 50 a month, with an a la carte menu of additional services. Bloomberg still costs $1,500 to $1,800 a month. This sounds familiar – Bloomberg has to watch out.

In the "dog house"

We have spoken a lot about movement from premium to commodity. Most subscription services, however, don't even make it to any of those quadrants. They are in the dog house from the moment they are born. The best examples are Internet newspapers. Several leading newspapers tested subscription business models on the Internet and failed. The *Los Angeles Times* tried charging a subscription for its arts section in 2005 but dropped this quickly. In the same year, "Times Select" was launched by *The New York Times* for $7.95 a month. After two years, they managed to sign up 227,000 people, generating about $10m in annual revenue. In contrast, the free, advertising-based web site had about 11 million unique visitors a month in 2005, making *The New York Times* the most popular online newspaper site. The web site of *The Boston Globe* added a further 4 million unique visitors for the New York Times Media Group.[2] Just compare the achievement of 200,000 subscribers to the base of 15 million (and growing) potentially interested monthly readers. Vivian Schiller, who ran the NYTimes.com at the time the subscription service was terminated, stated the predicament of her company clearly: ". . . our projections for growth on that paid subscriber base were low, compared to the growth of online advertising."[3]

Vivian Schiller was right about pulling the plug on subscriptions – at the time. In 2009, the New York Times Media Group generated roughly $200m annual revenue with Internet advertising, even without counting its About.com service. There is another problem with the subscription business model on the web – by closing off content to non-subscribers, it also limits the amount of information available for search engines. Many readers come to the site not directly, but through search engines and portals, mainly Yahoo! and Google. The more content available to these search engines to process, the higher the likelihood of a greater number of visitors coming to the site. Through the advertising business model these visitors then can be monetized.

Recently, *The New York Times* has developed a newer, more sophisticated subscription model, which includes some free access (for example, from social media sites) and some paid services. The final verdict on newspaper subscriptions is not out yet. Broadly re-establishing subscription for news in the digital world – if it could be pulled off – would require action not just by one media group but by many. This was why the helmsman of the newspaper industry, Rupert Murdoch, asked the newspaper as a whole to go for a paid model in a widely publicized appeal in 2009. The spectacular success of the Apple iPad came just in time to underscore Murdoch's call to action.

The current exclusivity of the iPad is breathing new life into newspaper subscriptions. For the sake of the publishers, let us hope this will last.

The future of clubs

If you have a unique and compelling service, subscription can be a fantastic business model. When everything is done right, membership paid by subscription can underline the premium nature of your service. Furthermore, the long-term relationship suggested by subscription membership can be positively associated with trust. Some exciting new subscription services are building on exactly this link between long-term membership and trust.

One of these services is called Hellohealth. Hellohealth offers online doctor's care by linking your personal physician to you in a secure web site. It cuts the administrative overhead created by visiting a doctor's practice. It remains to be seen if Hellohealth or other Internet start-ups can establish themselves in an area such as health, which is permeated by a high degree of complexity, many players and regulation. Subscription seems like a good business model choice for these new initiatives, however.

Another example of new subscription schemes comes from a completely different area. In the software industry, "software as a service" has been discussed intensively as the future of software. Salesforce.com is the best-known software as a service company. Salesforce.com offers CRM software to businesses as a hosted service over the Internet, in the "cloud." Companies wishing to store their customer data can do so without the hassle of setting up their own IT infrastructure and applications. It gets interesting when more than one company works together sharing customer data. To use Salesforce.com, businesses become subscribers. Of course, storing sensitive data with other parties requires a degree of trust. More and more companies and individuals are entrusting their data to cloud services.

In the consumer space, Google and Adobe are offering "software as a service," too. For consumer use, office programs, spreadsheet functionality or image processing software is provided not by subscription, but is funded through advertising. Adobe tried the subscription business model for its Internet version of Photoshop, but quickly changed its mind. Even though some of this functionality has taken a lot of time to program and contains a lot of value, selling subscriptions in the consumer space is difficult. Office and image manipulation software are simply not as unique as business CRM. All subscriptions have to pass the sanity check: do I really need this?

Getting people to subscribe

If you are thinking of offering subscriptions, think again. The real challenge with the subscription business model is not the business model itself. It is if you have the right service for the model. Perhaps you are planning to offer a necessity such as Internet access. Chances are that you will not be having a great time given the cut-throat price competition in these commodity markets. Unless you have massive scale and can compete better than others, commodity markets are not fun to be in.

With most likelihood, you are probably thinking of offering a premium service. For example, you have just finished developing a cutting-edge online game. Or an up-market travel information web site. Or a great image-editing software program. Your CFO has persuaded you that subscription is the right choice for your business model.

There is a huge amount of self-delusion in the premium segment. Many people think of their service as being unique and compelling. Sure, this is because they are working every day and night like a dog to provide the service. But just putting in effort does not mean that their customers perceive their service the same way. The great real-world brand *The Encyclopedia Britannica* also failed to establish a successful subscription model on the Internet.

And even if you manage to establish a premium service, the risks do not disappear. It just gets worse, because others will lick their lips seeing the margins which are being generated. We have seen how CompuServe slipped from being a premium service to being a commodity. It was AOL which initially started to take the bricks out of the wall that held both online service providers up. Even Bloomberg's premium pricing is being attacked viciously by its competitor, Thomson Reuters. Pornography, too, was hit – the big Internet business no one speaks about. From 2008 onwards, subscription-based pornography was attacked by ad-funded competitors. But if you happen to have the right service for a premium subscription model, by all means go for it.

CHAPTER 4

The third building block – retail

Don't treat online like offline

Many people underestimate the challenges of Internet retail. It consists of selling physical products in an Internet shop. It's about real things we can touch. It is far less fancy than its closest relative, digital license sales, because it does not require formats, interfaces or devices. Indeed, there are a multitude of shops on the Internet selling almost everything one can imagine. If you sell jeans, strawberry jam, chili seeds or books on the Internet you don't have to consider compatibility issues. But you still have to make money.

There are many Internet shops out there, but only a few people actually make a living from Internet retail; many of these are micro-businesses. Some Internet shops are the virtual storefront of a real-world shop, the owners of which are wondering on a daily basis why they are going through the troubles and expense of an Internet site. Other Internet shops are run in someone's spare time after returning home from work. Don't get us wrong, please. We love the Internet because it is open all over the world for all types of businesses, large and small. But there is a massive amount of frustration precisely with the Internet retail business model. And we have found that not just small business owners are frustrated, but big companies, too.

These days, it is easy to open a shop on the Internet. All the tools and help you need are there. But it is really hard to make money from it. Consider the basic steps required to sell an item. First, the potential customer needs to find your shop among thousands on the Internet. Second, the customer actually needs to find something in the shop he or she really wants to buy. Third, the customer needs to go through the checkout and sale process completely. The item then needs to be shipped out quickly and efficiently as a fourth step. Finally, the item may be returned, in which case the process starts again. The sale is only completed if every one of these steps is successfully carried out and the item is not returned.

The third building block – retail

And for each of these steps to be successful, a significant amount of time and money needs to be put in, in Internet marketing, in web site design and technology, in inventory as well as for shipment and returns. Oftentimes, Internet retail seems a limitless pit in which time and cash is thrown and very little comes back. And this despite the fact that the costs of launching an Internet shop today are a fraction of what they were in the past. For the business case to work out, every step needs to be just perfect, the shop needs to be compelling not just because of what it sells but how it sells. Succeeding on the Internet is a whole different game from the real world. And just because you are good at selling in the real world, does not mean you will be successful on the Internet.

The challenges to making money with Internet retail did not seem to bother anyone during the Internet retail hype period. In the end of the 1990s, every single possible type of Internet shop imaginable was funded with venture capital, from pet food to groceries. Some retail companies founded during the hype period actually crashed prematurely even in the midst of the New Economy bubble, which, given the euphoria surrounding the Internet and the willingness of investors to pour money into start-ups at the time, is quite something. An estimated $800 million was poured into building Webvan, an online grocer. To burn $800 million actually is an achievement – we are not talking about banking Ponzi schemes after all. Webvan went out of business in July 2001.[1] Pets.com folded in November 2000 after purportedly spending $300m. Its main claim to fame was its marketing campaign based on a sock puppet and an advertisement in the 2000 Super Bowl. An even more spectacular crash in terms of sheer speed actually occurred a few months before, in May 2000. You may not have heard of Boo.com before, a shop for trendy sportswear. The amount of money they burnt was less, only $120 million. But the web site was up and running only for six months.

There is one great success story in Internet retail. Amazon.com played the hype of Internet retail just right. Its timing was perfect, because it used the hype phase to fund the massive amount of pre-investment required to get its retail business going, build scale and to collect an unmatched amount of know-how. Amazon.com was founded in 1994, but generated its first profit only in Q4 2001. Unmatched Internet retail know-how is the key to Amazon's long-term success. Hundreds of thousands of Internet shoppers associate Amazon.com with a compelling shopping experience. There is a huge amount of trust in the brand, too. The management of Amazon.com is using its powerful consumer brand to extend the breadth of items sold and to transform it from a bookshop to an Internet megastore. One of the most ambitious projects of Amazon.com is to use the power of the brand to become less dependent of the costly retail business model itself and to extend into selling licenses for digital products, taking commissions on third-party business or selling software infrastructure as a service.

The million books project

The pioneers of Internet retail sold books. In fact, it would have been downright foolish to try to sell anything else in the early days of Internet retail. It probably helped that Jeff Bezos was a financial analyst working for an investment bank before founding Amazon.com, but going into bookselling was largely commonsense. And Jeff Bezos in 1994 was not the first online bookseller. For example, the company Amazon.com acquired in Germany to address one of the largest book markets in the world was founded two years before Amazon itself. The company ABC Book Service sold books on the German online service BTX, a subscription service comparable to CompuServe. In many other countries Internet booksellers were founded in the next few years. In Sweden, an online bookseller called Bokus was founded in 1997; we will hear more about their founding team because they moved on to start an Internet retail store in a different category and flopped miserably.

The reasons for choosing books are simple and practical. Books do not go stale and can be stored for a long time. Books do not have to be tried on to see if they fit. Dropping glass or porcelain is not a good idea. Dropping a book usually is fine which makes it easy to ship. Books are clearly identified by unique IDs, which makes them hard to confuse. People buy books many times a year; they are not singular, lifetime investments like a wedding dress. And if the wrong book was sent, then it is not a problem to send them back and sell them again. This is not the case with underwear or food.

But even the pioneers of Internet bookselling needed to proceed with caution. Just because books were easy to sell on the Internet did not automatically mean people actually wanted to buy books on the Internet. It just meant that the costs associated with selling books in Internet retail were lower than for other product categories. Costs definitely matter in this business but they are not the whole story.

Internet booksellers competed against other bookshops online, but they mainly competed against the classic bookstore. Most people love to spend time at a bookstore. It is nice to be able to physically browse a book before buying it. Sure, sometimes customers cannot easily get to a store. The classic Sears & Roebuck mail order business was a huge success in the 19th and early 20th centuries because it sold to customers who were sometimes days of travel away from all but the most basic types of stores. Because of this, Sears & Roebuck could sell things which were far more difficult to ship than books, like oil lamps or clothing. These reasons don't apply any more, most people live within close range of a bookstore – so why buy on the Internet?

The reason was selection. An average bookshop has about 100,000 titles on stock. ABC Book Service, the German online book company we mentioned earlier, already had 700,000 titles available in the early 1990s. And Jeff Bezos named his company Amazon because he had the objective of featuring the biggest ever number of book titles in his Internet store – one million titles. But selection is important to a customer only sometimes, it is not a killer argument. Bookshops will not go away any time soon. But it is valid and is a clear advantage that can be communicated. It turns out that selection and the ability to cater to specialist tastes is an advantage for many Internet businesses. As we will see, selection is central to "the Long Tail."

You can be sure that Jeff Bezos also did his homework by vetting the market size of his product category. The book publishing industry market is significant; in the US alone it was around $23 billion when Jeff Bezos started. More important than the overall market size is the actually addressable market. In the case of Amazon.com, the relevant subset was books that potentially appealed to the first Internet users. They were mostly male and technologically oriented, so computer books were an obvious category. Computer books were an incredibly successful specialist category of the book industry, with many new titles each year and strong sales. According to Amazon.com, the first book they ever sold was titled *Fluid Concepts & Creative Analogies: Computer Models of the Fundamental Mechanisms of Thought*. How much more specialized can you get?

There were, therefore, three important reasons why, in the beginning, it had to be books: books are cheaper to handle than other product categories, there is an advantage compared to real bookshops and the market size is significant. This is common sense, or so it seems – but common sense is the first thing to go in a hype phase.

Early death in May 2000

If, as an Internet start-up, you failed before the crash of the New Economy in 2001, you really did something drastically wrong. Actually, the company we are talking about now – Boo.com – had the right boxes ticked. They were experienced. The founding team had successfully started and sold a venture before. This previous start-up was Bokus, the Internet bookshop we mentioned from Sweden. It still exists today. There was more still. The founding team had an ex-model as CEO. They hosted glamorous parties, which participants still remember as the best in their lives. What more would one want. The only thing one could have criticized ex-ante was the awful name. But Boo.com would go down in history as one of the most spectacular failures of the New Economy ever. They went under in May 2000, after only six months of being online and having burned a whopping $120m in venture capital and strategic investment.

What the Boo.com management team needs to get credit for is for thinking big. But they made every mistake possible in Internet retail. They must have forgotten to analyze their addressable target group. Boo.com was supposed to be the ultimate website for trendy sportswear and dance fashion. At that time, the Internet was geek-dominated and mostly male. The average Internet user did not normally buy cool handbags and probably did not wear the newest shoes. Boo.com must also have forgotten to assess the impact that returns would make on their business case. Many products they sold were precisely those that get returned frequently because they do not fit. But these were not the worst mistakes. Nobody knows what the Boo.com team was thinking when they decided to offer shipping for free. The shipments partner of Boo.com obviously wanted money for the service. Since launching a global company from scratch is much more glamorous than just starting in one place, Boo.com probably was the first electronic commerce site that was launched in several countries at the same time. This added a huge amount of complexity to the challenges that already existed: Multiple currencies (this was before the Euro replaced several European currencies), multiple languages, multiple tax regimes.[2]

Almost a decade after the Boo.com crash, the ideal target group of Boo.com is finally online. The art student living in London but partying over the summer on an island in the Med would surely go shopping on Boo.com if it existed today. In all rich countries more than 50% of the whole population is on the Internet, making the addressable global market huge and diverse. There are many retail shops on the Internet today selling trendy stuff in several countries – and they are making money (for example, Natalie Massenet's Net-A-Porter.Com).

But the Boo.com team was too early – ten years too early. They were great fund-raisers, but they suffered from a severe reality disorder. At the time that Boo.com launched, the technology cost for even a simple retail web site was at least half a million dollars. Today, you can buy software for a tenth of that price. In fact, you don't even have to buy, install and run the software yourself; there are many cloud-based software services which are hosted remotely and charged on a subscription basis. Today, many logistics and shipping specialists offer specialized services for e-tailers. There are numerous payment facilitators which can be integrated easily into your website. Finally, you don't need a massive advertising budget. Thanks to Google, it is much easier to get found on the Internet than in the past. Friends can recommend your shop on Facebook. If costs are managed well, they are not the biggest challenge in Internet retail any more. You still need to create a compelling shopping experience from start to finish – that is the really hard part.

Being good at bricks is not enough

Severe reality disorder killed Boo.com. Before the Boo.com story becomes a complete joke, however, it needs to be said for the sake of completeness that Amazon.com's initial investment was massive as well. Amazon famously went on for seven years before being profitable. The Seattle-based company built a complete bookselling infrastructure of warehouses, inventory and web site technology from scratch. Wouldn't it have been much easier just to take an existing bookseller and add an Internet shop?

The major US book chain Barnes and Noble thought just that. So did many others. The term "bricks and clicks" became the battle cry of established retail companies against the Internet upstarts. In the late 1990s, Barnes and Noble mounted a massive "bricks and clicks" challenge against Amazon.com. Imagine the advantages: Barnes and Noble did not have preexisting mail order operations but they had the inventory. They also had warehouses to supply their bookshops. They had scale – they could buy books wholesale at much lower prices than most others. The most important advantage was in terms of marketing, however. Barnes and Noble was founded in 1917. Everybody knew Barnes and Noble – in the beginning, Amazon was merely a big river in Brazil. Bricks were a natural fit with clicks, right?

Wrong. Warehouse, inventory and shipping is the part that everyone can do. The problem is not the bricks, it's the clicks. Buying technology to power your web site is not enough. Barnes and Noble did that. You need to know exactly what to do with it. You also need to be paranoid, experiment constantly and get better each and every day. Amazon.com has a pure play Internet culture. They live, breathe, eat Internet. You can tell by the way customers navigate through the site. It is the way product categories are displayed and the way products are selected. Difficult trade-off decisions need to be made all the time. For example, the trade-off between helping your potential customer find exactly what he or she is looking for and making him or her see something else they may want to buy in addition. The shopping experience should not be like a navigating a medieval labyrinth with screens of stuff you are not interested in. At the same time, you want your customer to see other items which may be of potential interest, too. Amazon has always made the most out of the limitations of an Internet bookshop; on the Internet, you cannot walk the aisles and browse in the displays. Winning in Internet retail is not about warehouses, inventory and shipping, it is about creating the perfect online shopping experience. This is the only chance Jeff Bezos had against the onslaught of Barnes and Noble and he took it.

In hindsight, we know that Barnes and Noble did not manage to put Amazon out of business, despite all the advantages they had. On the contrary, Amazon prospered in coming years. Already by 2002, Amazon.com's revenues were $3.9bn (with 7,600 employees) – 3/4th of those of Barnes and Noble (with 50,000 employees).[3]

Today, if you have "bricks," however, there is no way to survive without "clicks." Many buying decisions are researched in advance on the Internet, even if it is only to look up the address of a shop. Luxury brands thought for the longest time that it would be damaging for their image to be present on the Internet. Today, Gucci, Hermes and Prada have some of the best-designed web sites around. They also combine their Internet presence extremely well with their flagship stores and their advertising campaigns as part of a combined marketing strategy. Flagship shops with their gallery spaces and cafés are excellent to convey an authentic brand experience.[4] The web is perfect at describing product features and value in detail. Luxury products, outdoor gear and cars – all these categories benefit from detailed explanations of their products and could not survive without a strong web site presence today.

But there still remains a lot of conflict inherent in "bricks and clicks." It gets messy when the brand manufacturers start to sell directly over the Internet. Retail brands selling online are a threat to their traditional sales channels, the "bricks" retailers. And it works the other way, too. "Bricks" retailers selling directly over the Internet are interfering with the Internet marketing presence of the brands. Channel conflict and cannibalization are further reasons why real-world retail operations are having such a hard time coping with the Internet. And this conflict between the manufacturers and retailers is heating up even though the majority of product revenue is still generated conventionally in real-world shops.

Why do brand manufacturers actually risk channel conflict with their most important partners for what still is a relatively small fraction of their business? They are not really dependent upon Internet retail revenues. The reason is the value of direct customer relationships and the value of data. Direct customer relationships help both the big gorillas and the small shops. Just take the example of Howies.co.uk, a small, organic cotton skate wear jeans maker. By selling directly online, they save the costs for a real store and also benefit from their direct customer feedback. If you are a gorilla and collect a massive amount of data, advanced analytics can tell you not only how successful you are selling your current product range, it can even help you make predictions about emerging product trends. Nobody wants to miss out on direct relationships and the power of data. We will describe later in this chapter how some of the upcoming Internet retail companies are using the power of data to generate a completely new retail experience which feels much more personal than ever before.

The "Long Tail" vs. "superstar economics"

In 2006, the renowned journalist and magazine editor Chris Anderson came out with a truly phenomenal book. *The Long Tail* is one of a small handful of essential books written thus far about the Internet and its impact on society. The book describes what one could call the democratization of consumption. The concept is actually quite simple, but the implications are huge. The concept applies to many business models on the Internet, one of them being Internet retail.

Anderson's concept starts with a particular understanding of society: a belief that we all are different and have our own individual tastes. The Internet provides us with a possibility we have never before had in our human existence – access to unlimited diversity on a global scale. Now that consumers have unlimited choice, they are not shackled any more to mainstream tastes. Anderson does not believe that mainstream will disappear completely, but he does think that the golden days of mainstream music, films and books are over. He dates the apex of mainstream to be 2001, when the boy groups were at the pinnacle of their success. From then onwards, the "Long Tail" takes effect.

Anderson based his hypothesis partly on previous research done on Amazon.com data, which sells a surprising amount of obscure and specialized books not available in a conventional store. This was Jeff Bezos' instinct from the very beginning, that selection was an important benefit of Internet retail. Even though books are easy to store, Amazon.

com is still restricted in the number of titles because warehousing costs have to be taken into consideration. For digital goods, incremental costs for additional products on sale is far less.

For this reason, Anderson's best example comes from Rhapsody, an online music streaming service. A normal music shop only can carry a small amount of titles, around 40,000. You need to be pretty old to remember the "Top 40," but even today a normal radio station only plays a very small roster of songs each day. Most people expected that on the Internet, too, people's buying would be restricted to the top titles. This was not the case. In fact, the more titles were added, the more were consumed. Rhapsody added more and more titles over time, expecting to get to the end of the "Long Tail" eventually. But even the 400,000th rated song – even if it was an obscure Japanese band playing Salsa music – would be streamed at least once a month (there is a very good Japanese Salsa band actually, called Orquesta de la Luz.) Welcome to the niche. Only 1% of the massive database of Rhapsody music tracks was so exotic that it did not get streamed at least once each month.

The term "Long Tail" is derived from the way a graph of purchasing data looks. Mapping popularity of consumer choices onto a chart results in a peak with the most popular choices and then a trailing off. The "Long Tail" itself is not a new discovery. What Anderson showed in a brilliant way was that significant money can be made with the "Long Tail." The "Long Tail" inspired a whole legion of entrepreneurs, marketing experts and public relations specialists and has changed their way of thinking about the consumer. Given the choices available today, it is not realistic to put people into boxes based on target groups any more. We are much more complex than the labels "baby boomers," "generation X" and "millenials." This is where heavy-duty analytics and viral marketing come in.

But we do not consume only Japanese Salsa bands either. We do like our Titanics, Harry Potters and our Avatars. Despite the "Long Tail," blockbusters are not dead. In fact, it is possible to argue that the Internet actually sometimes increases the blockbuster effect. Popular titles become even more popular in the networked Internet world of limitless communication. In 2008, Anita Elberse wrote a much-discussed criticism of the "Long Tail" theory in the July/August edition of the *Harvard Business Review* citing "winner takes all" and "superstar economics" on the Internet. In the previous chapter, we mentioned the related concept called "Metcalfe's Law" or "network effects." Actually, we all like bestsellers and we all like choice, too. Amazon makes money off both. So does Apple with iTunes. In the next section, however, let us explore those businesses that do not operate on significant scale. And which only cater to the "Long Tail."

Fighting the clutter

The Internet license shop iTunes sells hundreds of thousands of tracks. They make good money (even though that was hard, too). Amazon sells hundreds of thousands of books profitably (and that was a huge achievement). Both Apple and Amazon.com benefit from the "Long Tail" because that is one of their great advantages compared to real-world shops – they can cater to many more diverse and exotic tastes than any shop can. But behind iTunes and Amazon.com is the unknown band creating the music and the author writing a specialist book. And next to Apple and Amazon are a multitude of online shops which sell diverse things ideal for the Long Tail such as chili pepper seeds or natural pearl buttons. The question is whether the "Long Tail" actually works in the harsh world out there for the unknown music band and the small Internet shop owner.

If you have a small enough cost base, you can sell far less than an Amazon must to break even. But you still need to sell a certain amount. The problem small shops face is easy enough to describe. The more you sell, you can afford better marketing, design and technology. But to sell more, you need great marketing, design and technology. Getting found in the clutter out there on the Internet is the challenge.

In theory, this is where technology kicks in. Intelligent search and filtering technologies were identified by Chris Anderson as absolutely essential aspect of the success of the "Long Tail." Otherwise, nobody would find your unknown band or shop. The secret with these technologies is not in the processing power, it is in the availability of data about consumer choices. James Surowiecki, called this wisdom of the crowds. Amazon has so much data on book-buying patterns that not only can it recommend you a book based on what else you have bought or looked at, it can differentiate based on other factors as well. If you browse a certain book in one country, you are recommended a different title compared to browsing that same book in another country. What all of these systems do well is reward popularity. And they pick up on rising popularity – so that this becomes a self-enforcing virtuous circle. This is what "superstar economics" actually is about.

The intelligent search algorithms out there being run by Google, Apple or Amazon are the unknown band or small business owner's best friend but they are also their worst enemy. Google is a massive improvement compared to any search engines that existed before, but there also is a lot out there competing for Google's attention. Amazon's recommendations technology is probably among the best in the world. But the specialist book title is one in a million. Recommendations on Facebook are great, but 500 plus million people are recommending stuff every day. The question is, how does one get momentum in that self-enforcing spiral of popularity?

This is why for smaller entities on the Long Tail, nothing can replace old-fashioned word of mouth. Or at least word of email, word of blog, word of Wikipedia or word of Facebook. People have to recommend you to their friends. This is the only way to grow, despite what your search engine optimization consultant is telling you. Sure, you need to get the basics right and you need to be found on Google. You need a certain technical and Internet marketing savvyness and if you don't have it you have to acquire it. But this is not enough. You need loyal customers who will recommend you. Or readers. Or listeners. If you are not compelling enough to have a certain popularity, you will never make enough money with your band or your Internet shop to live off it. And no, the far, far end of the "Long Tail" will not sustain your livelihood. You need to edge just a little closer to where the blockbusters are to survive.

The future of the shop is personal

Let us go back in time for a moment. In the good old days, you entered your corner shop and the shopkeeper knew your name. He also knew your tastes and needs. Please note that this shop from the mythical past was not terribly large. It was probably not possible to even see all the products – a lot of items were tucked away in back rooms or the cellar. Buying was not a stroll through aisles and aisles of goods; instead, it was like having a conversation. If we would not move around so much and juggle our lives between different cities constantly, then perhaps this type of personal relationship with a shopkeeper could even exist today.

Back to the future: The corner shop we just described is the number one guiding vision for Internet retailers today. It is not the sprawling department store or the huge shopping mall. The corner shop appeals to all alike: to mega Internet retailers such as Amazon or Zappos, to manufacturers establishing a direct Internet channel for their brand and also to business people running a specialized Internet shop on the "Long Tail."

There is a technical reason why the corner shop is the guiding vision for Internet retail. No one actually likes aisles. People do not like to browse through screen after screen of products. Through their recommendation technologies, modern Internet shops are able to recommend products to its buyers with increasing accuracy. Since these recommendations are intelligent, they are not perceived of as annoying, which is very important. Netflix has a powerful movie recommendation engine called Cinematch that uses a large amount of data points to create a personalized web page for each customer.[5] You can be sure that the technical gurus at Amazon are perfecting their recommendation technologies all the time.

More important than navigation and screen sizes is the direct relationship to the buyer. Through this relationship, the shopkeeper encourages further purchases and can understand his or her customer tastes and requirements much better. With incredible foresight, Doc Searls and his co-authors wrote a brilliant book already in 1999 called *The Cluetrain Manifesto*. The book was based on 95 theses, the first of which was "Markets are Conversations."[6]

You don't need a ton of technology to have conversations with your customers. Owners of a small Internet store such as Howies.co.uk do not talk much about their vision or their strategy, having conversations with their customers is simply what they do. From the perspective of the customer, it is just fantastic that a real live person is just an email away ready to answer your questions and make helpful recommendations.

At big and small sites alike, the Internet is being used to reintroduce a very personal approach to shopping. This is the main advantage that clicks retail has vis-à-vis bricks retail. Some Internet entrepreneurs have pushed personalization even further. Their model is not the corner shop with the friendly shopkeeper but the shopping club. Gilt Groupe, Ideeli, Hautelook and RueLaLa are examples of U.S.-based shopping clubs for luxury brands. It was actually the French who pioneered the concept with vente-privee.com. If the French don't understand shopping, who does?

Vente-privee.com works like this. By using a simple membership concept, unsold goods inventory of brand manufacturers are sold via a closed club. In this way, the products, which are way cheaper than in the shops, don't interfere with the normal channels. But please don't think of these Internet buying clubs as a sort of Internet-based outlet store. Yes, the outlet part of the story is valid and explains why the stuff is cheap. But the real advantage of these clubs is their access to customer data. The more they sell to their customers and the more the customers click on individual items, the more targeted the offers can be. And this concept cannot just be applied to Gucci handbags but also to other high-value goods such as travel services.

Even though the retail business model is straightforward, there is a lot of innovation. We are convinced Internet shops will develop even smarter ways to become more personal. This means there is a lot of opportunity in Internet retail, especially also for small businesses. However, Internet retail requires stringent cash management and a well thought-out business case. The basic costs of opening a shop have fallen, but there is still the heavy-duty stuff, especially around customer data analytics. Warehousing and shipment can be provided by specialized partners, but there is still a cost here. Getting listed on the search engines and marketing the web site requires painstaking work in building a loyal customer base who frequently click on your site. And the importance of deep experience required to create the ultimate Internet buying experience needs to be taken into consideration. Just because you are good at selling things in a real shop does not mean that you can sell online. None of this is a piece of cake. But if you succeed, you are not just the big name on Main Street; you are selling to the world.

CHAPTER 5

The fourth building block – commissions

Don't believe your clients are stupid

In the past couple of years, ant scientists have been getting very excited. Through a series of discoveries, they have located ever-larger so-called super-colonies of ants composed of interconnected nests. Previously, it was thought that different ant colonies don't get along with each other. Now we know that some actually do. One super-colony exists along a 6,000 km stretch of Southern European Mediterranean and Atlantic coasts. It consists of millions of nests and billions of worker ants. In 2009, ant scientists found out that several of these super-colonies in Southern Europe, California and Japan actually form a global mega-colony. They are not physically connected (yet) but when introduced to each other, they are cooperative, not competitive.

Ant hills are superorganisms. Superorganisms are composed of many individual organisms, sometimes millions of creatures, functioning as true teams. Each individual would not be able to survive alone for an extended period of time. Individual creatures will even die for the sake of the colony. In the living world, superorganisms actually are quite rare. Next to ant colonies, we see such true teaming in beehives. Other animal groups, such as bison or fish, actually crowd together mainly to protect themselves from predators. They do not exhibit complex interdependency and an advanced division of labor. This is why scientists are so excited about super- and mega-colonies.

Knowledge from how ant colonies work has been applied to business problems – such as for finding out the optimized delivery route. There is no leader ant with a master map telling the workers where to go. Learning from ants, scientists have developed an algorithm called Ant Colony Optimization (ACO), a software called AntRoute and much, much more.[1]

In his seminal book *Out of Control* from 1994, Kevin Kelly compared complex technology-based systems to biological systems. Kelly's timing was perfect because the World Wide Web was just beginning its spectacular success story as a global mega-colony. Early Internet visionaries such as Kelly applauded the www as a revolutionary platform to enable cooperation. What was important about this network-enabled collaboration was that it developed without centralized control, neither through government nor through large corporations (although it should be noted that government financed the nascent Internet). The new opportunities this created for start-ups and individuals was the main theme of Kelly's work.

The next two business models we are discussing, commissions and advertising, are business models ideally suited to enabling true teaming between different parties. They are perfect business models for an Internet mega-colony made up of millions of dispersed interactions between writers and readers, game developers and gamers, sellers and buyers, bands and listeners. None of our other business models – let us ignore for a moment the emerging financial business model – are so ideally suited to spread collaboration and monetary flows across multiple web sites as these two business models are.

Commissions and advertising are agent-based business models. The job of an agent is to bring together two parties interested in an exchange. This is why these two business models require a minimum of three parties to work: the seller, the buyer and the agent. Marketplaces like eBay involve three parties. Sometimes, when the agent does not operate a marketplace itself, there are four parties. Commissions Junction in the U.S. and Zanox in Europe are affiliate marketing companies which develop a tracking system used by publishers of web sites making referrals. In this case, the four parties are the publisher of a popular web site, the potential buyer, the seller and the agent. Publishers try to get potential buyers interested in a purchase made on another web site; Commissions Junction tracks whether a sale actually is made or not. These multiparty business models are different from the previous three models we looked at in Chapters 2, 3 and 4. There, we had just two parties: the client and the service provider, the subscriber and the service provider or the buyer and the shopkeeper.

Agents thrive in complex mega-colonies like the Internet with a lack of complete information. Due to a lack of information, parties which are potentially interested in a transaction cannot find each other. If agents do their job right, they serve as intelligent traffic coordinators through the chaos of the Internet. The Internet is all about traffic, and if you find a way of directing that traffic you can print money. Agents have to strike a delicate balance, however. They have to watch out they that are not too obtrusive. At the same time, they have to keep proving to their clients that they are worth their money.

There is an important difference between the two agent-based models, however. The commissions model only generates cash when the transaction actually is successful, when an item is bought or a service purchased. The sales risk is spread among the agent, the seller and the buyer. The agent accepts this risk because the reward is potentially higher. The higher the value of the sale, the higher the proceeds from the commission.

Commissions models are therefore particularly appropriate when the agent is a significant part in the whole sales process. Many marketplaces for goods and services use a commissions model. The role of eBay in the sales process is huge. Not only does eBay need to make sure that it attracts a large number of potential buyers to its marketplace, it also needs to make the end-to-end sales process as easy and secure as possible. The commissions model is the right one for eBay and eBay pockets the whole commission. Where there is no marketplace, the work to attract potential buyers is done mostly by the publishers. In this case, the publishers get the lion's share of the commission. At the end of the spectrum is advertising with a fixed fee for referrals. Commissions Junction actually offers both business models, commissions and advertising, to its clients, depending on the involvement of the publisher and the ability to track sales end-to-end.

Agents always have to be afraid that their clients act behind their back. In theory, this can happen in both agent-based models, advertising and commissions. However, single commissions payments often are larger and this makes it more tempting to do the deal direct. It gets especially dangerous for agents when transactions occur frequently between the same parties. eBay knows this risk all too well. It has a love–hate relationship with its so-called Power Sellers. Power Sellers use eBay as their sales channel to sell popular items such as printer ink cartridges or baby products. They are responsible for a large, recurring volume of sales and have clout on eBay. As they gain their own popularity, it becomes attractive to go direct and move off the site. Power Sellers then get to keep the commission for themselves. Or they threaten to take their business elsewhere, for example, to Overstock or Amazon which also allows third-party sellers on their web sites. This puts pressure on the commission margin.

More than the regular eBay customer, Power Sellers have negotiation clout and demand value in return for their commission. The agent needs to provide top service, such as easy automation in placing items on the site. The crux for eBay is that it needs to balance the needs of two very different sellers, Power Sellers who sell popular items over and over again and private individuals who use eBay as a global flea market to sell unique and used items.

In recent years, "Power Buyers" have appeared who purchase used items such as used media (CDs, games) or used electronics directly from consumers, saving them the trouble of listing the items on eBay. SecondSpin.com for used media or Gazelle.com for used electronics are examples of Power Buyers.

Life is not easy if you are earning a commission – but it can be very rewarding too. As long as sellers and buyers feel that the agent has delivered value, the commission is not a problem.

The beauty of C2C

It is a story told many times, including in an enjoyable book about eBay by Adam Cohen, but deserves to be told again because of its beauty. Zoom back to 1995, Bay Area. At that time, Apple still called itself Apple Computers and was not a media company yet. Pierre Omidyar was a young programmer at Apple Computers. On weekends, he developed an Internet platform which allowed people to sell used items through a private auction. Omidyar discovered the power of the platform when he offered a broken laser pointer for sale. Someone actually bought it – a huge surprise to Omidyar. He wanted to know if the buyer had understood the tool was broken. Yes, someone out there actually was collecting broken laser pointers.

Pierre Omidyar never ceases to mention that he never saw the people he developed his auction platform for as his clients. He wanted to create a tool, which would help the community because it would provide clear value: it helped people sell their stuff for a fair price. The idea of community has been hyped so much on the Internet that it has been largely forgotten what it means. Community does not divide the world into sellers and buyers, or into any other groups for that matter. It means that everyone benefits from each other. In terms of media consumption, it means that music is created by the listeners themselves. Or blogs written by readers. If applied to a marketplace, people are a seller one day and the next they are a buyer. Mutual benefit of all is the key aspect of all so-called consumer-to-consumer (C2C) platforms.

The beauty of C2C on the Internet is its scalability. A community on the Internet can grow to a massive, global size. People with very precise interests can find each other. They do the work, they even spread the word for you, you simply need to provide the platform. In the retail chapter we spoke about the "Long Tail." Well, the community populates the "Long

Tail." Without the power of C2C, the broken pointer would never have been found by the one person who collected this otherwise useless item. Today, eBay connects 90 million people worldwide in a global flea market with over 200m live listings. In 2009, the total worth of goods sold over eBay was $60bn, eBay calculated this to be $2,000 every second. But the really surprising number is that already in 1996, only a year after the platform was launched, 1,000 new auctions were listed on the platform each day.

There was a true need out there that was previously met by highly dysfunctional mechanisms in the real world. A flea market is fun to walk through – especially if it is warm and the flea market is in Paris. But chances are higher you will buy something you don't need than find exactly what you are looking for. In the previous chapter, we discussed why Jeff Bezos chose the category books – to have the advantage of selection that real-world bookstores don't. Well, selling books online is a bit better in terms of selection than selling books in a shop. Opening a global flea market is not just a bit better than the banks of the Seine; the sheer power of C2C creates something that simply cannot exist in the real world.

An Internet service that simply takes off like a rocket because it fulfills a need is a beautiful sight. We saw similar growth a few years later by watching Google, Facebook, Zynga and then Groupon take off. The next step is finding a way to monetize this popularity without destroying it. This sometimes is very, very difficult. In the case of eBay, it was not difficult at all because the auction-based marketplace concept fit so well with the commissions business model. The business model just kind of tagged along.

Pierre Omidyar initially did not take a commission for his community service. In fact, as the lore goes, Omidyar did not even think of money initially. What really bothered him, however, were the rising costs of his Internet service which quickly went up to $250 a month because of traffic. To cover these costs, Omidyar introduced a small commission which he could pocket when a sale was carried out successfully. Already in the first month after introducing the fee, he broke even. Very soon his business developed so well that he enjoyed profit margins of 80%. Running the platform cost very little and there were no marketing costs. The money – in the beginning in forms of cheques sent to his home – just poured in cramming his mailbox. Omidyar knew he was onto something big and quit his job at Apple Computers.

Living in the Bay Area, Omidyar was surrounded by the best venture capitalists in the world. Initially, they were not impressed by the concept of an Internet-based flea market. None of them understood the power of C2C. What was missing was one personal, enlightening moment – call it the laser pointer moment. According to Adam Cohen's book about eBay, only one venture capitalist actually tried the service himself; this was a Partner at the Benchmark fund. Once he tried it, he got it immediately. Benchmark invested $5m for 21.5% of the company. These $5m were later worth $4 billion. eBay actually was instantly so profitable that they never needed the money from Benchmark in the end.[2]

In 2005, *The Economist* published a fascinating graph created by two scholars who studied business models for many years, Raffi Amit from Wharton and Christoph Zott of INSEAD. This chart showed the stock value of different flagship Internet companies and how they fared before and after the crash of the New Economy. Almost every player – even successful companies such as Amazon – went through a massive hype bubble before 2001 and then declined rapidly. The only company which hardly was dented over this time period was eBay (the success story of Google came a little later). From 1999 to 2004, the profit of eBay grew year on year by more than 40%.[3]

This stunning growth in times of economic hardship shows that people like to look for better deals in bad times, including buying used items on eBay's global flea market. It also shows, however, something else. eBay was able to scale incredibly well in those years. Once its platform was set up and running in an automated way, growth simply meant more and more profit. eBay did not have to deal with shipments, nor with warehouses – all this was handled by the sellers themselves. eBay profit margins for a long time were at 40% or more. This is the beauty of a C2C business.

Listings * ASPs * Conversion Rates = GMV

The strength of the commissions business model is that the interests of the agent and the seller are aligned. Both can only make money once the sale goes through. This is not the case with the advertising business model, even if it is tweaked to reflect success-based metrics such as clicks on advertising links. Some agents working with commissions seek an upfront fee to engage, such as eBay, which requires a listing fee. Usually, however, the listing fee is low because it would otherwise dilute the powerful message that the agent sends to the seller – "I don't get any money until you do." The reason for the listing fee is to prevent marketplaces such as eBay from getting cluttered with completely hopeless and low-value stuff.

In their best-selling book *Freakonomics* from 2005, the economist Steven Levitt and the *New York Times* journalist Stephen J. Dubner famously prove that real estate agents actually don't have an interest in selling a client's house for the maximum value. They instead try to maximize their overall turnover of all their house sales. This means that agents generally try to sell houses quicker so that they can move on to the next one. This means that the selling price on average is a bit below the highest possible market price. Yes, this slight difference in alignment between agent and seller applies to all kinds of agent deals which are similar, also on the Internet. Overall, however, we are sure that even Freakonomists would agree that the commission model is a great way to incentivize an agent to do his or her best to make the perfect sale happen: fast and for a good price.

eBay invests a huge amount of experience and money into providing the right conditions for the perfect sale. This is all about how products are searched for, appear in the catalogue, how items are displayed up to the whole choreography of the auction process. eBay allows buyers to automate the bids in advance – much like sophisticated traders on Wall Street can. Levels and alerts can be set. eBay allows you to scan for auctions where no one has bid yet – here you can make a potential killing.

The ingredients of success are described in a simple formula called Gross Merchandise Volume (GMV). Morgan Stanley uses it to evaluate eBay's performance. GMV is made up of the number of listed items (Listings) multiplied by the average sales price (ASP) multiplied by the conversion rate. All three factors are immensely critical to eBay's success as an agent.[4]

Fraud

One of the strongest factors influencing the success of a marketplace is trust. Especially in a C2C environment such as eBay, where people sell to other people, trust is absolutely essential. A buyer will not participate in a bid if he or she suspects fraud. Thus fraud has an impact on sale prices as well as conversion rates. Through these two metrics, which are part of GMV, fraud influences the revenue line of eBay directly.

The most important ally that eBay has to combat fraud is the Internet community itself. The star-based rating system of eBay is the best-known self-regulation mechanism on the Internet. It is the pride of eBay. People love to collect things – game developers picked up on this, too – and a history of cute stars with different colors means you are a good Internet citizen. In the eyes of analysts, the eBay's ratings database is one of the main barriers of entry the company has to shield itself from competitors. In fact, without it, eBay would not work. According to Adam Cohen, Pierre Omidyar invented the system out of necessity in the early days of eBay because he could not deal with the sheer volume of questions and complaints by members of his community.

The rating system has its weaknesses, however, which eBay is trying to fix by continuously tweaking the system. One popular approach is to sell many lower-value items on eBay truthfully to build up a solid reputation. With his or her exemplary report card, the seller then puts up a fraudulent higher-value item for sale. A further weakness of the system is that many buyers don't give negative feedback because they are afraid to get negative ratings themselves in the future. eBay has tried to solve this problem by making ratings anonymous.

Cute stars alone cannot make the world a better place. Tough policing is necessary, too. It is a well-known secret that eBay employs its own fraud-busting team and it isn't small. Also, eBay probably uses some sophisticated fraud-detection analytics software. You can be sure that anti-fraud measures are a significant cost item that even the CFO of a company with annual revenues of approximately $8bn notices. Next is its community ratings database, eBay's ability to fund a fraud team is another barrier to entry vis-à-vis competitors. So don't forget that item in your own Internet business plan – venture capitalists won't buy the fact that community self-enforcement alone solves all trust problems.

The B2B trap

The picture-book success of eBay in the late 1990s attracted a huge army of entrepreneurs. The thinking at the time was pretty easy. If an Internet-based flea market for consumers can be so successful, then a "serious" marketplace for companies must be the absolute killer service. Think of all the markets where a lot is traded at high frequency: used industrial machines, specialty chemicals or used office equipment. The list goes on and on. What an opportunity compared to a flea market.

The thousands of entrepreneurs and the venture capitalists that financed them could not have been more wrong. Established enterprises from many different industries pitched in, fearing they would otherwise miss a once-in-lifetime opportunity. They were also wrong.

One of the biggest blow-ups was VerticalNet, a marketplace that actually made it to NASDAQ. Most other B2B marketplaces didn't ever make it that far. In 2000, VerticalNet – it's stock ticker was VERT, was valued at $10bn. The results were more than dismal. In Q2 2001, for example, VERT generated $33m of revenues on a loss of $219m. VerticalNet managed 59 industry specific marketplaces, including e-Dental.com, which sold equipment for dentists. After the massive loss in 2001, VerticalNet announced it would shift its business toward supply chain software.

What caused the failure of the many hundreds of so-called B2B marketplaces at the end of the 1990s and the early 2000s? It is not immediately obvious why a commissions-based marketplace would succeed in a C2C context but would fail in B2B. The B2B failure teaches us an important lesson which applies to all commissions-based marketplaces. It has a lot to do with the advantage of the Internet relative to the real world. There is less comparative advantage of the Internet compared to the real world in B2B businesses for three reasons: high efficiency in the real world, established mechanisms for trust and the importance of associated services.

Real-world competitors to eBay are flea markets, classified ads in newspapers or pin boards in schools. All these real-world competitors are not terribly effective. The Internet makes a real difference in terms of the pure size of the participating community, the ease of search and the fun of the bidding mechanism.

In the cut-throat world of business procurement, however, where a 0.5% margin difference is a lot, this is not the case. Predating the Internet by centuries, B2B exchanges have existed for a long time, such as the Chicago Mercantile Exchange (CME) which originated in the so-called Chicago Butter and Egg Board. The Butter and Egg Board was founded in 1898, but was based on Chicago-based trade that itself already was decades old. Suppliers in the business world employ legions of representatives with deep know-how in their respective areas. Business buyers are armed to the teeth with advanced supply chain and procurement software. Efficiency already is very high in the real world. The Internet can improve things, but only by a bit.

Next to the high level of efficiency present in real-world B2B procurement processes, there are powerful, existing relationships based on trust in the real world. In many industries, specialized ways have been found to control fraud. The supply of diamonds, for example, is controlled by a handful of families. These families conduct trade in a small handful of places like Antwerp, in ways largely unchanged since the Middle Ages. There, buyers and sellers literally walk around the streets with pockets full of diamonds. A computer is not required, let alone the Internet.

A third explanation for the failure of B2B Internet marketplaces is that in many industry segments, buying and selling is not enough. The procurement of industrial and business supplies more often than not is linked to complex processes and services related to expert knowledge on valuation, logistics and installation. For this reason, companies often prefer to work together with two or three suppliers which they know can cover the whole range of services required. The Internet is just one part of a comprehensive service. NASDAQ-listed Dealertrack, for example, provides 17,000 automotive dealers with financing and offers its own sales and inventory solutions to its clients.

All this does not mean that the Internet does not provide advantage in B2B trade. However, it is absolutely critical to understand not just the precise sales process but the pre-sales and after-sales services required in the specific industry segment. Many VCs and entrepreneurs just did not do their homework in the late 1990s and early 2000s.

Beware of the smart client

We have described some reasons why B2B Internet marketplaces frequently fail. However, we have so far left out one of the worst threats. Since this threat actually applies to all agent businesses, it is worth exploring in more detail. This threat robs an agent's sleep at night. It is the fear of their own clients becoming too smart. Although contracts between sellers and their agents try to create a legal bind for that specific item sold, there is often very little preventing a seller to take advantage of the relationships of the agent in subsequent sales. Smart clients remove the middleperson, splitting the commission between seller and buyer. The higher the frequency of recurring sales to a given set of buyers, the higher the risk.

On many B2B marketplaces, the risk is very high. Take machine tools, for instance. Let us assume there only are a few potential buyers of a specific type of powder-coating machine used in automotive parts production worldwide. The initial sale of the first used machine to a new buyer is brokered by agent. Once the seller has persuaded the buyer that his or her machine tool is reliable and trustworthy, the seller would be foolish if he or she did not offer to sell directly to the automotive parts manufacturer, splitting the commission with his buyer. This is why understanding the structure of that specific market and industry are absolutely critical to the success of an agent-based business.

The problem of so-called Power Sellers is one of the greatest challenges eBay has. Power Sellers may have special access to good and cheap products, for example, electronic toys. Or they are particularly smart at packaging, labeling and marketing their products or services, such as sets of gardening tools and seeds. Perhaps they are specialists in one specific area where they have deep know-how, such as antique furniture. What Power Sellers want is actually quite simple – they demand a lower commission and threaten to move their business to another platform or "go direct." One Power Seller leaving eBay won't make the world go under. But since they sell large volumes over the platform, if many Power Sellers move, it does hurt financially. Obviously, eBay is in a difficult situation. There is a lot of temptation to lower the commission just a little for those making large sales. But where do you stop. Every fraction of a percent has a significant impact on eBay's earnings. How much of this can eBay actually afford is the real question.

The negotiation power of the Power Sellers increases with the likelihood of the threat. In the past, it actually was quite difficult for Power Sellers to move their business elsewhere. In the past, eBay has been very lucky to be the number one gorilla. Second-ranked marketplaces have a hard time, because buyers and sellers love to congregate in the most popular places. There are only a few countries where eBay is not number one. Yahoo! outsmarted eBay in Japan with its own eBay-like offering. Tim Jackson, a British entrepreneur with a platform called QXL got to Poland first with huge success. And China is dominated by Alibaba, where eBay has a minority stake.

Today, however, even in markets traditionally dominated by eBay such as the U.S., Power Buyers can move their business elsewhere. In fact, there really is a war going on between the different platforms competing for the business of the Power Sellers. One destination is specialized marketplaces. There is a significant secondary market for concert and sports events tickets which is addressed by some successful marketplaces focused exclusively on tickets. eBay acquired one of these, called StubHub, in 2007 for $310m. Another competitor in this segment is RazorGator; it is financed by one of the best-known venture capitalists in Silicon Valley.

Then there is Amazon. Amazon.com for some years now allows smart sellers to sell directly on its platform. Starting with used books, Amazon is expanding its third-party business since it enjoys the inroads it is making into the commissions model. Amazon loves the attractive profit margins and does not have to deal with logistics, warehouse costs or shipping.

Potentially the biggest threat to eBay is Power Sellers going direct. What has been very difficult in the past – namely to set up one's own shop on the Internet and sell to consumers – is now becoming easier. Shop technologies which used to cost an arm and a leg in the past are virtually free today. Most importantly, perhaps, is that smart sellers who are benefiting from rising popularity accelerate their ratings on Google. If they are lucky, their rise to fame can be a self-enforcing spiral of popularity, courtesy of Google algorithms. We have spoken about the challenges of the retail model in the last chapter. Retail is what Power Sellers do and as tricky and dangerous the game with Google is (we will see this in the next chapter), the option of running a small shop on the Internet has become more attractive. Everyone has more options these days. Sellers can work with an agent like eBay, but can go direct, too.

All this, specialized marketplaces, flirting with Amazon and going direct, adds to the negotiation power of the Power Seller on eBay. And as we said, eBay can't just lower its commissions for big sellers substantially even if it would really like to do this. What eBay tries to do instead is increase the value of its services as an agent. eBay has a special executive position in all its major markets called Head of Seller Experience. This executive has a whole team just dedicated to improving the seller experience though technology and services. eBay has put in considerable effort to improve the ways that sellers with a large amount of simultaneous sales can manage their activities through a type of seller's cockpit. Life is not easy, even as the dominant C2C marketplace gorilla.

Reports of the death of the intermediary

When the first businesses appeared on the Internet, there was a lot of discussion regarding the death of the middleperson. The pet term everyone used was disintermediation. What the debate referred to at the time were intermediaries from the real world. One powerful example comes from the travel industry. Twenty years ago, people planned their trips in the offices of travel agents. Even the student backpacker with the Eurail pass and no fixed plans would trudge down to the STA travel agent – at least to book his or her flights. The Internet hit the travel industry like a tsunami. Today, when we book travel, we have many different options. We can go direct completely, using the Internet to book hotels and flights directly at the hotels and airlines themselves. Since so many local services are online today, we can go down to a microscopic planning level, such as reserving and paying for a train ticket directly from home – perhaps thousands of miles away. When we book directly at the provider, we engage services sales transactions. We discussed this business model in Chapter 2. This is disintermediation big time – because the traditional agent loses out.

But reports of the death of the intermediary have been exaggerated. Despite the fantastic possibilities to buy direct on the Internet and go directly to every manufacturer of products and each provider of services, intermediaries still seem to persist. We frequently book our flights and hotels using travel web sites such as Expedia or STATravel.com which sell travel packages or offer us price comparisons among several airlines. The old intermediary has died, but a new one has appeared in his or her place. This new intermediary is a completely different animal from the old. It is truly last-minute, providing almost real-time access to newly available offers. It is powerful in the sense that it equips us with advanced analytical price comparison capabilities. And it is personalized in the sense that it can suggest to me very individualized travel ideas based on my previous choices and those of thousands of others who booked trips before me.

The commission that these travel web sites make is hard earned. There is a massive amount of competition, and while there are a few exclusive travel services, the emphasis in the travel industry is on low price. In fact, there are price engines comparing different travel price engines. Effectively, these comparative price engines are disintermediating the new intermediator. eBay tried to sue such a comparison engine when it appeared. The battle to offer better and better services from analytics to personalization is really tough. The greatest prize is scale. With scale, an agent can afford lower margins, which in turn means lower prices and this again, more customers. Even more importantly, scale can provide negotiation leverage to achieve better prices from sellers such as travel service providers.

Cut-throat competition among agents applies to many B2C Internet services, not just in travel. The Internet is full of financial service agents such as Lendingtree, where buyers can compare different mortgage offers or apply for loans. Services such as Mint.com compare a whole range of financial services. A moment of sympathy for the agent is called for. The agent will not die because of the Internet, but survival is a lot tougher than it used to be. And the agent will always need to prove that he or she is providing value to earn their commission.

CHAPTER 6

The fifth building block – advertising

You force it, you lose it

Advertising seems at first to be pretty one-sided – great for one party, bad for the other. The publisher of a web site receives money for the advertising on his or her site regardless of whether the ads are successful or not. Even so-called performance-based Internet advertising only takes clicks or other consumer actions into consideration, not actual sales. The company paying for ads has no certainty that the ads will actually lead to more sales – but has to pay anyway.

However, what seems to be a good deal for the publisher on first glance actually is not. Advertising is a tough business model. The reason is fierce competition. This is the Internet, not the golden age of television a couple of decades ago when the broadcast spectrum was tightly controlled. On the Internet, the number of web sites is unlimited – and so is potential advertising space. Publishers and their agents have to break their backs to differentiate themselves from all the other web sites selling ads. Mostly, this means having the biggest reach and the best target groups. Differentiation also means finding better, increasingly sophisticated ways to get consumers to engage with an advertisement. One company, Offerpal Media, gives money to people who are willing to look at Internet ads. Therefore, advertising is not an easy game to play; publishers and their agents share sales risk too, not directly like in the commissions model, but indirectly. Advertisers will often test different web sites and abandon those that do not yield the desired results.

Creating value in advertising is so tough because the seller and his agent are caught in a classic catch-22 situation. The seller and his agent need to prove to their clients that their advertisement will lead to success. The more they push their ads on the visitors of their web sites and try to force engagement, the higher the likelihood of achieving the opposite effect. People will find the ads horribly annoying or, worse still, an intrusion on their privacy. This catch-22 situation does not just apply to obvious situations such as large, obnoxious banner advertising on a web site. It can be more subtle, too. It is often claimed that targeted advertising is less obtrusive because it is actually tailored to a potential customer's interests. However, the more personalized the ad is, the greater the risk that people will have privacy concerns. And people don't like disguised ads either.

The best way to avoid the Internet advertising catch-22 is to create a situation where an implicit agreement is reached between the publisher, the agent and the end customer. This happens when the customer knows what the deal is and actually supports it. We call this "advertising as a service." This type of dream deal happens on well-crafted classifieds ads sites, such as Craigslist or Monster.com. Here, the customer seeks out the web site on purpose to find ads. The content of the web site are the ads itself. Google tries to offer its search customers a useful mix of information and subtle, but clearly labeled targeted advertising. Creating ads that the end customer sees as a service is the ultimate goal. But usefulness is not the only way an ad can be a service.

The opposite of information-based, utilitarian approaches are advertisements that themselves are entertainment or become part of a customer's lifestyle. Certain cleverly made YouTube videos have become classic Internet favorites. One of these was a video of babies on roller skates celebrating the Evian brand. People love to send these lifestyle ads to their friends because they love them so much. Some sponsored online games have the same effect. To be clear, however, a lot of this marketing activity actually does not involve the advertising business model. The business of Evian is selling water. Placing a video on the YouTube or publishing an online game is not advertising because no one, apart from Evian, is making money.

To be advertising, there have to be more parties involved, not just the consumer brand and the consumer. An appealing banner ad on a lifestyle web site is advertising – and if it is really attractive it can work even without algorithms. Social networks such as Facebook are a part of the lifestyle of hundreds of millions of people. Facebook explored advertising for several years in order to find non-intrusive ways in which ads can become a part of social network lifestyle.

Advertising involves three different parties if the publisher and the agent happen to be a single company. The three parties are the publisher selling the ads, the advertiser buying the ads and the consumer engaging with the ad. Classifieds web sites such as Craigslist and Monster.com are great examples – they create content and sell ads. Google does this, too, with its search advertising offering. Here, Google mixes search results which are the main content piece with ads ("AdWords") on the right side or on top of the results. Facebook is a part of the three-party ad camp, too.

Sometimes, the publisher and the agent are separate entities. Now we have four parties: the publisher providing the reach, the agent selling the ads, the advertiser and the end consumer. Google plays this game very well, too. Its "AdSense" offering is an agent-based service which places AdWords on third-party publisher web sites in an automated, context-sensitive way. DoubleClick, a company Google acquired in 2007, is an agent which runs banners on publisher's web sites and takes care of the important backend stuff such as ad delivery, reporting and payment.

We did make a little pitch for lifestyle, but, let's face it, lifestyle often is not enough. It is not smart showing a skateboard ad to an elderly farmer. Unless he wants to buy one for his granddaughter. One of the main areas of investment by publishers and their agents – in the competitive battle to win over advertisers – is data crunching and analytical capability. There actually is a virtual arms war going on as sellers of advertisement inventory everywhere are rushing to upgrade their technologies. Several technology companies and start-ups are the arms manufacturers; they are focused on providing software and services in the area of analytics and ad management.

Initially, sellers of ads offered simple reporting of clicks on their web site and on ads. Today, automated customization technologies are commonplace. This means that a consumer's own personal click pattern on the web site is driving content and ads selection. Based on what you do on the web site, you see other content and ads compared to someone else. Customized content is as important as customized ads, because the longer you keep people on your web site, the more ads they will potentially engage with.

It gets really interesting when different types of data from different sources are combined and ad data becomes part of a whole new way of doing business. Data is fundamentally changing business today. Imagine the following scenario. The web site you are interacting with is not static but completely responsive based on what you click on. It makes predictions about which types of products you may be interested in. For example, it predicts color preferences or travel destinations. The color of the car you see in the display ad has been customized to your preferences. Or, the advertisement for a travel service already shows a photograph of your favorite destination. But it does not end with the advertisement. Your click on the ad and subsequent clicks in the car manufacturer or travel provider web site in turn leads to a better understanding of your consumer preferences – and those of thousands of others of consumers like you. This information is being used by product development and research.

Production of certain car types is increased to meet rising demand. New, upcoming travel destinations can be identified. Internet advertising is part of a much bigger story where different, previously isolated business activities are now fused together.

In the previous chapter we mentioned the true teaming behavior of ants and bees. The two agent-based business models, advertising and commissions, are perfect business models to enable new models of partnership between different companies in a world of complex data flows.

Spam and pushy banners

In the beginning of the World Wide Web, search was pitiful tragedy. Search results on the Internet were so bad that when by chance a good result came up, the link was bookmarked and saved for future use. Why? The likelihood was high that otherwise you would never find it again. Even the best search engine at the time, Altavista, delivered mediocre results. This was because search engines were highly susceptible to manipulation, so-called spamdexing, which consisted of embedding web sites with hidden key words. Bookmarks and human-made link collections actually were the best way to navigate the Internet at the time.

Yahoo! started in 1994 as a link collection of two Stanford University students. The acronym Yahoo! stood for "Yet Another Hierarchical Officious Oracle." The main term here is "hierarchical," signifying a well-sorted collection of web site addresses. The first links came from the founders David Filo and Jerry Yang themselves, but Internet users could also send in their favorite links. These did not get placed in the catalogue, automatically, however. Humans sorted out and organized the links. Despite the fact that Yahoo! used a lot of technology to support this selection process and to keep it continually up-to-date, the company was a media company more than a technology start-up. In the beginning, the main value of the company was its editors – the Yahoo! employees who selected and combined content.

The contribution of Yahoo! in the early days of the Internet is not to be underestimated – it made the World Wide Web accessible for millions of people by pointing out quality content among a mountain of useless trash. Yahoo! was among the first Internet IPOs when it listed in April 1996 – only eight months after the legendary IPO that initiated the Internet business era in the first place, that of Netscape.

Like established media companies, Yahoo! is financed by advertising. In the beginning, this was banner advertising. Display advertising was not much different from conventional advertising, such as in a magazine. Internet users hated banner ads as soon as they appeared. The Internet community saw the Internet as a means to democratically liberate information and to change the world. Banner ads seemed like a sell-out. Internet users would probably not have had such a big problem with banner ads, however, if they did not take up as much valuable screen space as they did. Here are some of the terms used to describe different types of banner ads when they are sold to advertisers: "Bigsize Banner, "Skyscraper," "Wide Sky" and "Wallpaper." Yes, being obtrusive is the point here. The first banner ads were not targeted – the likelihood that a farmer would get the skateboard ad was high. And the service did not know about the granddaughter, either. In general, people hated display ads – and still do. Tech savvy people download and install software that deletes display advertising from web sites. One of the most popular advertising blockers, the Firefox extension Adblock Plus, was downloaded 90 million times worldwide from the beginning of 2006 to the end of 2010.

Search revolution

In 1998, a web site was launched that would revolutionize how information would be found on the Internet. At first quietly, and then with a roar. Behind the stunningly simple Graphical User Interface of Google – with only an input field and not much more – was something absolutely extraordinary: an Internet search technology that actually worked. Google was the first search engine that with full consequence did not base its search on information found in the target web sites themselves, but on contextual information around the web site. Web sites could easily manipulate the information they featured on their web site – this is what spamdexers did – and this data was no indication of the quality of the site. Contextual information is much harder to manipulate. How often is the web site in question linked to by other sites on the web? More importantly, what kind of web sites link to the site? Are they trustworthy, highly popular sites of high standing or are they themselves "fake" sites created by spamdexers? To improve its results further, Google evaluates the click patterns on its own search results and a host of other data.

The difference between Altavista and Google was how computer intelligence was applied. Altavista used processing power, which was massive for the time, to analyze the content on the web sites according to set algorithms. It relied fully on artificial intelligence. As it turns out, this is not enough. Google founders Larry Page and Sergey Brin understood this very well. Google uses a massive amount of artificial intelligence but it also taps what some have called the "Wisdom of the Crowds." This is the title of a book by James Surowiecki published in 2004. The main thesis of the book is that the collective behavior and choices by many, many people (the more, the better) are a highly reliable source of information – provided the decisions are independently made. By tapping on the "Wisdom of Crowds," Google has become one of the best-known brands of the world, not just of the Internet world but of all brands. It also redefined how traffic flows on the Internet by making search work. It is impossible to understate the importance of Google.

By far most Internet searches today are carried out with Google. Because of this, Google has an unbelievably rich and broad understanding of which topics interest the world today. Google summarizes these topic trends and publishes them in it's "Zeitgeist" section. For example, the topic that moved the most people in 2009 was Michael Jackson's death, more than any natural disaster or political development. The fastest rising sports topic in the world in 2009 was not any US team or event, but the Spanish premier league soccer team Real Madrid. This shows how international the Internet has become. In his book *The Search*, John Battelle describes Google as a "Database of Intentions" and discusses the huge amount of power that this database confers. The data does not just point to what people do today, but what they may do in the future. The ability to make social predictions is the holy grail not just of marketing and advertising, but has massive implications for society, economics and business.

Google is aware of its power. The leitmotiv of Google, "Don't be evil" was chosen by the founders for a good reason. Public perception is clearly one of the main concerns that keeps Google managers awake at night. Google.org, the nonprofit organization of Google, uses the Google database, for example, to make predictions about possible global outbreaks of flu. There is a connection between the use of certain search terms and an approaching flu outbreak. This service is called Flu Trends. In early 2010, a decision by Google to pull out of the Chinese market in response to censorship brought the company right into the heart of an international political controversy. This was a brave move by Google given the importance of the Chinese Internet market.

Beyond doubt, Google has done a lot of good – especially for Internet business. What Google does in its search results is reward quality. Rewarding quality has helped a lot of small Internet shops, as we discussed in the retail chapter. Without Google, small enterprises would have a much harder time selling directly to Internet consumers – simply because no one would find them. Amazon and eBay would be even stronger than they are today in a world of imperfect search.

But while Google has perfected search in a revolutionary way, there still remains more to do. A whole industry has been established around so-called Search Engine Optimization (SEO) and Search Engine Marketing (SEM). In fact, these specialists are modern-day spamdexers. What they do is tweak web sites with the objective of achieving a higher page rank in Google. This has moved from a shady to a legitimate business by becoming a commonplace, even mandatory activity for any web site owner. Google actually recommends using SEO and SEM.

However, getting SEO or SEM expertise is expensive for a small business. It is not uncommon for an experienced consultant to charge US$4,000 a day for his or her services. The knowledge is so difficult to come by; it bestows "unfair" advantage. To keep the SEO and SEM people on their heels and shift the balance back, Google occasionally changes the way its algorithms work; sometimes this happens without any warning. As a result, highly ranked web sites are sometimes thrown way back in rankings and require time to reestablish themselves at the top. What is called the Google Dance actually can mean a tornado for small businesses. In his book on Google, John Battelle tells the story of 2bigfeet.com, an online retailer specialized on selling shoes made for very large feet. 2bigfeet.com almost lost its complete Christmas business in 2003 due to a very badly timed "Google Dance".[1] Without an occasional "Google Dance," however, spamdexers would slowly and surely degrade the quality of Google searches; dancing is a necessary evil.

"The wisdom of money"

Let's zoom back in time again to the early days of Google. While the Google founders Page and Brin were working on solving the problem of search, another entrepreneur was doing the same, but with a fundamentally different approach. Let us introduce the "other" search entrepreneur, Bill Gross. Gross is one of the few persons in the world who can work on several start-up ideas at the same time successfully. But he is not a venture capitalist. Bill Gross gets deeply involved in developing and executing a new business idea. He is a true modern-day inventor – and a multitasking one. Many businesses have emerged from his incubator IdeaLab, be it Internet ventures or solar energy companies. A significant number of these have been successful, even hugely successful. The problem is, however, IdeaLab is based in Los Angeles. For the pampered venture capitalists of Silicon Valley who love to point out that they invest only in a radius of a few miles, IdeaLab is worlds away.

In Silicon Valley, the Google founders perfected search using the "Wisdom of Crowds," an approach that trusts the opinion of large groups of people making independent decisions. In the incubator in Los Angeles, an approach was developed based not on wisdom but on money. A search result using the "Wisdom of Money" would work like this: the person paying the most for a specific search term appears in the top slot in the search results, using an auction mechanism. Charging for search results is a true spam killer. Now all need to fight the battle for attention with the same means – money makes honest. Gross called his new search engine "GoTo.com." But don't bother looking up GoTo.com on the web, you will find something completely different under that address. The history of the GoTo.com's search turned out very differently from that of Google.

The idea to take money for search placement was almost as revolutionary as the context-based search approach used by Google. Effectively, Bill Gross had dropped a neutron bomb on spamdexing. And Gross did not stop with this basic idea, he added two others. First, companies only had to pay when their search entry was actually clicked on. This performance-based payment scheme made his service more valuable for advertisers. But an even more important consideration for advertisers was that the GoTo.com web site needed to be popular in the first place. This is where Gross' second idea came handy. Bill Gross believed that companies would pay more for clicks on specific search results than for general banner advertising. In this way, Gross figured he could pay for his own marketing. He would place a banner ad for GoTo.com (for a bulk price) on a completely different popular web site (for example Yahoo!) and pay the equivalent of ¢10 per click. He would then sell the keywords on his site for ¢50 per click. To make money, he simply had to make sure people would keep clicking. These may not have been the actual figures, but that does not matter. Gross knew he had to pre-invest, since he started his auctions at a low level of ¢1, but he also made a business bet that the price for his success-based advertising offering would rise with time. And it did.[2]

Why was the invention of Bill Gross almost as revolutionary as Google itself? GoTo.com itself is gone; the company was renamed Overture and was sold in 2003 to Yahoo! But the invention of Bill Gross lives on stronger as ever because it is the idea behind search advertising. You can find an adapted version of GoTo.com on the right side of your Google search results – it is called AdWords. At the beginning of the 2000s, Google adapted the concept and improved it by combining it with their own search results. Many books on the topic of search cite a legendary meeting between the Google founders and Bill Gross in 2001 where a possible partnership was discussed, but collaboration never happened. Search advertising provided Google search with a business model. Since Google search results in the center of the screen are clearly differentiated from the advertising on the right side of the screen, end customers don't really mind because the ads are both relevant (to the search results) and also not intrusive.

While Bill Gross did not fare badly from Yahoo!'s acquisition, the winners were the Google founders who combined "The Wisdom of Crowds" with the "Wisdom of Money" to create a truly phenomenal web service and an ideally tailored advertising business model. Today, search advertising makes up more than half of all Internet advertising revenues – and Google takes the lion's share of this market.[3]

The death of the newspaper

So far, we have discussed two of the three main categories of online advertising: display and search. We also mentioned the companies most closely associated of each of these, Yahoo! for display ads and Google for search. The third ad category is classifieds. Craigslist is the champion of classifieds.

The name Craigslist is straightforward. It actually is the list of a guy called Craig. Most Internet users love Craig because his classifieds list is so comprehensive. About 50 million new classifieds ads are published on Craigslist every month. The web site ranks among the top 10 English-language web sites of the world. Craigslist remains down to earth, not only in terms of its minimalist, heavily retro ASCII-based user interface. Craig Newmark charges only for a fraction of the classifieds he lists, namely the categories real estate and jobs. All other categories are a free public service for the Internet community. This all fits to the person Craig Newmark, who is often described as a private, down-to-earth person himself. On his web site, Newmark describes himself in this way: "Craig continues to embrace his inner nerd, though he no longer wears thick black glasses that are held together with tape, and he retired the plastic pocket protector some years ago." No one can really hate this guy, right? Wrong.

In the media world, Craig Newmark is known as the person who killed newspapers. Let us assume that Mr. Newmark never set out to destroy newspapers when he started an email list of San Francisco events in 1995 (as a hobby while working as an IT consultant). But his unconventional, anti-establishment attitude is not making things easy for the media industry. First of all, this man refuses to sell his business to a newspaper company, although many tried to remove this troublesome competitor. Secondly, he has thus far stubbornly refused to carry out an IPO. The pressure of quarterly results would surely have led to a more business-like approach, rising prices for classifieds on Craigslist and a reduction of the proportion of free listings. If Craigslist were publicly listed, it would be easier for newspapers to compete with their own online classifieds offerings. It drives media executives insane that a simple Internet list, run by about 30 people out of the Bay Area, achieves placement in the top 10 web sites and cannot be tempted by all the money in the world.

Newspapers face several problems. With the exception of a few top brands, it seems very difficult for newspapers to make money on the web. In 2009, according to the annual Pew report, 90% of U.S. newspaper revenues still came from their print editions. And their overall revenues collapsed by 26% in 2009 alone. This is, of course, not just the fault of Craig Newmark. Hoards of other classifieds players have contributed as well, such as Monster.com, Autotrader.com and many, many others. Classifieds was always a safe provider of revenue for newspapers. It has moved online, but in doing so has shifted to specialist providers and away from the newspapers themselves.[4]

But online classifieds is only one of the problems that traditional newspapers face. Despite the popularity of citizen news web sites and Internet reporting sites such as Huffington Post and Drudge Report, which draw upon a large amount of citizen news and commentary, a majority of the news on the web still comes from legacy media, which produces original reporting. This content is financed by conventional TV or print activities. But almost half of total online ad revenues – the total pie of $22 billion in the U.S. alone according to the Pew Report – flows to search engines which aggregate the news. In a nutshell, even though a large part of the content on the Internet comes from traditional media, they are not getting paid for it. Their content is being aggregated by search engines and other Internet sites. There is much talk among the newspaper industry about blocking out the aggregators or charging for content, which would be a license sales or subscription business model. This is more a threat than reality, however, since newspapers need the aggregators and they need the online advertising – even though their overall share is small.

Too bad traditional newspapers missed the boat with Internet classifieds; their financials would look better today if they had not. Online classified web sites are very simple and straightforward; the ads are the content. People are not annoyed because they go to these sites explicitly to browse ads. Simplicity and honesty are the success formula of online classifieds. Why did newspapers miss this golden opportunity? Because they realized too late that classified ads work much better online than on paper. On the Internet, classified ads are more up-to-date, they are searchable and they can be just as local. The newspaper industry hung on to their old ways far too long; by the late 1990s, it was too late.

The sexiness of statistics

It would be interesting to compare who is lamenting the passing of the golden days of media more, media executives themselves or their counterparts in the advertising industry. Working for an advertising agency used to be utterly glamorous. It was as close to stardom one could come without actually being a star. This is so hard for us to believe today that "Mad Men," an award-winning TV series, had to be made to recreate those days. The complaint from the legacy admen can be summarized as follows. Well into the 1990s, advertising was about creating lifestyle. It was a world of mass consumption ruled by a couple of top brands. Back then, it was a colorful world full of promises set as a vibrant capitalist counterpoint against the drab greyness of communism behind the Iron Curtain. Today, advertising has descended into boredom, say the admen. It is only about science, statistics and efficiency. The Internet is to blame for this change.

Even in the golden days, some statistics were needed. At the top of the hierarchy in an ad agency, however, sat creative people who did not concern themselves with numbers. At the bottom were the media buyers, they had to work the spreadsheets. The instruments were very crude. It was all about Gallup polls, reach and target groups. The broadcast industry used samples of population to estimate how many people in which age groups, sex and with what economic background saw which programs. Newspapers and magazines had better access to data since many had subscribers in addition to anonymous newsstand buyers. In general, advertising in the past was a guessing game. While reach could be reasonably well measured, the effectiveness of an advertisement itself could not be confirmed. There was nothing to click on, no interaction. Even if product sales rose subsequent to an ad campaign, this did not necessarily mean that the ads were responsible for the success. Was it the ad or had some celebrity photographed pulled out a branded product on a red carpet somewhere? Consumer brand companies spent billions on ads with no way of measuring their direct effect. Working for an ad agency must have been loads of fun in those days.

By the late 2000s, the high times were finally over for traditional media and ad agencies. The volume spent on Internet advertising rose continually more than 20% each year. Traditional broadcast and print advertising, on the other hand, declined year on year. Traditional advertising still makes up the lion's share of the advertisement market with a global size of over $400 billion, but Internet advertising now stands worldwide at over $40 billion.[5] Especially in times of economic crisis – such as the late 2000s – Internet advertising benefits from the advantage of being much more measurable.

Ad pricing schemes on the Internet are variable and performance-based. Take Google ads, for example. The price of an ad is determined by a transparent auction mechanism – not in a back room of a hotel suite. The buyer of advertising only pays if the ad actually is being clicked on by a user – which is a pretty good indication of interest. What this means is that risk is shifting increasingly from the advertiser to the agent and the publisher. The more success-based advertising becomes, the more it will be similar to the commissions business model, which pays only on actual sales success.

Our bet is, however, that the two models will never fully merge. This is partly because businesses find the distinction between advertising and commissions useful. We know it from our real-world experience. There are many different situations, which favor fixed fee approaches such as advertising as there are those better suited to commissions. Classifieds, for example, work very well with a fixed listing fee. Fixed ad fees are straightforward and easy to understand. If you are a third party selling on Amazon's web site, however, expect to be charged a commission since your host is significantly involved in the sales process. What we are saying is that hard data and the measurement of effectiveness have made the demarcation line between the two business models less clear. Risk is distributed more evenly than before between advertisers, publishers and their agents. Affiliate marketing companies such as Commissions Junction actually sell their leads according to either an ad or a commissions model, depending on the particular situation.

Hard data on advertising success enables risk sharing and new commercial models between the involved parties, but, in addition, it opens up a far greater opportunity for advertisers. It gives advertisers, publishers and their agents an on the fly ability to change and adapt their approach during an ad campaign. In its advertising exchange for display ads, Google allows advertisers to bid in real time for banner spaces. It then switches banners in flight. The banners on Google's DoubleClick AdExchange are targeted according to geographic locations, target groups and times. More or less anonymous data such as click patterns or IP domains can be combined with data from personal services such as Google or Yahoo! email or from social networks such as Facebook or LinkedIn. Ads are tested in a certain environment; if they don't work, a switch is made. The objective of all this real-time adaptation; targeting or personalization is to make advertising more and more effective.

But this is not all. Hard data and in-flight experimentation has the potential to change the role of advertising in business. The Marketing Department used to be a separate entity in the company which was given the job: "Help sell this." One of the things Marketing did was to set up advertising campaigns. This has changed radically. Through the power of online advertising, the Marketing Department has now moved into the center of the organization. The better measurable advertising is, the more it can be used as an input for core business activities such as manufacturing, supply chain management or R&D. If people click on the ads of certain products or services more than others from the company, this probably means demand for those products or services will rise. People can be asked to interact with advertising, not just through online questionnaires but through more playful and sophisticated means. People will try on different clothes virtually in an ad.

So-called sentiment analysis is a widespread business intelligence approach which can be used to detect the "mood" of Internet discussions in blogs, forums and in Tweets. The technology was originally used for fraud detection. Brand managers use it to better understand how their brands are perceived by consumers. Data from advertisements can be combined with other data from call centers, real-world shops, GPS location-based information to reveal what people are thinking about certain products and services, as well as when and where they are thinking this.

Data helps us understand what people think today, where they think what they are thinking, and most importantly, what they will probably think tomorrow. We are only at the beginning of massive changes in the way advertising is integrated into business processes.

Hal Varian, one of the pioneers of the Internet, famously said that: "The sexy job in the next 10 years will be statisticians."[6] Is it then true that creativity will be replaced by statistics? The complaints of the older generation of advertising executives show that they don't understand what is going on. Data will not mean the death of creativity in advertising. Instead, there will be a burst of creativity enabled by analytics. Statisticians are becoming sexy precisely because their work will be deeply integrated with creative approaches. We will see this more and more as advertisers find out how to work with Facebook and other social networks.

Advertising as a service

Advertising as a service refers to advertising that itself offers value to the consumer. Finding the right information at the right time and at the right place can be such a service. The people at Google work nonstop on improving the value of the advertising Google carries. Google offers Gmail and office programs on the Internet to extend the possibilities of advertising further. The right ad bar on Google search is controlled; Google uses algorithms to insure that the web sites behind the links are of good quality. In fact, the ad only shows up if it is somehow related to what the consumer is searching for. But Google does not stop at its AdWords. Google Maps opens up a whole new domain for advertising. Location-based ads appear in the maps and provide helpful information about restaurants, shops or hotels close by. All over the world. On the mobile phone, location-based ads become even more powerful. Facebook's "Places" is another location-based service. In fact, whatever Google and its top advertising competitor Facebook do is powered by the idea of smart advertising as a service.

But the quest for relevance and usefulness can also turn into the opposite. When Facebook first experimented with advertising on its social media site, it made some really bad mistakes. The most classic example is the ad partnership Facebook set up with Fandango, an online shop for movie tickets. The two parties thought that if information about who bought which tickets were published to their Facebook friends, this would be perceived as a useful service. A feed would be sent out: "Nick bought 'No Country for Old Men' on Fandango." Instead, people such as blogger Nick Antosca were incredibly annoyed and disturbed. Facebook management – and these are some of the brightest people around – had completely misjudged the issue of privacy.[7]

Facebook stopped integrating user data without explicit "opt in" permission and has since concentrated on selling a more conventional ad formats on its pages. Facebook ads can be targeted based on user profile data, down to location, sex, age and other details, but the ads stop there now. Google also blundered when it made its first steps in social media. Google analyzed the email data of its users and then sent out automated information about its users to those people it supposed were friends. Google realized too late that not everyone I write emails to frequently is a friend. These examples of blunders by companies in advertising show how important it is to get the balance right.

Although Facebook and Google made mistakes, at least they made the right mistakes. The mistakes they made came out of a desire to make their ads more valuable for their users. Their problem was that they went too far. Others simply flat out do not understand what the Internet is about and plaster their ads everywhere with no relevance at all. On of the worst displays of ignorance made by an ad-financed Internet company was that of MySpace.

MySpace was the first really big social network site. Initially, it was bigger than Facebook, much bigger. It had 45 million unique monthly users. And it was growing at an astonishing rate of 70,000 new users each day. In 2005, at the peak of the hype, MySpace was sold to a global media company, News Corp, for $580 million. NewsCorp is the company behind the Fox television network, the Wall Street Journal and other media brands worldwide. When it bagged MySpace, NewsCorp was ecstatic. Everyone had wanted MySpace, including Google, Yahoo! and Microsoft. To impress everyone at MySpace headquarters, the Google founders purportedly flew in by helicopter. But traditional media saw its chance and took it.

Coming from traditional media, the new owners saw the pages of MySpace instead as "AdSpace." They had a very limited understanding that social media pages actually belong to the users themselves. Users invest a huge amount of their time to fill their pages with content and photos and to acquire friends. The people are the pages; the company merely a provider of technology. Well, the new owners did not think of social media in this way. They decided it was time for their baby to make some money. They sold banner ads on the pages of their users, any ads as long as they paid. The MySpace community, however, did not think that their pages looked good with "in your face" ads for teeth straightening, cosmetic surgery and diet pills. Most people like the way they look and don't need an upgrade of their body, thank you.[8]

Don't get us wrong. Every company needs revenue. Advertising is a great business model to finance services which would otherwise have to be charged directly to consumers. But there is only so much advertising a user will want to live with and finding the right balance is the key to success. Unfortunately, MySpace management did not get it and the number of members declined proportionally to Facebook, which rose like meteor. A huge chance was lost. MySpace has since concentrated on music to differentiate itself from Facebook – basically accepting a less dominant position in the market. Social networks such as LinkedIn and Facebook are careful and conservative when it comes to ads – an approach which users actually can live with quite well. Balance is so critical for Facebook today that they think long and hard about every type of possible interaction between its members and possible business interests. In March 2010, for example, Facebook changed its "Become a fan" button (which is used to express support for a music band, social cause or brand) to a "Like" button. This was very important for Facebook because the concept "fan" expresses a greater allegiance than "like." In September 2009, Google launched an initiative called Data Liberation Front, and is introducing technologies allowing Internet users to revoke personal information from Google's sites. Why would Google do this, *The Economist* wondered, and then concluded that people will rather share information when they know they can take it back easily.[9]

However, this is definitely not the end of the story. Social network sites possess a particularly attractive type of data which search engines like Google do not have, despite the algorithms and the "Wisdom of the Crowds." Facebook, LinkedIn and others know who is friends with whom and what people talk about to each other. In combination with the power of mobile phones, they also know where people happen to be – for example, near a shop or a restaurant. Facebook and LinkedIn have the power to strengthen the emotional, lifestyle-based side of advertising. Recognizing this, Google launched its own social network, Google+, in June 2011.

The best form of advertising is that which "pulls" people instead of "pushing" them, to use terminology used by John Hagel III, John Seely Brown and Lang Davison. "Pull" is created in special creative, congregated environments, in which serendipity causes people to discover things they are interested in or complementary talent they would otherwise have missed. The authors especially mention the social networks Facebook and LinkedIn.[10] The race is on to further experiment with social media and the advertising business model and to find approaches which users will like because they add value. We are also convinced, however, that the mistakes made in Internet advertising will continue – without experimentation there is no progress. Especially on the Internet.

CHAPTER 7

The sixth building block – license sales

You will need all your friends

License sales is the dream business model of the new creative class. We kindly borrowed the term "Creative Class" from Professor Richard Florida. In his best-selling book *The Rise of the Creative Class*, Florida uses the term to describe just about everybody in the knowledge economy, about a third of the US national workforce. In his book, he argues that diversity encourages creativity and innovation.

We are using the term creative class more narrowly to group together a "digital generation" of video producers, music bands, animation artists and software developers. We are referring to anybody who creates intellectual property on the computer and distributes it digitally over the Internet. The new creative class is working all over the world; wherever their MacBook Pro is, is their home. They are using the newest software tools for producing content or software; some of these tools are themselves provided in the cloud as Internet-based services. As digital purists, they are fascinated by the fact that their work can exist entirely in a digital world; it is born on computers and is consumed on computers and devices, traveling the world in digital streams. Payments follow these streams in an equally ethereal way.

However, selling digital creative work successfully over the Internet is very difficult if the creator is alone. Music or software can be downloaded and copied easily if unprotected. Digital Rights Management (DRM) software, however, complicates consumption of music, especially if different systems are incompatible. Payments are a further challenge, adding complexity – even if people actually want to pay for music. But incompatible DRM and different shop systems are not the worst challenge. The main challenge probably is that there is such a massive amount of creative work on the World Wide Web that it is hard for even very gifted creators to differentiate themselves.

Consumers don't want to search, figure out DRM and puzzle over payments. They want to find, use and enjoy. For this reason, platforms have emerged which combine devices, players and online shop technologies. The most successful of these digital download platforms are very influential since they manage to create a virtuous self-enriching exchange between owners of creative content to the consumers of this content. They split up the fees generated by the sale of licenses between themselves and the owners of content. Apple defined the success formula for a digital download platform in the 2000s, starting out step by step with the iPod in 2001. In that decade, Apple sold hundreds of millions of devices to consumers and provided income to tens of thousands of content owners. These content owners were not only traditional players such as record labels but also members of the new creative class, especially freelance game developers.

Intellectual property 300 years after Queen Anne

Most countries protect creative or scientific work as intellectual property. From a legal perspective, any piece of intellectual property – it can be a video, a song, a game or software – comes attached with a license. A licensed piece of intellectual work can even be a digital sword a player creates in an online game. A license is an agreement over conditions of use. It does not have to be documented on paper. We click to accept license agreements on a web site all the time. If we don't agree to special terms, national laws are applicable.

Buying a license can mean many things – there are no limits to what a license owner can dream up for his or her business. As the owner of digital property, you could sell a license that allows the single use of an item before it expires. This could mean listening to a song once and then having to buy it again. While the song would have to be really great for people to strike such a deal, people do buy licenses in this way for a single viewing of a film on an entertainment service. A license could also be defined according to time usage; it could terminate after a year of use, for example. Often, a license allows ownership of a digital item which never expires. A really interesting aspect of licenses is that they can incorporate rules limiting or promoting the distribution of digital items, too. Licenses can stipulate that the buyer can gift the digital item to seven other people, for example. The people receiving the license may like the item and buy a different piece from the same content creator or owner.

The concept of intellectual property long predates the digital world. Most probably, the world's first copyright law was the "Statute of Anne," named after Queen Anne of England, Scotland and Ireland, whose reign the law was enacted in. It came into force in 1710 and protected authors for 14 years. After that, the creation went into the public domain and anybody could copy the work without payment. While Queen Anne had some flexibility in determining aspects of her license law such as the duration of protection, she was restricted in many ways by the fact that, in 1710, creative work always had a physical form. It made no practical sense to try to prevent someone from selling a used book, music record or a painting, for example. A physical book also does not expire and does not normally disintegrate after a year. A buyer can also not easily make seven books out of one and give these copies to their friends. All this has changed in the digital world. Three hundred years later, there suddenly are an almost infinite number of possibilities surrounding a license for digital works. This makes things complicated. The good news is that digital licenses can be designed to reflect the exact business needs of the content owners and creators.

In fact, license sales is such a flexible setup that it should technically make the subscription business model redundant. A provider of a video entertainment service, for example, could define a monthly recurring license that works just like a monthly subscription. But, as we mentioned in the beginning of the book, the seven business models are useful in a practical sense because people have set expectations about how to pay for things or services. A subscription connotes access to something, whereas a license implicitly means some form of ownership, even if it is restricted in many ways. This difference in the way the two business models are perceived by people is useful for entrepreneurs and companies. The seven business models don't work when dissected and analyzed, they work because this is how people actually think about payments and value.

The digital world has been both a friend and a foe to the creators of intellectual property. On the one hand, the flexibility that digital items provide and the distribution possibilities of the Internet allows content owners and creators to sell their work faster and across many more borders than ever before. They can craft very intelligent license models which maximize their revenues. On the other hand, digital items can be copied very easily and the risk that people bypass the license is very, very high. The smartest license setup is useless if it cannot be enforced, in one way or another.

At one point in time, companies selling digital goods put their trust in DRM and anti-copy protection. Or, more accurately, they put their hope into anti-copy protection. Companies installed copy-protection software, but soon found out that hackers could break it. They made the software tougher and hackers broke that, too. Owners of intellectual property also spent millions suing those who broke their protection and illegally used their content. The best example was the war the music industry waged on illegal Internet music distribution networks like Napster. But they did not just try to hurt Napster, which was fairly easy; they went for the people who distributed their music over the Internet using these platforms. This was a rather blunt way of ensuring compliance with the license sales. Napster was just one service among many, and each time one was closed down, another one like Kazaa would come up. And people don't really like being sued. The image of the music industry was badly hurt.

Innovative companies have shown that the key to successfully selling digital licenses is the best platform, not the best copy protection. A platform is a user-friendly environment set up for the consumption of music, games or software. It is often linked to some devices which exist in the real world, such as a gaming console, a specific computer or a smart phone. Cynical people could say a platform is simply a very elaborate setup for copy protection. Practical people (like us) would instead point out that not every platform is successful, and there are many. Those that are successful don't just ensure protection, they actually offer value to consumers because of some unique aspects such as ease of use, practicality or they are just great fun. In fact, Napster and Kazaa were popular in the early days of online music because they were so easy to use – compared to the alternatives provided by the music industry itself.

Today's commercial platforms extend the license sales business model to at least three parties. There are the owners of digital content. Then there are consumers buying the content or the software. But they are not buying licenses directly from the creators and developers, they are buying via the third party, the platform provider. A platform can mean any hardware or software framework that allows software applications to run. Sometimes the platform provider will also themselves create content or develop applications such as games, but it makes a lot of sense to try to involve further companies. The more content or software available on the platform the better. It is a virtuous circle, because the more consumers use the platform, the more creators and developers will be attracted to it.

Once this virtuous circle kicks in, it can be very lucrative to provide a platform. No wonder many device manufacturers are so interested in this model, including Apple, Nokia and Nintendo. But software developers such as Google or Microsoft are also keenly interested in being leading platform providers, working together with manufacturers such as Intel, Nokia and HTC. In August 2011, Google supercharged it's platform ambitions by announcing it's intention to acquire Motorola Mobility.

Even though technically the platform providers earn a commission on the sales of licenses over their platform, the content and applications are so deeply integrated with the platform that it makes sense to simplify and group all parties together into the license sales business model. Remember, a platform often involves devices, players, search, interfaces, data exchange and much, much more. Content providers to a lesser extent and software developers to a greater extent need to specifically adapt their products to a specific platform. They certainly think twice about which platforms to support with their digital products. A successful platform is a very powerful integrated ecosystem of interdependent players.

In a nutshell, people don't like to buy licenses, they want to use digital products. This is what platforms are about. And to be successful, platforms have to be outstanding to attract both content partners and end-users. This is anything but easy. There are many, many failed platforms littering the history of the web and even before that the history of computing.

The indecisive history of computing platforms

These are two very different philosophies to providing platforms. When we hear the word "platform," we often immediately think of device manufacturers such as Apple, Nokia or Nintendo. But then there are software-only platforms such as the mobile computing platform developed by Google under the name Android. Or Microsoft's PC-based or mobile platforms. The software-only platform providers join up with hardware partners. To understand these two approaches better, we need to go back to the beginnings of the computer industry. The main themes are always: dominance, protection of intellectual property and innovation. To say that one approach is better than the other would be foolish, since the verdict of history goes back and forth, as we will see.

What we will do in this section is describe briefly how computing platforms changed from the early, IBM-dominated "vertical" era, to a more "horizontal" era dominated by Microsoft. Bear with us as we go through the history of computing very, very quickly – and please remember we have left out many of the fun, geeky parts because we simply would stray too far from our topic.

The original computing platform setup was vertical. This meant that the same company sold the hardware platform and the software running on top of the platform. The company which was most successful during this era was IBM. And the most successful platform was the System/360 – introduced in 1964. Software applications were not sold separately, but as a part of the computer hardware. Periphery components such as keyboards, punch cards and power supplies as well as maintenance and financing; everything came from one single manufacturer. What made the S/360 into such a powerful platform, however, was that parts and software were compatible to run on all six computers of the S/360 family. The S/360 was an enormous product development effort by the most powerful computer company at the time. The S/360 also was a huge risk for IBM – it cost more than $4 billion to develop and 50,000 IBM employees worked on it. In the end, it was worth the risk. The S/360 became such a huge success that the US Department of Justice initiated an antitrust lawsuit against IBM in 1968. And it was a resounding success for the innovation strategy of IBM, which relied on in-house Research and Development. The R&D Department of IBM was one of the best in the world, racking in massive amounts of patents. IBM researchers won several Nobel Prizes. The innovation expert Henry Chesbrough describes the vertical computing approach of IBM in his book about innovation. He termed the IBM approach "closed innovation" in order to contrast it to "open innovation," the domain of subsequent computing pioneers.[1]

IBM managed to retain its position as dominant player of the computer industry into the early 1980s. IBM was replaced not by a single competitor but by a radical change in structure of the IT industry. Chesbrough calls the period of change from 1980 to 1992 the time of "shifting sands." Although even after this time very powerful, new vertical platform players emerged in IT, none did it entirely alone. Pure vertical in computing was dead after the "shifting sands." This would not be the case with a purely horizontal approach, which entered into its golden era, under the leadership of Microsoft.

The Microsoft operating system, Windows, which in itself relied on an Intel hardware base, enabled many a successful software product. Many of these pioneering software applications are forgotten today, but they were all pioneers in their specific areas: WordPerfect for word processing, CorelDraw for diagrams and, most importantly, Lotus 1-2-3 for spreadsheets. A very dynamic landscape appeared on the "Wintel" platform in which competitors could become partners and then competitors again. Change was fast-paced. A parallel "horizontal" transformation took place in the business world with SAP shaping enterprise resource management and Oracle redefining the database. The horizontal platform was a catalyst for innovation and this led to new ways of doing business. New approaches were created to manage interoperability between different business processes, data and technical systems – allowing data and products from different companies to work together.

But the openness of the horizontal platform also ushered in new possibilities to copy software. Copy protection of its intellectual property already was a problem for IBM during its heyday as a dominant gorilla. But it was a comparably small problem. One had to clone an IBM computer to get the software to work. With Wintel and the horizontal era began the real age of software piracy. Since software was sold independently of hardware, consumers could avoid spending a lot of money through software piracy. They only needed to buy the computer.

Copy protection programs, which software companies rushed to install, were ineffective because they were soon hacked. Another sort of copying was just as treacherous if not more so – since it was determined to be legal. This was the nabbing of software ideas without copying the code. Lotus, the company behind the original, breakthrough spreadsheet program Lotus 1-2-3, tried from 1987 onwards to sue several companies that had developed similar spreadsheets. Borland was one of the companies which was sued, for example. In the end, Lotus failed. The so-called look and feel trials went all the way to the US Supreme Court. The American judiciary system did not want to prevent innovation from taking place and decided that the arrangements of menus in software was not protected by copyright. As long as you wrote new code, you were fairly safe from copyright infringements even if you borrowed some good ideas along the way. This makes a lot of sense; the world would not have benefited from the same degree of innovation in software if "look and feel" protection would have been successful. But while Borland was being sued because of its spreadsheet Quattro Pro, Microsoft raced ahead and improved its own spreadsheet program Multiplan (renamed Excel).

Microsoft was clever. It did not put its trust in copy protection – sure, its programs were protected but the company always knew this would not save them. They also did not put too much trust in the U.S. judiciary system which – wisely so – backed away from an overly rigorous interpretation of copyright on software. What Microsoft did is to make sure their platform offered value to the consumer: through ease of use, compatibility and above all by allowing partner companies to participate. An ecosystem was created and nourished by Microsoft which – despite all the pestering by computer geeks along the way – actually was very valuable for the end consumer. The horizontal platform strategy was the winner – not by going it alone but by going together. For this reason, a purely vertical approach does not exist any more. But the approach by ambitious device manufacturers – Apple being the clear leader – to bundle a device with a platform for applications and content is a vertical approach combined with the "best of" horizontal.

Thus, the two different philosophies still exist. History's verdict is indecisive; device manufacturers seem to be very successful again today with a vertical approach, as we will see in the rest of the chapter. Going it completely alone without partners, however, has proven a dead end. If the media industry would have been more alert and had carefully studied the history of software platforms, they could have avoided a lot of pain in the 2000s.

Distributed distribution

Many consumers do not bother with license rights. To be fair, the concept was abstract and was not really relevant for consumers in a pre-digital world of real products. Back in the old days, you needed to buy an album to enjoy high quality music. License and product were one. Once the Internet became available, consumers used the network to share their favorite music using digital formats ensuring that there was no degradation. Thousands of people shared their music with millions of others. They were supported by platforms; free-of-charge music distribution platforms. These platforms were based on so-called peer-to-peer technologies, meaning that the music was not actually stored on the platforms themselves but was distributed directly from the hard drives of the participants. In this way, popular platforms such as Napster tried to avoid legal implications. Technologically, they were simply directories pointing to people's hard drives. However, the centralized directory function of Napster was an easy target for the music industry. Subsequent sharing platforms such as Kazaa, Gnutella and BitTorrent distribute even their directory, which makes it almost impossible to turn off. Other services index the files available on these sharing services. The most prominent example is The Pirate Bay, an advertising-funded Swedish-run index for BitTorrent files. Throughout the late 2000s, it ranked in the top 100 of global and U.S. web sites.

From the perspective of the music industry, sharing platforms were heinous breeding grounds of illegal copyright activities. They started to sue the platforms, turn them off and when that did not work started to sue the consumers – their own clients, effectively. This activity did not really enhance the popularity of the music industry. The platforms evolved and continued anyway, just under different names and using even more difficult to track down technologies. Money flowed back to the music industry through the lawsuits. But even the US$100 million of settlement fees that Kazaa founders Niklas Zennström and Janus Friies paid to the music industry in 2006 jointly with the company they had sold Kazaa to,

Sharman Networks, is nothing compared to the billions lost year on year through revenue erosion. $100 million is a lot for an Internet start-up, but very little for Universal Music, Sony BMG, EMI and Warner Music. Side note: luckily, Zennström and Friies themselves had made $2.6 billion from selling Skype to eBay in 2005. The global retail value of music sold in 1999 was US$39 billion, in 2008 it was merely US$28 billion (according to the music industry association IFPI – the International Federation of the Phonographic Industry). More than $10 billion of revenue wiped out in ten years – that is something. No doubt, this massive shrinkage really hurt the people working for record companies. If it is such a disaster for musicians as a whole is debatable, since the Internet opens up completely new opportunities for the creative class.

Let us move beyond legal battles and settlements a bit and focus on what the peer-to-peer music distribution platforms actually offered. They were not just free, or ad funded, they were really easy to use, too. Their interfaces were well designed and self-explanatory. It was obvious that Napster or Kazaa were far better than any legal alternatives provided by the music industry. The music industry protected its content with Digital Rights Management (DRM) technologies to prevent copying. DRM actually was not one standard, but many incompatible technologies, meaning that music could not be transferred even if the consumer had legally bought the music. This made buying and listening to music digitally really, really complicated. The Swedes, whose contributions to the development of the Internet included peer-to-peer initiatives with significant impact such as The Pirate Bay, Kazaa as well as Skype (OK, one of the founders, Janus Friies, is Danish), have a way of interpreting the acronym DRM: "Dina Rättigheter Minskar," which means "Your Rights Minimized." A certain proportion of kids would have been willing to pay for digital legal downloaded music (we will see this proven later by the company Apple) – if the legal alternative platforms would only have been simple to use and well designed. The sad fact was that the music industry in the 2000s actually never managed to understand how to build and run a platform on the Internet. They would have loved to remain in a world forever where consumers bought CDs in a shop. With the heads of the music industry stuck in the sand, it was a computer company which would take the initiative.

"Stay hungry. Stay foolish." – the rebirth of Apple

Enter Steve Jobs in the picture. An extraordinary person such as Steve Jobs is bound to be controversial. He is both admired and hated. Many books have been written about Jobs, with titles ranging from *Return to the Little Kingdom: How Apple and Steve Jobs Changed the World* to *iCon Steve Jobs: The Greatest Second Act in the History of Business*. *Return to the Little Kingdom* itself is a 2009 sequel to a book about Apple by Jobs and co-founder Steve Wozniak, published in 1984 by Time reporter Michael Moritz. Moritz later became a well-known known venture capitalist in Silicon Valley; he was the person behind Sequoia's investment in Google. Despite its global significance, Silicon Valley is a tiny place full of gossiping villagers. We will try to ignore this discussion, wait for an official biography of Steve Jobs by the former Time editor Walter Isaacson and in the meantime do our best to stick to the story. The story is how a computer company showed the media industry how to make money from license sales on the Internet.

Apple is known for simplicity, ease of use and great design. The Apple Macintosh, released in 1984, was the first commercially successful computer with a Graphical User Interface (GUI). The Mac with its GUI was revolutionary because it was a truly "personal" computer that people could instantly relate to and directly work with in a human, intuitive way. It was the coolest computer in the world at the time. Every other broadly available computer was command line-based, including Intel computers running the Microsoft operating system MS-DOS. The Macintosh development team at Apple Computers had not invented the GUI and the associated elements such as windows, icons, menus and the mouse. The GUI was developed in the Palo Alto Research Center (PARC), the R&D department of a big technology company, Xerox. The work at PARC was itself based on experiments of the inventor Douglas Engelbart at the nearby Stanford Research Institute. But the computer Xerox released in 1981 based on the PARC GUI did not go far enough in thinking the revolution through. The team at Apple Computers did. In 1984, Apple Computer Inc. launched the Macintosh – taking a huge business risk with a massive marketing campaign which included a famous Superbowl ad. In this ad, a heroine liberates humankind from a totalitarian future ruled by machines.

People initially underestimated the power of the Mac and called it a toy. But Steve Jobs and the teams working with him never built anything that was simply pretty, like the ancient Chinese who invented gunpowder for use in fireworks. (The Chinese since have seemed to have woken up as well.) The Apple Macintosh became a platform for applications which revolutionized media production. These applications, software such as Aldus PageMaker, and later Quark, Photoshop and others, were essential to the success of the Mac. Desktop Publishing (DTP) redefined the way that newspapers, books and posters were made. It is hard to imagine that creating layouts was previously done with strips of paper and glue on a big table. It was fun in a way; one of the authors of this book glued together the newspaper of his high school for a couple of years. The GUI and mouse enabled the digitization of this activity. Even when Microsoft Windows came on the market with essentially a cheaper version of the Mac GUI, Apple Computer survived because it was the de-facto standard computer platform for DTP. For many years, most serious media and graphical applications ran only on the Apple Macintosh platform. This was the first upheaval Jobs caused in media. It redefined how media was made. DTP allowed newcomers to enter publishing- and design-related fields. Calling Steve Jobs and his devices simply "cool" is inadequate. Jobs took gunpowder and put it in a gun. Then he left Apple Computers, in fact, he was booted out by management. It was 1985.

While the 1980s continued to be great for Apple, the 1990s spelled misery. The company was shrinking and verging on becoming meaningless. Even the supreme bastion of the Mac, DTP, was seriously threatened by the much cheaper Wintel platform running the same applications with the same performance. It was time for Steve Jobs' return, who in the meantime had dedicated much of his attention to his animation film company, Pixar. And return he did.

Steve Jobs is an entrepreneur, not an inventor. Entrepreneurs seek out unique, disruptive opportunities to change industries and markets. And Jobs is specialized on media industry disruption. Whereas the Apple Macintosh changed how media is created and Pixar was a live example of how computing can change animation production, Jobs' newest efforts focused on how media is distributed. Jobs started this effort in 2001 with a flash memory based MP3 music player. Michael Moritz describes the launch of the iPod – which went from design start to the store shelf in eight months – as a "madcap effort" to save Apple when computer sales were falling.[2] Portable music players existed already a while. And there were dozens if not hundreds of models. The most popular player at the time was the Rio. The Rio PMP300 had been released in 1998. It was the size of a cigarette pack and held a dozen songs.[3] Sales grew after a lawsuit by the Recording Industry Association of America against the company making the Rio, Diamond Multimedia, failed.

But the iPod was not any old MP3 player. As a device, the iPod looked much cooler. The navigational concept was based on a wheel-like button. Battery life was much longer than for other players. Up to 1000 songs could be stored. The entry-level device was carefully priced to be affordable. The most important difference to the Rio, however, was that the iPod was part of a platform. It had its own embedded computer operating system. iPod was synched with iTunes, a software which allowed consumers to manage their media. And the iTunes shop, launched a little later in 2003, offered music tracks which could be obtained legally from music industry partners participating on the platform – at first with DRM, and then without. Taking all these elements together, Apple offered a great end-to-end experience for the user, which started with the Apple real-world shop itself, including the white "Designed by Apple in California" box holding the iPod to the music downloaded over the iTunes shop. Media partners got a fair revenue split of the sales, with Apple keeping around 30% and 70% going to the artists and the label.

The success of the iPod, although it came up from nowhere in a market teeming with competing devices, was resounding: 200 million iPods sold and a billion iTunes songs downloaded by the end of the 2000s. Steve Jobs' credo – movingly told in a commencement speech he gave at Stanford in 2005 – was "Stay Hungry. Stay Foolish." (In the Stanford speech, Jobs talked about the huge challenges in his life and credits the 1960s counterculture for his perspective including the antiauthoritarian, yet life-affirming, attitude of the Whole Earth Catalogue. "Stay Hungry. Stay Foolish" was the 1974 farewell message of the Whole Earth Catalogue. The Stanford speech video is on YouTube.[4])

While others struggled or floundered, Steve Jobs excelled at building platforms and making the vicious cycle virtuous. To finalize the shift from computing into consumer platforms and media, Jobs renamed his company. Apple Computer Inc. became just Apple Inc. in 2007. After the iPod and iTunes success story, Apple moved into mobile computing with the iPhone. The launch of the iPhone and the renaming of Apple were both timed to take place on the same day. The iPhone became a platform for so-called Apps. "Apps" are specially designed software programs for the iPhone and other Apple products. Apple sold the licenses in its Apps Store. It was a huge success, overtaking all the efforts of Microsoft and Google in the early days of the mobile Internet. Some of the most popular Apps are games which take advantage of the unique touch sensitive screen of the iPhone. Touch sensitive screens have existed for a long time, but the Apple touch experience is perfect, taking advantage of electromagnetic sensors. Once more, the device was not something that did not exist before, it combined existing technologies in some of the best ways possible. What the iPod was for music, the iPhone and the compatible iPod Touch was for games and other small pieces of mobile software. In the first 18 months after launching the App Store, two billion software applications were downloaded, most of them frivolous but fun.[5] Among the top sellers in 2010 were "Koi Pond" and "Super Monkey Ball." Not to forget "Crash Bandicoot Nitro Kart 3D."

These two mobile devices, iPhone and iPod Touch, together represent the fastest growing new computing platform in history, according to the star analyst Mary Meeker from Morgan Stanley. Runners-up were the gaming consoles Nintendo Wii, Nintendo DS and Sony PSP.[6]

Steve Jobs did not rest on his laurels. Next, he extended the iPhone platform to a new computing category, the tablet computer. Also in this area, Microsoft had sunk a lot of money. Amazon was slowly building its own platform focused narrowly on books license sales called the Kindle. Apple made the tablet computer work by attracting thousands of partners. The iPad became a resounding success where others had failed.

Despite the heroics surrounding Jobs' return to Apple, his eagerness to take business risk and the spectacular success of the new consumer platforms, Apple could not have done it alone. It needed friends. Without partners, a platform cannot compete. From 2008 to 2010, partners created the overwhelming majority of the over 185,000 available applications in the App Store and helped realize the four billion plus downloads. The days are over when a single company could be successful with a vertical platform approach built end-to-end. All providers of Internet and computing platforms seek to build a strong and growing partner base. Partners may be huge, global corporations or freelancers working on weekends. Acquiring partners is not easy, even for savvy companies. Often, efforts fail because the platform and the device is not accepted by a sufficient set of partners. Microsoft's first efforts to build a mobile platform were disastrous. Or Google's Android, for that matter, which struggled at the beginning, too. Take care, however, the final verdict is not out. It never will be.

But partners alone are not enough. As important as partners are a platform's end users – the consumers of content. They are picky; they are paying hard-earned real money for digital stuff. There is a lot of free content or software on the Internet, so money is expected to buy value. Sometimes, end users are active participants as well. They don't just want their voice to be heard, they seek to create content as well. The scary part is that the business of building platforms is a vicious circle, without partners you won't attract end users, without end users, partners are not interested.

Platform building best practice

What is the magic of Steve Jobs? How does he manage to join up thousands of partners with millions of end users when so many have failed?

Many believe Jobs creates a fervent fan community because he is a master of hype. Sure, the Apple conferences at which new products and platforms are announced are legendary, with people doing almost everything to get in. These conferences are orchestrated to perfection. Already months before such a conference, pundits ponder what the next announcement could be. Nothing seems uninteresting enough not to be discussed. There still is not enough clarity, for example, whether or not the signature black mock turtleneck Jobs wears is an out of stock item made by the Japanese designer Issey Miyake[7] or if it is from a Minnesota boutique store called St. Croix. The way Jobs handles details at the conferences is legendary. To present the iPad, for example, he sat down on a couch specially set up on the stage. More than anything he said, Jobs sitting on the couch and using the iPad as a personal entertainment device was the message that came across.

Sure, Apple conferences with Steve Jobs are stunning, but there actually is what can be called an Apple success formula for building a successful platform – we already mentioned the points. This success formula was adhered to with the iPod, iPhone and iPad breakthroughs. Let us look at the formula in a bit more detail: great device, fantastic user experience and fair revenue share for license sales.

Firstly, we have already mentioned the devices with critical details such as the fly wheel navigation on the iPod and the special touch screen on the iPhone which monitors the movement of electric current caused by your fingertips. But it is not enough just to assemble the coolest, snazziest technologies. The price has to be affordable for an entry-level model. To make sure that the first iPad was priced at under $500, it had to leave out several items such as a built-in camera for communications. A camera would have been cool, too, and competing tablet computers models had a camera. Making that call, camera or not, was probably really hard for the decision makers. A side note: we already mentioned that Apple as a brand device manufacturer has a vertical platform strategy, combined with the "best of" horizontal. Apple partners very successfully with application partners and content owners.

Let us move to the second point. User experience is much more than just a nice GUI. Apple originally thought through the GUI more than any other company, but never stopped thinking – at least not with Steve Jobs. End-to-end user experience covers a lot of ground. It includes, for example, the easy-to-use shop for license sales. It seems obvious today, but many previous portable devices did not come with a good shop, meaning content or software partners had to sell their licenses separately to consumers in some other way. In this area, too, decisions are never simple. Consumers seek advanced functionality in their iTunes music management and shop software, but they also like simplicity. End-to-end user experience à la Apple is applied to other areas, too. Apple has shown us that the retail box that contains the product is supremely important. Jobs started what every management consultant in the world would have strongly cautioned against; he started his own real-world retail chain and launched the Apple Store.

Apple seeks to control as much as it can. The strong control Apple exercises in vetting the content and software it sells in its offline and online stores certainly is controversial. Apple knows that its cool Californian image and its reputation for doing great things is what prevents a mauling by the unforgiving tech community. But the control Apple exercises also is part of the signature end-to-end user experience which so many people love. As the operator of a global platform, Apple has to think about which content may be offensive in one country but completely normal in another.

Not just content and design but also technical quality and security are checked. For example, Apple does not allow certain software functions, which could have a potentially negative impact on platform functionality. Many people love the Apple world because everything just works. But the software programmers who love to try the newest stuff and get the most out of a new device need to be given some room to play – otherwise there is no innovation. Again, it is all about balance.

Finally, the revenue share model for license sales is an important aspect of Apple's success. We mentioned the magic numbers already: 70% goes to the owner of the content or the developer of the software, 30% to Apple. Given the history of revenue splits, especially in the area of telecommunication services, this split is fair and increases the attractiveness of the Apple platform considerably. Remember, Apple needs those content providers. They need to feel a strong incentive in order to support the platform with their best content.

For years, telecommunication companies in the States and Europe tried to incentivize content partners with meager revenue shares of around 20%. Assuming that a whopping 80% for themselves was their birthright, telcos did not really have an objective view of their own value contribution. This was the status quo until Apple came along in most countries except Japan. There, the mobile carrier DoCoMo created its own mobile content revolution – well before the iPhone. Launched in 1999, iMode was DoCoMo's data service at the time. It attracted 40 million subscribers in Japan as well as 3,000 official content suppliers and many more unofficial ones. Monthly subscriptions and airtime data fees were charged, but the share for license and e-commerce transactions was absolutely revolutionary at the time: 9% for DoCoMo, 91% for the content and services partners.[8] It is was probably one of the most important reasons behind iMode's success and it probably served as a major inspiration for Steve Jobs.

In terms of charging for licenses, Apple kept everything as simple as possible as with everything else it did. 99 Cents per song. The music industry realized too late that the model of selling individual songs actually was a disaster for them because, in the past, they sold CDs for over $10 each. Many CDs contain only one or two truly good songs. If consumers now bought only these one or two songs, the overall revenue going to the record company was much less than before. Regardless of this, the experience of the music industry with digital downloads and license sales was so dismal that any working Internet-based model would be welcomed as some light at the end of the tunnel. The music industry could not afford to boycott iTunes if they wanted any future at all. For software developers, on the other hand, a 70% revenue share was perfectly all right because it matched revenue splits in bricks-based real-world shops. The bottom line for the Apple platform was that the partners were on board and the revenue split set the incentives right.

Looking back on the success of Apple with entertainment content, mobile applications and games, it all seems rather easy. The Apple formula for success in license sales was a great device at the right price, an awesome end-to-end user experience balancing simplicity, functionality and innovation and a fair revenue share. But putting these pieces together in the right way is anything but easy. To be successful so many times in a row – iPod, iPhone, iPad – surely must qualify Steve Jobs for once in a century genius status. But we will let others decide that.

The "Battle of Platforms" in entertainment

In the 2000s, starting with the iPod/iTunes combination, Apple defined best practice how to go about building a license sales platform. Apple enjoyed fantastic success. Apple's share price multiplied forty-fold under the leadership of Jobs and sales rose from $6 to $33 billion. By 2010, Apple had collected a war chest of $42 billion, which was larger than that of all other tech companies including IBM, Microsoft and Google.[9] This success story went anything but unnoticed. It was not just big; it was in everyone's face. The success of Apple seems to indicate that if you are in the entertainment business, you want to own the platform, not the content.

Many others began to work very hard to emulate this success with their own platforms. These were not small companies, we are talking about

Google, Microsoft, Amazon, Nintendo, Nokia and others. They also tried to put together their own package including great devices, fantastic user experience and fair revenue share for license sales. As we know, getting the right mix is anything but easy.

These powerful contenders leveraged their own strengths, created their own interpretation of platform building best practice. While Amazon launched its own book reader with the Kindle, Google instead partnered with a mobile device manufacturer, HTC. Amazon used the license sales business model – delighted to be able to benefit from the scalability of a fully digital business model. Google instead transplanted its advertising-based approach onto its platform which was focused not on entertainment content but consumer software, such as office applications and communications programs. Competing in the office area, Google analyzed the much older fully horizontal Microsoft platform model just as intensely as the hybrid iPod/iTunes setup. Google even launched its own operating system for mobile phones called Android. Both Amazon and Google used analytics to realize powerful additional services for its users, such as content recommendations in the case of Amazon or advanced spell checking for Google. The strong heritage of analytics in both companies meant that their services were superior to the "Genius" service on iTunes which provided music recommendations.

How will this "battle of platforms" play out, with so many powerful companies trying to push their own offering? Big names do not mean big success. Not all will be successful, because platforms, like many other Internet services, are subject to network effects. Content owners, which include music labels, book publishers and game developers, cannot afford to be on every platform. They will select those with the most consumers. And consumers will tend to select the platform with the best content. It is the virtuous circle we already talked about earlier.

It will be interesting to see if in this "winner takes all" world, Apple retains its lead or if other companies manage to wrest the top position from Apple. The top platform would be able to dictate its conditions to content owners. The top platform will probably also control customer relationship and customer data. Relationship and data is pure power, augmented by advanced analytics and with the ability to provide recommendations, it is here where future sales are generated. The new creative class, such as freelance game developers, may benefit in this scenario because they can directly market their products and do not need to negotiate with a major content publishers. The game would be played according to the rules of Apple – or whichever other player achieves the supreme position.

A different scenario also is possible. Since there are many different variables, network effects may not come into play the usual way and a single, uncontested player may not emerge. One platform may offer the best devices, but may lag in ease of use due to a lack of analytical capabilities and deep data. There may be one platform slightly better suited to music and another mainly for games. In this scenario with many multiple and overlapping platforms, the owners of entertainment content may emerge as the winners in the long term, not the platform owners. Here, the content owner, let's say Pixar Entertainment, provides its blockbuster film with the associated games and soundtracks to many different competing platforms, dictating its terms. The revenue share for license sales gets reduced for the platform providers. To what extent content owners get to control the customer relationship and customer data is an open question. The scenario would be similar to the balance of power in cable TV, where cable TV companies either are mere distributors of blockbuster content or are outright owned by content companies. The most outspoken cheerleader for the content camp is Rupert Murdoch, the owner of News Corp, which in turns owns Fox, The Wall Street Journal and many more media companies. On 2 February, 2010, he stated in the News Corp Earnings Call with analysts that, content is not just king but the emperor of the digital universe. He also asked his listeners to pardon his lack of humility.

The "battle of the platforms" does not only have to be based on the license sales business model. Just when the license sales business model seemed to be the only game in town for music consumption, other players lined up with a different approach. The iTunes music platform competes as a license-based model against subscription or advertising based services such as Spotify or LastFM. Apple bought its own subscription-based music service called Lala in late 2009; it shut it down later and incorporated its services into iTunes. These so-called cloud-based services seem to do a better job with analytics and recommendations, too. The Founder of Spotify, the subscription-based competitor to Apple, was quoted as saying: "We know that this is a huge shift. People are used to owning music – but more and more people are becoming comfortable with accessing music and services in the cloud."[10] Whether license sales or subscription wins the day for music will depend on how people wish to consume it.

In general as applied to media and entertainment, both approaches license sales and subscription will continue to persist. People will seek to "own" some media – for example, books – and at the same time will want to consume media – such as a role-playing online game – as a service. How the consumer pays for something shapes his or her most basic thinking about the nature of the transaction – ownership versus membership.

Micro license sales – evolution continues

While the "battle of platforms" rages in entertainment and different business models are explored, the license sales business model itself keeps evolving. An exciting hotbed of innovation is how the license sales business models is mixed in with free-of-charge services. In Chapter 9 of this book, we will explore all sorts of combinations of business models with the free foundation of the Internet.

An example is the sale of digital items within free online role-playing games. The game is played free of any subscription fees, but players can upgrade their own status by buying licenses for digital items such as a big warship, a diamond-encrusted sword or nifty clothes. The Chinese online gaming company Tencent generates millions of Yuan in revenue through these "micro" license sales embedded in its free games. The U.S. online game developer Zynga has been very successful with the same approach of selling digital items.

It is also possible to have players create digital items, and sell them in the game with the platform provider receiving a commission. This is a consumer-to-consumer (C2C) variation of license sales, which benefits players of the game directly. This C2C variation of license sales feeds into

---

Heyzap – building value in the gaming ecosystem

There was no sudden, single eureka moment. The Heyzap concept was derived from a systematic appraisal of different business ideas. Nine start-up ideas were narrowed down to three and then to the final concept: A widget for discovery and play of casual flash-based browser games.

The widget addresses a two sided-market. On the one side, web site publishers can integrate the widget into their site, allowing them to feature online games on their site. On the other side, game developers can distribute their game to a large number of publisher web sites with a single partner. Heyzap is hugely successful with both sides. 460,000 publishers are working with Heyzap tools. The company supports 25,000 games from 2,700 developers.

Heyzap is constantly improving on their original idea. Just a few days before our meeting, the company launched an iOS and Android application for social discovery of new games. The business model itself, as we will describe below, has undergone three permutations. To be able to keep the company focused while going through constant change requires strong leadership.

The two Heyzap founders, Immad Akhund and Jude Gomila, knew each other already in school in Britain. Both attended Cambridge University. They then went their separate ways, starting several companies in the US and Europe. Akhund and Gomila knew, however, that they would to work together one day. Anyone who sees them at work would not be surprised. Everything the two do is incredibly synchronized with each another. In the middle of an explanation, one of the two will stop talking, knowing that this is where the other will carry on.

Initially, Heyzap's business model was based on a distribution of advertising revenues among the ecosystem partners. This model was a good start, but as many other web businesses have realized, it is difficult to build an online business only on advertising.

For game developers, in-game sales of digital items have been a major source of revenue growth. Several game developers such as Zynga in the U.S. and Tencent in China have generated significant license revenues from sales of virtual goods. Inspired by these successes, Heyzap's business was pivoted to provide game developers with a virtual goods engine. The Heyzap engine worked as a type of web service and could be integrated into an online game. The proceeds would be shared out between Heyzap, the game developers and the publishers.

The problem with this virtual goods engine was that it was in some cases "bolted on" without really being part of the original game experience. If a game is not originally designed for in-game virtual good sales and the items are not part of the overall game orchestration, then people won't buy them. People don't buy stuff just because it's there. Zynga and Tencent both develop their games specifically to make digital items compelling, they don't add them at the end. Furthermore, those game companies that excel at virtual goods have their own engine that they have used for a long time and have already integrated into many of their games.

A final issue with the virtual goods engine business model was differing revenue expectations of the web publisher compared to the game developer. In-game license sales mean that revenues flow throughout the lifetime of the game, which averages about three to six months, with a peak in the middle. Web site publishers – who usually work with advertising – want to be paid up-front for traffic that they provide, and not with a time delay.

Time for the leaders to put their heads together and for the business model to pivot again. The third permutation of Heyzap has proven to be the right one. The company now offers an arbitrage-based model, which is perfect for both sides. Acting on behalf of the game developers, it negotiates a CPI price with its publishers. CPI means "Cost per Install," a very relevant success indicator for game providers, far superior to CPM or CPC (which measure traffic or clicks, not actual installations of the

> game). Game developers pay this CPI price, plus a spread for Heyzap. The game developers then concentrate on recouping these investments with in-game license sales over their own engines. Web publishers are happy, because they get up-front money for traffic, but they are incentivized to actually convert this to installs.
>
> The business model seems less sophisticated compared to the virtual goods engine service, but it is very straightforward and well matched with the expectations of both sides in the ecosystem.

a big debate about the value of so-called user generated content (UGC). The creators of UGC are also called "prosumers" because they produce as well as consume content. Media executives love to point out the low quality of UGC. Maybe they haven't noticed yet that many Internet users don't care about the quality of a YouTube video, if it is original and funny. Most importantly, UGC has achieved a new dimension by moving into games and evolving into a significant source of income through the digital license sales business model.

And there is more, too. "Micro" license sales are enabled by virtual currencies, which facilitate "micro" payments. But virtual currencies don't just support digital license sales; they also create financial liquidity in the Internet – which supports a very innovative, emerging business model in itself. And this development goes way beyond media into the world of finance.

CHAPTER 8

The seventh building block – financial management

Making money with money

In the real world, there are many different ways of making money by taking financial risk. Welcome to the world of investors and loans, but also to hedge funds and derivatives. And welcome to the gambling casino, too. The approaches we are concerned with in this chapter share one common trait: they are always about taking a financial position in anticipation of a predicted outcome. What we are not talking about are agents earning a commission or fee on a financial transaction with no position themselves. This is the commission business model we spoke about already in Chapter 4.

In his fascinating book *Against the Gods*, Peter L. Bernstein makes the point that quantitative risk management is what distinguishes modern times from the past. According to Bernstein, calculated risk taking is one of the prime catalysts that drive Western society: economic growth, quality of life, investments and technological progress. The word "risk" comes from the Italian "risicare," which means to dare.[1]

Before focusing on the Internet, let us take a short detour through real-world financial business models. An investor, for example, will buy real estate, commodities or stocks in anticipation of rising prices. The investor may have been provided a loan. The amount of risk exposure a fund or bank has in these cases can vary a lot. It may be zero if they are just acting as an agent. Or the bank many have made a so-called principal investment on its own balance sheet. And everything in between zero and full exists, too – one needs to consider the setup, contractual terms, collateral and a whole lot more like securitization. The practice of securitization, for example, was part of the problem in the Subprime Mortgage Crisis of 2007. Securitization essentially means loans and risk are repackaged and sold to third parties. For simplicity's sake in this book, we will not try to differentiate by the amount of risk exposure, as long as there is one, even if tiny and well managed. By the way, loans don't have to be cash; they can be stocks, too. A trader anticipating falling prices takes a short position by borrowing an asset from a lender and then selling it. Since she has to return the asset to the lender, she needs to be sure that she can buy it back later at a lower price. But taking a financial position does not always mean an involvement in the acquisition or sale of an asset.

Recent history has seen unprecedented low interest rates and a huge amount of innovation in the financial system. This has led to the development of derivates, which work like "bets" on predicted outcomes. Derivatives are contracts between two parties with a value linked to an expected price of an asset. The underlying asset actually is not touched, it is neither bought nor sold, it merely provides an outcome, which then triggers the contractual obligation. The trigger can be almost anything with a variable future outcome: the future price of cocoa beans, success of a movie or whether a country will default on its debt. Derivatives can also be used to provide insurance (for example, to the media company financing the movie).

Financial markets have become very sophisticated in the real world – some would say too sophisticated. There are many estimates about the size of the global market in derivative trades, for example. These estimates are all very large; we are talking about trillions of dollars. In the aftermath of the Subprime Crisis, the regulation of banking was reviewed as part of a frenzied effort to reduce systemic risk. Government has always regulated financial business. There were numerous laws on interest rates in the Middle Ages. If you are getting into this business, approvals of some kind are almost always necessary; it does not matter if you are running a gambling operation or a brokerage.

In contrast to the real world, one has to search for a long time to find leading Internet companies making money by talking financial risk positions. There are many agents offering third-party financial products or services on the Internet. Some of these are great companies, running very sophisticated data-driven engines to compare offers. Take Mint.com, for example. WePay is a useful service helping people collect money. They don't expose themselves to financial risk. These companies are not what we are primarily looking at in this chapter. Agents are not making money through financial positions themselves; they are merely selling real-world financial products and services and earning a commission. We are also not considering banks and brokers which are mainly based in the real world and merely use the Internet as a sales channel or for client communication. The discount broker Charles Schwab, for example, runs its business to a large degree via 300 branches spread across the United States.

ING Direct is one of very few pure online banks in the United States with a government banking license. But also here we are cheating a bit. Elsewhere in the world, ING is a real retail bank – a huge one. Paypal is a pure play Internet payments provider and qualifies; so does the online broker E*TRADE.

We are looking for enterprises that seek to exploit the liquidity of people and companies on the Internet and take financial positions. There is one exception to the relative lack of top players in this space. One type of service fits our description and is very popular: online gambling. Whereas in online poker, bets of players always cancel each other out, online roulette, for example, involves (a very, very small) financial risk for the house. Sports betting also involves theoretical financial exposure for the bookie. One of the main success factors of this business is the ability to navigate strong governmental regulation in this space.

Then there are a few, very innovative emerging start-ups outside of gambling which make money with money. One of these is Wonga, a company offering short-term loans to customers on the Internet. Or Weatherbill, which sells small and medium-sized companies weather derivatives. Wonga and Weatherbill are both pure play Internet companies.

Expect the financial risk business model to gain momentum in coming years with the spread of virtual currencies on the Internet. Here, providing a payment option itself becomes a business; we will look at payment systems as well as virtual currencies. PayPal provides an Internet payment mechanism. Square applies Internet payment to real-world transactions. Facebook Credits is the best-known Internet currency. Virtual currencies started their existence in online games as player awards. But the more widespread beyond games these virtual currencies get, the more they will provide opportunity for innovative financial business models. We will discuss virtual currencies in the next chapter.

Companies taking financial positions can build up losses. They could potentially experience financial bubbles or a crash. But the financial risk management business model offers exciting opportunities for experimentation. Virtual currencies and mobile micropayments may kick-start many innovative uses of this business model. We are still at the very beginning.

The mysteriously slow growth of financial services online

Most banks are accessible over the Internet. Retail banks use the Internet as a distribution channel and communications medium to allow their clients easy access to their services. Increasingly, online self-service is perceived by banks as a way to reduce personnel and branches. In general, the Internet is not used to change or improve the business model of retail banks, their main activities are firmly established in the real world.

Pure Internet banks and online discount brokers are different. They have very different cost structures from established offline competitors because they have no branches. Often they offer their clients very diverse and sophisticated financial services, which would otherwise only be offered in combination with high service costs. Online discount brokers originally made self-service brokerage services available to wide numbers of people – services that previously had been accessible only through banks and were much more costly. The customers of online banks and brokers are people with experience in investing and different financial products. As such online brokers and banks were part of a wave of emancipation of personal investing. Educational books and guides such as Fool.com were crucial as well to create this new generation of investors.

Judging by the impact that online banks and brokers had, it is surprising there are so few of them. Many disappeared with the end of the dot com era – the lucky ones were bought by established financial services firms. ING Direct is a pure play online bank in the United States. Outside of the States, ING is one of the largest banks in the world with very much of an established, offline presence. ING simply made the decision to enter the US without branches as an offline player only.

E*TRADE Financial Corporation has a long, long online only history. It was founded in 1991 to offer trading over AOL and Compuserve. In the late 1990s and early 2000s, there were many, many other discount brokers on the net like Ameritrade and Scottrade. E*TRADE almost did not survive the aftermath of the subprime mortgage crash. In November 2007, a Citigroup analyst pointed to the risks associated with E*TRADE through subprime assets, causing a substantial drop in customer deposits and posing a major risk for the online brokerage. Billions of subprime assets were taken out of the balance sheet of E*TRADE through a deal with a hedge fund, Citadel Investment Group. Citadel now owns part of E*TRADE. A new era has begun for E*TRADE.

We have discussed the development of a pure play online bank and a discount broker offering diverse financial services. Missing from the list is the last of the three well-known financial services companies on the Internet, the payment transaction provider PayPal. PayPal is the result of an early merger in March 2000 between two electronic payment companies based in Palo Alto and founded in 1998 and 1999. PayPal was acquired by eBay in 2002 for $1.5bn after it became very apparent that eBay's own payments system could not compete with the volume of PayPal and the attractiveness of a payments system that was far more universal than for eBay only use. Today, PayPal is hugely successful as an independently operating entity under the eBay Umbrella. Its total volume of transactions was $71bn in 2009. It is present in 190 international markets and services over 70 million active accounts. It services 19 currencies.

Other financial services players on the Internet frequently only compare different financial service products, such as mortgages. Some of these are quite sophisticated comparison engines, using very intelligent data analysis. Mint.com provides a personal financial guide based on a large set of personal financial data. Mint.com was sold to Intuit. These companies, clever as they are, clearly have a commissions-based business model and are not offering financial services themselves.

WePay – helping people collect money online

Which one of you is Rich Aberman? There are no obvious hierarchies here, no corner offices. The WePay open floor space in Palo Alto is full of desks, people and teams; it is not easy to find Aberman, the co-founder. Rasmus Lerdorf, the creator of the PHP programming language, works there as well. Not just Aberman or Lerdorf but everyone at WePay is working hard to make it easy for anybody to collect money online.

Everybody has to collect money at least once in their lives. Whether it's collecting dues for a soccer team, or selling tickets to an event. WePay simplifies the process to collect money. Payments can be made using bank accounts or credit cards. Collected money can, in turn, be spent with a WePay debit card, which is useful for managing shared expenses.

The company makes its money by charging a small transaction fee for each payment made through the service. The company also makes money when people make purchases using their WePay debit cards.

Like all companies engaging in financial services, WePay must heed its fiduciary and regulatory duties, including the USA Patriot Act.

The questions to ask when describing the development of ING Direct, E*TRADE and PayPal is why so little, why so slow? In the last one or two decades, we have seen nothing less than a revolution in personal investing; a liberation of small investors from financial institutions that had charged dearly for their services. Financial services are perfectly suited for the Internet, because they consist only of information. And yet, we have very few online only banks, some discount brokers which are not strong enough to survive by themselves and a single payments provider. $70bn is a nice sum for PayPal, but compared to the volume of cash transactions over conventional credit cards or other forms of bank transfer this is miniscule. What is going on here? Do people want the security of knowing there is something real out there which can be touched when it comes to financial services? Is this the reason why ING Direct has launched its Cafés in major metropolitan areas and E*TRADE its Financial Center in San Francisco?

Another reason probably is a far more important explanation for the slow growth of online financial services. The providers of online financial services originally thought they would tap a client set that was sophisticated and financially strong. The Internet would provide access to new liquidity. The expected online financial services revolution did not happen so far. Financial services on the Internet are on the discounted low end and volumes on this very low end have not risen fast enough to make it worthwhile. So far, banks, brokerages and payment providers can make much, much more money outside of the Internet in the real world. This explains the relative strength difference between the established, real world and pure play Internet companies and the fact why real is still very much in control and the virtual is but a sales channel.

George W. Bush wrecks the party

Online banking and brokerage is regulated by financial services authorities. But the most tightly regulated financial activity on the Internet by far is online gambling. In fact, online gambling is so dependent upon loopholes and licenses that the history of online gambling regulation is the history of online gambling. Period.

By far the largest market for online gambling was the United States. Please note the use of the past tense. Ever since the first online gambling outfits offered its services to US citizens, individual states as well as groups in the Federal Government have tried to ban it. For years, online gambling navigated difficult regulatory waters, exploiting every possible loophole. The European gambling operator Bwin uses an ancient gambling license from the former Communist German Democratic Republic (GDR). Many of the operations offering their services in the United States were based overseas, for example, Antigua, Cayman Islands or the UK Commonwealth island state of Gibraltar. Next to gambling, Gibraltar is known for its monkeys. Occasionally the managers of these operations were arrested in U.S. airports. But it was worth it. From 2001 to 2005, online gambling grew worldwide from $3.1bn to $12.1bn – most of the market was in the United States (estimates from Christiansen Capital Advisors[2]).

The SAFE Port Act signed by George W. Bush in October 2006 authorized the use of high tech detection equipment in U.S. ports to prevent smuggling of nuclear, chemical or biological weapons into the USA. It also banned U.S.-based banks and credit card companies from processing payment transactions associated with online gambling. This put an end to the U.S. online gambling market growth overnight. One of the largest players in the space, Gibraltar-based PartyGaming faced a huge, instant revenue loss due to the SAFE Port Act bill. Gambling regulation in the States had sufficient loopholes to exploit, but without payments, the whole house of cards collapsed instantly. In 2006, PartyGaming had revenues of $1.1bn.[3] In 2007, annual revenue was $458m.[4]

Online gaming companies needed to refocus on markets outside of the U.S. In order to more effectively address these opportunities, PartyGaming and Vienna-based Bwin merged in July 2010, creating a $890m unified poker, casino, bingo and sports betting group – still not the level reached by PartyGaming in 2006. But the United States Market still remains "the holy grail" according to Jim Ryan, PartyGaming's chief executive.[5]

The brave and few

The barriers to entry faced by Internet start-ups intending to make money by taking financial positions are higher than for other business models. Firstly, regardless of the type of business, there almost always is regulation to watch out for and licenses that need to be granted. This is especially true for all gambling-related ventures, but also for any types of business involving banking activities. Secondly, start-ups in this area need to have detailed knowledge of financial markets. People with this knowledge have a far easier time making money on the payroll and bonus plan of a bank, fund or insurance company compared to an Internet venture. In rare moments of a financial crisis people may move into the Internet segment, but even then, one cannot really speak of a mass migration. There is a third potential reason discussed in the section about online banking – the general ability thus far to make more money elsewhere, outside of the Internet.

For these three reasons, regulation and know-how there are very few companies using this business model today. There are some innovative start-ups in the finance space, nonetheless, overcoming the barriers to entry.

We feel that the financial risk management business model is still "emerging." We are on a permanent lookout for Internet-based financial activity, which takes advantage of the liquidity provided by the Internet. We have not found the financial risk management flagship company yet, like we have for the other business models.

Just selling regular financial services through the Internet channel without taking a position – think web sites of banks – usually is a commissions-based Internet activity and does not qualify for this business model.

Differentiating commissions-based financial businesses from companies and individuals carrying out investments and taking financial risk on the Internet is far from easy, however. Regarding many of the companies we mention in this book, we do not really know if they are actually taking a financial position or are passing the risk on.

The Internet loan providers we discuss here are almost all acting as intermediaries either for financial institutions or private lenders. Some peer-to-peer lending sites which act as intermediaries for consumers lending to other consumers have actually created secondary markets for debts, allowing lenders to offload their own debt to further third parties.[6]

This business model is not just "emerging," therefore, but also "tricky." Nevertheless, we are delighted to introduce a few companies here, which are using the Internet either to directly take financial positions or are acting as intermediaries for those who are.

Investment in Internet real estate

One of the first Internet-based financial business models actually were investments into Internet "real estate." Domain brokers like GoDaddy.com serve as agents for this type of business, some of them actually making investments into thousands of domains themselves. Generic domain names are popular among so-called squatters, because they cannot be legally seized by brand owners. $7.5m was paid for business.com in 1999 and $16m paid for insure.com in 2009. Then there are unique opportunities. The trade association American Farm Bureau benefited from such an opportunity in late 2010, when it sold its domain fb.com to Facebook for $8.5m. Oversee.net estimates the domain name market to be $500m a year.[7]

Investment in Internet traffic

In 1998, Bill Gross, the Founder L.A.-based Idealab, started GoTo.com. GoTo.com was a search engine, which sold rankings using an auction process. The GoTo.com concept was very similar to the one adopted later by Google for monetizing search. Here, we do not want to elaborate on the advertising business model, but instead mention what Bill Gross did to direct traffic to his site. He bought traffic for 5–10¢, targeted it and sold it again for a higher price.[8]

Some affiliate marketing and search engine marketing companies do the same today. They try to benefit from price differences by buying Internet traffic in volume at a low price and reselling it again at a premium to their customers. Since this business benefits from secrecy about price differences, there is not much public information about these companies and how they apply the financial business model.

Spread betting services

Then there is a great variety of betting and gambling taking place on the net, despite restrictions introduced in the era of President Bush. The established spread-betting specialist IG Group moved into sports betting in 2006 by starting Extrabet. Turning the table, the sports betting company Betfair in 2010 launched its own spread-betting service LMAX (Goldman Sachs holds a 12.5% stake).

Through the Internet, foreign exchange spread betting is being carried out by people who would previously never have engaged. In the UK, for example, foreign exchange trades rose threefold on one service from 2008 to 2010. Lisa Baum at Cantor Fitzgerald stated: "Our clients are not [financial professionals] … but people interested in current affairs." She added the memorable comment: "Everyone's got an option these days."[9]

Internet-based B2B, B2C, C2C and even C2B loans

Despite the occasional news item for a particular domain such as fb.com, domain name investments are not going to grow beyond the current level. In fact, search engines and social media should eventually make domain names on the web far less important as they are today. Betting is closely linked to regulation and will surely go through its ups and downs according to the political climate in different countries.

One area which is particularly interesting on the Internet is loans – it may very well be that our future financial flagship company comes from this area. We have four varieties of loan providers: B2B, B2C, C2C and even C2B.

AliLoan is a B2B loan service providing cash liquidity for small- and medium-sized Chinese companies, which frequently use Alibaba, Jack Ma's trading platform. By serving as the primary Internet trading platform for 57m registered business users, Alibaba provides data and transparency about smaller companies – which is used to manage lending risk. The proportion of defaulted loans provided by AliLoan is at a low level of 1%.[10]

Wonga uses the Internet to provide short-term, small loans to consumers. Wonga has developed a sophisticated credit risk assessment system which provides very quick results whether a consumer can receive a Wonga loan or not. 1,500 data points are checked; money is transferred in 24 hours and can be on the borrower's account even at 2 AM. Interests rates are very high at 1% a day. But the loans from Wonga are designed to be used to overcome short-term liquidity problems, such as a broken washing machine, which needs to be fixed before the next paycheck.[11]

The most innovative loan offer over the Internet surely must be C2C loan platforms. These are intermediaries and do not take risk themselves; however, they enable a very novel lending business which would have been impossible without the Internet.

C2C loan platforms are provided by Prosper.com, Lending Club, Zopa (in the UK) or Smava (in Germany – Disclosure: Jörg Rheinboldt, one of the authors, is an investor in Smava). As of December 2010, one million lenders provided $211m in loans on Prosper.com. Major venture capitalists and angels have funded Prosper.com, including eBay's Pierre Omidyar and Accel's Jim Breyer. In order for peer-to-peer lending to work, many applications are denied because they fail credibility checks, as in the case of B2C loans. Lending Club claims that it denies 86 per cent of its loan applications.[12]

Kiva is a peer-to-peer lending platform supporting small businesses in poor countries. Since Kiva links up private lenders in wealthy countries to small companies in emerging economies, it is a C2B lending platform. Kiva provides daily data on the volume of its loans. As of December 4, 2010, Kiva enabled $177m in loans provided by 508 thousand people to 463 thousand people.

Kiva has been spared the criticism regarding tax evasion and improper conduct that has been made against the microfinance industry in general these days and against the pioneering Grameen Bank specifically.[13] In March 2011, the founder of the Grameen Bank and Nobel Peace Prize laureate Muhammad Yunus was removed as head of his bank in a financial regulatory conflict with the Central Bank of Bangladesh.

Substitute for the informal economy

None of the loan services mentioned – B2B, B2C, C2C or C2B – would have been available before the Internet. The small Chinese companies receiving loans through AliLoan previously were not served by banks in China. Small companies in China are traditionally dependent upon family members or loan sharks. In fact, family members also were the only resort consumers had, too, previous to Wonga, Prosper.com or Lending Club. The same applies to Kiva's loans in emerging economies.

This is what we mean by rising liquidity on the Internet. Rising liquidity will enable many more financial businesses than we have today. In the case of the loan services, they are helping move a previously informal economy (at times with benefits but oftentimes with major drawbacks) into the management sphere of professional business.

Our favorite so far: Weatherbill

Our favorite so far in the financial management category is Weatherbill. Weatherbill was started by two ex-Google employees and provides weather insurance to farmers (as well as other clients – such as travel providers) over the Internet. Weatherbill exploits a weather algorithm which is based on 20,000 years of weather data. It uses the Internet to access a previously untapped new client base for weather derivatives. Previously, weather derivatives were a financial product reserved for very large enterprises.

It gets fun when you think about what happens when you throw in the liquidity that the Internet offers. If true liquidity on Weatherbill can be achieved, then the weather insurance of the farmer who seeks rain and the concert provider needing some dry days can cancel each other out. Then the whole venture might get really, really interesting.

CHAPTER 9

It's a freemium world

Paying nothing

In the space of a few months in the late 2000s, two interesting commercial experiments were carried out by two music groups involving digital downloads and the price of their albums. Radiohead offered their album *In Rainbows* as a digital download in October 2007 and NIN digitally served up *Ghosts I–IV* in March 2008.

Both bands had the advantage of being very popular previously. NIN actually is not really a band at all, but a music project by the multitalented artist Trent Reznor. Both bands were started in the 1980s. Both were fit in the alternative rock genre, with a wide range of work in other musical styles. The first six Radiohead albums sold more than 25 million copies by 2007. During the 1990s, NIN, with a permanently changing cast of musicians performing with Reznor, became a highly celebrated act – winning two Grammy awards and selling 20 million records.

Radiohead provided their album as a digital download, telling fans they could pay their own price as they wished, it was an honor-based system. The CD of *In Rainbows* was released a few weeks later in the regular retail channels. There also was a luxury edition worth US$80. Radiohead was quoted in *Time Magazine* as saying: "I like the people at our record company, but the time is at hand when you have to ask why anyone needs one. And, yes, it probably would give us some perverse pleasure to say 'F___ you' to this decaying business model."[1]

NIN's *Ghosts I–IV* was sold according to five different fixed pricing models from free to an "ultra deluxe" edition for US$300, limited to 2500 copies. A CD was available for $10.

NIN's experiment was a success. The "ultra deluxe" edition was reportedly sold out in three days, grossing $750,000.[2] The maximum amount of customers bought the "ultra deluxe" version, even though the music itself was available for free. The expensive version was clearly seen more valuable by some due to the artwork and the limitation. They were willing to voluntarily pay.

The results of Radiohead's honors-based experiment were never published, but one can suspect there were too many free riders who took advantage of the offer without paying their dues. In February 2011, Radiohead released their new album called *King of Limbs*. The honors-based system was abandoned for this record.[3]

NIN's experiment closely matched the approach that several of the smartest web businesses were developing at the time: "freemium" business models, which include a mix of free services as well as paid options. These approaches meant an increasing sophistication in the development of business models on the web.

You can live on love alone

One of the most interesting debates we had when developing the *SimplySeven* framework was whether or not "free" actually is a business model. The Web 2.0 era after the crash of the New Economy was marked by an intense period of innovation and was characterized by openness, accessibility and modularity. The term "Web 2.0" itself was popularized by Tim O'Reilly. The first Web 2.0 conference was held from October 5 to 7, 2004 in San Francisco.

Many of the most ambitious new companies were free services, which cleverly included an unobtrusive, seamless business model – often advertising, but also alternative schemes, such as the sale of consumer data. Some of these were so unobtrusive, as we will see in this chapter, that a normal consumer may never have to pay anything, ever.

While it seemed for a moment at the height of Web 2.0 that one can indeed live on love alone, our conclusion was that a business exists to make profits and therefore a business model has to result in actual money being made. This is why the term "freemium," coined by the entrepreneur Jarid Lukin, is so shrewd.

For us, freemium solved the problem whether or not free is a business model. Freemium is a business model combining a free service with one or more of the *SimplySeven* building blocks. Determining what should be free and what should be paid for is one of the most important Internet business model decisions to make.

Here, we will not just describe several smart freemium business models, we will discuss free itself. Free is far more than a trick to attract people to a web site. Free is the basis of what the web stands for. We would argue that businesses that do not respect the free foundation of the web do so at their own risk of alienating their community of customers.

This has resulted in a very long chapter. We spend a lot of time on free, starting with an introduction to the important concept the journalist and editor Chris Anderson called the 5%/95% rule. We will then dive deep into the world of donations, only to return to 5%/95% again and then to continue with privacy issues and how they impact Internet business.

Chris Anderson's 5%/95% rule

The Internet is filled with products and services that are free. We mean really free – gratis. For example, there is a lot of software on the Internet that is entirely free of charge. In fact, much of the Internet actually is run on this type of software. There is valuable and interesting content on the Internet which is free of charge and even without advertising; Wikipedia is the best example of this. Finally, there is a lot of free stuff in combination with another business model. We have discussed many of these combinations in detail in this book. In Chapter 7, for example, we looked at free online games microfinanced by the sale of digital items. The game can be played, however, without ever having to buy anything. Here, we explore how come there can be so much valuable stuff on the Internet for free.

In the real world, we are suspicious of anything that is free. Call centers call us pushing free credit cards. Garages provide routine inspections for free. We know that these things are not actually free. We pay for them because they are priced into something else we buy from these companies. As consumers, some of us are put off by these schemes. Most of us cannot care less, but we see right through them. Should we apply this suspicion to the Internet? Is the Internet a bottomless digital pit of desperate con artists using the worst tricks in the book? Are we paying left and right for things we do not really want on the web? It does not seem that way; digital free seems to work differently.

Low to zero distribution costs, low cost storage and cheap computing power enable free Internet services. Companies and people can provide things for free because they themselves don't have to pay much for distribution, storage and computing. Sure, the Internet does cost something to run. However, these costs are borne by many different parties, such as Internet Service Providers (ISPs) or search engines – each with their own business models. YouTube, for example, is part of Google, which generates much of its revenue from search advertising. Google spends a lot of money setting up and maintaining high-performance video distribution on the net. Imagine what would happen if people would have to pay for the distribution of their YouTube videos. Most would not be able to afford not to charge something. They could not afford to be free.

In his book *Free*, which is the sequel to ground breaking *The Long Tail*, Chris Anderson spends a lot of time talking about how distribution costs, storage and computer processing power have nearly dropped to zero. Anderson then points out that these near-zero costs turn around what he says is the 95%/5% rule. In the real world, companies sell 95% and give away 5% as a loss leader. On the Internet, if a company sells just 5% and gives away 95% for free, it may already make a killing. Today's Internet has 1.8 billion users.[4] Turning 95%/5% around really does change things substantially.

Anderson also refers to this approach as the freemium model – citing the venture capitalist and blogger Fred Wilson.[5] We have used the term frequently in the book already. It turns out that Wilson himself did not come up with the term either, as he is at pains to point out. Wilson described the concept in his popular AVC blog asking for suggestions for names. The CEO of one of his portfolio companies, Jarid Lukin, came up with the term. Freemium is extremely useful for understanding free on the Internet. In fact, the way free works is so unique to Internet business that Chris Anderson notes only half jokingly that most people over the age of 30 will never get it. Anyone above this age has simply spent too much time in the real world. 30 plus is too suspicious that everything costs something in the end.[6] This is bad news for us authors, too, given the fact we have passed the age barrier quite a while ago.

Scribd – freemium sharing of written works

"I want to have exactly what I had yesterday," Trip Adler, co-founder of Scribd, says to the French-accented waitress in the chic bistro-style restaurant in San Francisco's SOMA district. Adler's day is perfectly organized like clockwork, he moves from one meeting to the next, always giving himself exactly seven minutes time for a quick advance briefing with his team. The lunch has been timed in the same way – on the way back from the restaurant to the office, Adler discussed the next meeting – a press event – with Scribd Communications Director Christine Schirmer.

Even though every single minute is valuable for Adler's venture, he is right there in the conversation – mentally extremely present and quick to react. Scribd offers a way to upload documents to the web – in any format such as Microsoft .PPT and .DOC. This is in itself not terribly unique.

> What Scribd does do – and here Adler steps up a gear in the conversation – is to make this experience as seamless, social and easy as possible. The technology that Scribd develops to enable this is anything but trivial, it includes full Facebook integration, copyright protection and automated conversion to the HTML 5 format. The numbers of users – 65 million and growing – and uploaded pages – over one billion of them – proves that this is working. World-class publishers have placed their books into the Scribd shop such as O'Reilly, Wiley and Simon & Schuster. Leading thinkers, teachers and researchers place documents on Scribd, including Mary Meeker (one of the best-known Internet analysts in the world and now with the Silicon Valley venture capital firm Kleiner Perkins Caufield & Byers).
>
> The business model of Scribd is currently a freemium service supported by advertising. Similar to other leading freemium services, the value offered to users essentially free of charge is significant, including technology and hosting. They have also tested a Scribd shop, which charges a 20% commission on sold items. The company is working on business ideas for its Float.com mobile service, which are not public yet. Adler reveals it may offer different options to users, depending if they wish to see advertising or subscribe to premium titles.

So let us go through the argument again for ourselves and the benefit of our aged readers. Under 30s need to bear with us for a while or else skip over this section. Is the 95% really provided for free on the Internet with absolutely no strings attached? Often, yes. Adobe's PDF reader is not made of cheap glass beads. It is valuable software with a ton of advanced data compression techniques. Since its launch in 1993, it has been continually improved upon by some of the best software developers. The same applies to many "light" versions of software we can use for free on the web, too. And to services. Skype is an excellent Internet communications tool with lots of embedded intelligence. Many have used it without ever paying a cent.

Ah, the 30 plus reader will say, this is about giving away oil lamps to the Chinese and selling the oil. It is like the shaver or the printer scheme. The product is designed in such a way that one needs to buy the equivalent of expensive blades or cartridges because of compatibility requirements. Actually, this is not about oil lamps, shavers or printers. The free PDF reader on the Internet is a completely functional piece of software. The consumer never needs to buy the priced version ever. Adobe does benefit from the fact that everybody has a free reader, because it wants to sell its PDF creation software. This is where the 5% comes in. But the point is that the light versions of many software products are completely sufficient for most of us. And most people don't ever have to use the paid subscription service of Skype to call into regular phone lines. 5%/95% makes a huge difference to us as consumers. The difference is simple; on the Internet most of us don't pay. We will return to this rule later in the chapter with more specific examples.

A web powered by small deeds of heroism

But this is not the whole story. That would be too easy. As Anderson also points out in his book, there are many valuable products and services on the Internet available for free and there is not even the possibility to buy a "professional" version. Take Linux software. Or Wikipedia. This stuff is not 95%, it is 100% free. There is a huge amount of useful content, services and products that is simply donated on the net. Something else is happening here.

We call the "something else" the donation economy because it is a cycle of reciprocity, which does not involve money. A programmer investing many, many hours of her time and her coding knowledge improving an Open Source operating system (OS) gets recognition for her work by her peer community. The 1,700 admins of the English edition of Wikipedia – without whose caretaking Wikipedia would not work – get back the satisfaction that valuable knowledge is available to all. This voluntary work is being done because we know the world is being improved. It is not any type of work, it is meaningful work, it is carried out in a community and it is also fun (ok, everyone has their own perception of fun).

We are talking about a cycle. Because people contribute, people can also take. While the Linux programmer only donates a fraction of the code, she can benefit from the whole OS. The Wikipedia folks benefit from their knowledge base improving through other contributors. Donations are about giving something back to society. The reciprocity is not an obligation. I can take without ever giving. But I know that if everybody would just take, I would not get anything.

Acts of donation make us feel good about ourselves as humans. In recent years, philosophers and economists have gone into great efforts to explain that we actually do want to do good in the world – and are not exclusively motivated by money. The philosopher Susan Neiman in her book *Moral Clarity* pulls long forgotten and misused terms out of the closet and attempts to revive them, such as "heroism" and "nobility".[7]

Previous generations of academics – especially economists – had brushed this aside as kitsch and wobbly frill. Neiman does make the point that being a hero does not always mean we have go out each day to slay monsters (Neiman is talking about the real world). The web cannot be explained without small noble deeds done every day.

The reciprocal donation economy and innovation

The donation economy is not entirely isolated from the monetary economy, however. The donation economy interacts with the monetary economy in diverse and subtle ways. We have already mentioned the 5%/95% rule, where 5% paid is combined with 95%. Interestingly, donations are crucial in the 5%/95% environment as well. For example, people put up with buggy software and give feedback, which is very valuable for improvements. Reciprocity may be in the form of usage data, which tells a company exactly how a service is being used. The most important form of reciprocity may be the improvement of a service through voluntary data input. For example, people adding locations and places of interest to a digital map. This gift of data is incredibly valuable. Not the specific microscopic data speck of one individual contribution, but added to lots of other data specks like it, it amounts to a vast treasure chest of donated value. The donation of data is fundamental to the web in many ways. Newer ventures have found ways to reward people for their work – creating what we call personal business models. This will be the subject of the final chapter. But these are only specific initiatives; much of the web consists of donations of time, data and knowledge.

There are other ways, in which the donation and the paid economy interact, however, which may not even directly relate to the Internet economy. A programmer's work on Open Source software may help her land a freelance job or employment in a software company. Not just people give back, but whole companies, too. In return for using Open Source in some of their commercial software, for example, IBM donates back code work to the Open Source community.

In his work, the Harvard law professor Lawrence Lessig has summarized all this in just one brilliant concept: the right balance of protection and openness is necessary for innovation. To explain this, we need to briefly review the arguments behind intellectual property protection. Intellectual property protection exists to provide an incentive to create something new. This goes back to the days of Queen Anne and one of the first copyright laws enacted.

Lessig says there is another side to IP protection, however. Innovation always builds upon past achievements – also achievements of others. By putting her software into the open, the programmer is getting free testing and free bug fixes in return. Without the smartly crafted legal T&Cs of Open Source or GNU software, there would be a far lower level of software innovation. Patent lawyers would earn even more than they do today. By contributing his knowledge on Wikipedia, the contributor can see over time how good his own knowledge is as others improve and correct the texts. Lessig says an "Open Commons" of freely flowing data is a requirement for innovation. In a very constricted intellectual property regime, it is very difficult to innovate. Lessig is concerned that today the pendulum may have swung too far on the side of protection and the inhibition of innovation.[8]

Thus, free does not just mean unpaid, free means free to use. One of the pioneers of open software development, Richard Stallman, referred to free "as in free speech, not free beer."[9] Free data – software, testing data, points on a map – all these lead to improvements and innovation. This applies also to other creative areas such as music or literature. There are non-digital examples, which Lessig cites, too. The 19th century "Open Source" stories of the Brothers Grimm have been used to inspire countless Disney films. The best example Lessig uses comes from Japan: Doujinshi comics. These self-published cartoons copy and use well-known manga cartoon characters, mostly in an adult context. Even though it is illegal to copy cartoon characters, the Doujinshi are tolerated because they are a creative space for new ideas, which then sometimes find their way back into mainstream manga.[10]

We will not hide from the reader that there is a lot of controversial discussion precisely when it comes to free. Some people get really worked up discussing whether free is good because it is good in itself or whether free is good because it yields practical value and innovation such as tested, powerful software. Just to provide some labels, this is a discussion taking place between the Free Software Foundation versus the Open Source movement. In fact, the Free Software Foundation warrior Stallman, who has made a huge contribution to the development of the Internet, surely would cringe if he would see himself quoted in the above paragraph where free is discussed in the context of innovation. We will avoid this discussion because we believe both camps are right. Maybe it does not even make sense to dissect what is right from what is useful.

In his otherwise great book *Free*, Chris Anderson is at his weakest when he calls Stallman an "extremist" and "anticapitalist" who "muddied" the word "free."[11] Maybe he got up at the wrong side of the bed when he wrote this, but Anderson should really know that there is no secret conspiracy out there trying to wipe out private property.

Let's be honest, without the long-haired, bearded Stallman-types fighting their heroic battles, the Internet would not have turned out in the way it did. Most of us would still be contained in the walled gardens of CompuServe and AOL. Lessig is right in being alerted when more and more data is shifting from the open Internet into domains legally owned by companies such as Facebook. Through his Open Commons initiative, Lessig and others are experimenting with alternative, open legal domains on the Internet. It is very important that these initiatives exist. Some people just don't seem to understand the value of a continued dialogue about intellectual property and the Internet. It is legitimate to discuss how 95% of the Internet will still remain "free" in the future, in the "muddied," Stallman-like sense of the word. We would like the Internet to remain a hotbed for new services and innovation. We also want to the Internet to keep inspiring personal acts of heroism – like donating small specks of data. Plus, everyone should know the fairy tale with a GNU.

A fairy tale with a GNU

Once upon a time, a company existed which owned wires going into every single house all across the land. These wires allowed everybody to speak to everyone else. The wires made the company so powerful that it needed to be watched very closely by the ruler of the land. The ruler did this very diligently.

And so it came that when the big company developed a very useful software OS to run on its computers and its network, it was not allowed to sell it. It had to give it free of charge to the military, to universities and research institutions. The software was very cleverly designed for use in networks; it used a client–server architecture. The scholars and researchers used this software to experiment and try many new things. They developed many great programs to run on it. Wonderful things were achieved with the software, not just in the land itself but all over the world. The OS was used to run servers on the early Internet. Since the software was free, no legal counsel or financial officer cared and no one interfered. This fairy tale environment existed from the early 1970s all the way up to 1983.

Effective January 1984, the fairy tale was abruptly shut down by the U.S. Department of Justice. Not because the officials had a problem with the experimentation and innovation that was going on based on the

UNIX OS. They probably did not even know about the wonderful coding that was being done. There was something going on that seemed far more important at the time, the deregulation of the telecommunications industry. AT&T lost its monopoly and was broken up. The various assets of the company now were commercialized, including UNIX. The motley crew of academics and researchers using the software should go somewhere else or buy a proper license.

Enter Richard Stallman. Stallman, who had studied physics at Harvard, was a programmer at the MIT Computer Science and Artificial Intelligence Laboratory (MIT AI Lab) in the early 1980s. Stallman was a part of early hacker culture and embraced open programming environments. As a reaction to the shutting down of the open UNIX environment, Stallman started the GNU Project in September 1993. In 1984, he quit MIT AI Lab to work full time on the GNU Project. GNU stood for: "What's GNU? GNU's Not UNIX." The supporters of the GNU Project immediately set to the task of developing different parts of an OS as a free alternative to UNIX.[12]

It was brilliant of Richard Stallman that he did not just begin coding straight away but that he developed a legal framework, which served as the basis of an influential social movement. The "General Public License" (GPL) was a set of terms and conditions that ensured that any software developed under it would always be free of charge and freely available to everybody. What Stallman anticipated was that a small group of programmers could trust each other to develop and share code together, but that this loose arrangement would never work for a movement consisting of hundreds or even thousands of people. Such a broad movement required a solid legal structure.

By decisively acting on this idea, Stallman proved that he had phenomenal foresight. In the early 1980s, the GNU Project was indeed nothing more than a small handful of people working on a smart compiler called GNU and a neat editing program called EMACS. But even Stallman, who had the incredible farsightedness to set up terms and conditions protecting the community's software, could not have envisaged what was later achieved by many, many people working together voluntarily. As brilliant as Stallman and his friends were, they had underestimated the power of the Internet. We will excuse this – it was the 1980s after all.

According to Eric S. Raymond, also an influential programmer and open computing advocate, the GNU group had a clear vision but never thought it could be applied to the full scope of a complete OS. A complete OS, which required more than a million lines of code, could only be developed with the funding and organizational structure of a large corporation, so the thinking at the time went.[13]

One million lines of code

Achieving something that the world believes is not possible requires one important first step. Believing it can be done. Maybe because of sheer naïveté. It does not matter. One person did believe that a complete OS could be developed informally through freely contributed effort. This was Linus Torvalds. He started with the announcement on an Internet newsgroup asking for feedback and input: "I'm doing a (free) operating system (just a hobby, won't be big and professional like gnu) for 386(486) AT clones."[14]

Torvalds belonged to a new developer generation which used the Internet as a platform to exchange code writing efforts with people all over the world they had never met. Torvalds himself lived in Finland. His belief and fervent work triggered a wave of enthusiasm across the globe. Very soon releases for the so-called Linux OS were developed in breakneck speed. One new patch was released about every week.

In his book *The Cathedral and the Bazaar*, Eric Raymond describes some important principles for massive, free and co-operative software development.[15] These principles are important, because they can be applied to any project, which is based on voluntary input from a community.

(1) At the beginning, there has to be an initial set of code, the beginning of the program. It can be basic. It can even be faulty. But the future potential of these lines of code needs to be apparent. Raymond has a beautiful expression for this: "Plausible Promise." If there is "Plausible Promise," many others will help to improve and to test. Only about 2% of the Linux OS code was written by Torvalds himself – but it was the base. The original code piece was posted by Torvalds in August 1991.

(2) The movement requires a cheerleader. The motivator of the group needs to be able to choreograph and encourage. But this cannot happen in a classical hierarchical leader and follower relationship. Orders are taboo. Fellow programmers are partners, not employees or disciples.

(3) Releases need to happen in short sequences, so that momentum is not lost. There has to be constant attention on the project.

(4) The initiative needs to be fun, needs to be interesting and has to have a purpose. Why otherwise would anyone work on something for free, donating their time. We are talking here about changing the world with a million lines of code, not about an entry in the Guinness Book of Records. A free computer OS empowers the people. It frees up intellectual property and changes the way we work in and open,

co-operative society. Programmers know that an OS is the steam engine of the next industrial revolution.

When it comes to the Linux phenomenon, we always remind ourselves to sit back and envision what's really happening here: hour after hour thousands of programmers sit in front of their screens. Without getting paid. All around the world. Understanding this phenomenon is an important key to understanding the Internet. Next to changing the world, the "Free Agents" improve their programming skills, make new (virtual) friends and acquaintances and demonstrate their work to the public. Perhaps this will lead to a paid job or to a freelance assignment. But there is no guarantee in the donation economy. What all these programmers know is that in the "Knowledge Economy" their own skills need to be honed and improved all the time. One also needs to be seen as a loyal and dependable partner in the community. Raymond called them "happy hoards." In the perspective of the social researcher Richard Florida, the Linux community is part of the "Creative Class" together with designers, journalists, filmmakers and scientists.

Change the world, yes, but in a smart way. The Linux generation adopted the heritage of their predecessors, the GPL and GNU folks. Linux was securely enshrined in a legal framework. The legacy of Richard Stallman – the fusion of code and law – was absolutely essential. Linux was not part of the GPL license, but adopted a slightly different framework called Open Source. Slightly different is important, since Open Source, in contrast to GPL, allows the commercial use of code. In other words, while Open Source is free to use in the public domain, it can be part of a code set that is sold commercially, too.

The term Open Source was created in a workshop held with Eric Raymond and others shortly after the announcement by Netscape in January 1998 to release its source code into the public domain. From the beginning, "Open Source" was meant to allow commercial use and encourage co-operation between the community of programmers and corporations. This makes the Linux movement slightly less idealistic but in many ways even more effective. It is a 5%/95% idea. Linux Torvalds embraced the new concept immediately for Linux.

"Open Source" was not only a set of terms and conditions but also a marketing concept. With the strong and active support of heavyweights like the publisher Tim O'Reilly, Eric Raymond and others communicated the concept as a new model for a new world mixing business with free. This is important, because Linux is a template for other initiatives combining non-commercial and business objectives.

Linux and similar projects such as the Apache Web Server initiative thrived. The Apache Web Server is one of the most important building blocks of the Internet. Many companies use Open Source software as an embedded part of their own commercial software. IBM, for example, sells its WebSphere Application Server, which contains parts of the Apache server. In this way, IBM does not have to develop the complete code base of its application server itself, but can simply add parts to differentiate itself. What IBM needs to do is to strategically select those parts of the software which will help differentiate the product and those parts which can be open commodity. Next to the software, IBM sells implementation services, support and hardware. To give back to the community, IBM has reported to have invested over US$1 billion in Open Source projects.[16]

There is a further important logic behind the commercial adoption of Open Source software. Since the code is open, companies that use it cannot be attacked for software copyright infringement. Specialized companies, so-called Patent Trolls, have hoarded software copyrights and patents and run lawsuits against major software companies. This is a relatively new phenomenon. In the past, what one could call a ceasefire existed. If a major company believed another had infringed a copyright, they would usually back off because the other company would also be able to prove another infringement. As long as each company was a major software developer itself, this worked. The new lawsuit specialists cannot be held back in this way, however. Given today's dangerous environment, Open Source software promotes innovation by securely putting developments into the open domain for use by all and open for improvement.

What a story. A million lines of gratis code. Thousands of people and hundreds of companies that donate time and money into co-operative development. *Wired Magazine* drew the right conclusion from all this. Such a thing was never meant to happen. It could never have happened. Linux breaks too many of our preconceived ideas how the world works. The title of the *Wired Magazine* issue in August 1997 was "The Greatest OS That (N)Ever Was."[17]

Three million articles

The next thing that was also never meant to happen was Wikipedia. Every day people put in a huge amount of work and knowledge into the web for free. Alone the English edition features over three-and-a-half million articles and the online encyclopedia is available in many additional languages too. 78 million visitors use Wikipedia each month (as of January 2010, according to Wikipedia). Wikipedia does not only rely on donated work to create articles, much more important is the voluntary work required on an ongoing basis to check the quality of articles. While thousands of new articles are created each day, tens of thousands of edits are being made.

Wikipedia's usefulness depends on these quality checks and revision work. Anybody can change a Wikipedia article or add new articles. Unfortunately, we live in a world with a lot of knowledge vandalism. This can come in many forms. Supporters of politicians or political parties seek to publish a highly subjective view of their candidate or cause. Or some people may just want to make a prank, by changing an entry. Knowledge vandalism cannot be prevented on Wikipedia because it is an open system by design.

Wikipedia does feature an ingenious mechanism to combat vandalism, however. New edits can be removed with a click. It is easier to remove new work than to place new work on the site. The custodians of Wikipedia are informed by email when changes are carried out. In fact, about 1,780 administrators take care of the English language Wikipedia. Vandalism is usually removed from the site within five minutes.

Only some very controversial entries – mostly with religious significance such as "Jesus," "evolution" or "abortion" – have to be "semi-protected" with open editing barred to anonymous users. The entry "Obama" also is "semi-protected." By the way, as Chris Anderson points out, there are really, really few caretakers and authors of Wikipedia compared to the number of visitors. One in ten thousand is the ratio between contributors and visitors. What a multiplier. Massive value is created by a few individuals donating their time and knowledge. The impact is real and powerful, which is probably the reason they contribute in the first place.[18]

This well-balanced and powerful system promoting free knowledge was never meant to happen. Wikipedia was only a "Plan B" when it was conceived, "Plan A" was called Nupedia. Nupedia was launched in March 2000 with the objective of creating a free encyclopedia. Its content was supposed to be comparable to that of a published encyclopedia. Contributors were preselected experts in their particular field of knowledge; they were academics, scientists and researchers. Contributors had to have their entries checked through an extensive peer-review process. Nupedia was a flop. Before ceasing operations in 2003, Nupedia featured only 24 articles which had passed the peer-review process.

Wikipedia was created in 2001 as an offshoot of Nupedia, in part due to frustration with slow progress and a lack of funding for the coordination of the elaborate peer-review process of Nupedia. By the end of 2003, the year of Nupedia's closure, Wikipedia already featured almost 180,000 articles. Per day in 2003, about 250 new articles were added. That is more than 10 times the amount of articles that completed the peer-review process of Nupedia.

In contrast to Nupedia, Wikipedia was an instant success. The story of these two "free" projects, Nupedia and Wikipedia, illustrates an important aspect of the donation economy. Donations don't usually come from those who are part of an established and recognized group. They come from people who have knowledge and skills but are often not heard. Let us go back to Linux development. In his book *The Cathedral and the Bazaar*, Eric Raymond describes the power of an open and free environment, in which anybody who can create good code can contribute – it does not matter where he or she lives, what their background or formal training is. Jimmy Wales, the founder of Wikipedia, stated in *Bloomberg BusinessWeek* that "If you are doing good work, you will gain trust. If you do bad work, it will get reverted. We don't care about your personal name or what your previous credentials are."[19] Quality appears through the open collaborative effort of the bazaar, not the formal and structured processes of the cathedral. The excitement behind the donation economy is the chance to get one's voice heard, to make a difference in the world and contribute something meaningful – despite your formal credentials.

In Chapter 4, when we discussed the retail business model, we mentioned James Surowiecki and his research into the "Wisdom of the Crowds." In fact, the open system of contributions behind Wikipedia is remarkable in its quality. In December 2005, the highly respected British journal *Nature* compared the quality of Wikipedia to that of Britannica. 42 articles were compared. Whereas *Nature* found four errors, omissions or ambiguities per article in Wikipedia, Britannica had three.[20] The difference in quality between the 200-year old flagship of encyclopedias and the collaborative effort of Wikipedia was minimal. The same thumbs up for quality applies to Linux and other Open Source software, too.

There are a lot of other community projects on the Internet that work with voluntary donations of time and knowledge. Open Street Map, for example, is a collaborative effort to create a free, editable map of the world. Here, thousands of volunteers collect data on streets and geographic landmarks using portable GPS devices. Ground surveys are conducted by mappers on foot, bicycle or on a boat. Once the raw data has been uploaded, it has to be identified and named. Volunteers are encouraged to add more than street names and rivers, but also places of interest such as restaurants or bus stops. This map information is free to use for all – unlike a lot of other cartographic data which is proprietary.

In fact, most of the Internet has been donated. Chris Anderson estimates that 40% of the web has been created by people for free. To better describe the size of this contribution, Anderson has done some back-of-the-envelope calculations to arrive at the whopping number of 13 million people working full-time per year – representing a value of more than $260 billion a year. That is the GDP of a medium-sized country.[21]

Donated power for business

The Open Street Map is not the only place where volunteers are asked to contribute geographic data. On Google Maps/Latitude, people are encouraged to add places of interest. The mobile service Foursquare thrives from user-generated content linked to geographic locations. Unlike the Open Street Map, the resulting work is not entirely free for use. Companies such as Google or Foursquare collect voluntarily donated geographic and localized data and augment it with their own business model, in this case, advertising. It is these hybrid free/paid models that are of special interest for this book. In this section, we return to the 5%/95% rule with more specific examples.

There is a huge amount of value in data. In fact, many several free services explicitly are free in order to encourage the contribution of data. In these examples, free enables business. Josh Kopelman, co-founder of the venture capital fund First Round Capital, has coined the memorable term Data Exhaust.[22] What he is referring to is data that is amassing on the web and which is not utilized properly. A number of Internet start-ups founded from the mid 2000s onwards have focused on mining these gold nuggets previously disregarded by the wayside.

One of the most successful approaches in Internet data mining is the personal finance site Mint.com. Mint.com also is a 2006 seed round investment by First Round Capital. In 2009, the service was acquired by Intuit. What Mint.com does is access your financial information and spending patterns from various locations and match it with the spending patterns of its other users. Since Mint.com is used by one million people, it comes up with very detailed information. It tells you if you spend too much on car insurance or if you are having too many Frappuccinos at Starbucks. What Mint.com does do is use your passwords to log automatically into your online banking accounts. People who use it, therefore, trust that Mint.com does not misuse this access or this personal information in any way. The founder of Mint.com Aaron Patzer, wants to help America save.[23] Mint.com is free but refers people to online financial services, taking a commission. Outright.com, another First Round investment, does the same that Mint.com does for small companies.

The mining of "data exhaust" is not only possible with financial data but all data which can carry value. Two of the authors of the book, for example, are investors in Linguee.com. Linguee.com is a translation tool that is based upon the data available in tens of thousands of bilingual, previously translated web pages. In his book, Anderson mentions the company Practice Fusion which was founded in 2005. It is a doctor's practice software and electronic health records application, accessible online and for free. Usually, this type of software to manage a doctor's practice costs around $50,000. 30,000 doctor's practices use the service to manage their patient's health records. The data stored there is worth a lot – pharmaceutical research accesses the anonymous data to analyze. Aggregated and anonymous patient records can fetch serious money and can be resold for various specialist research – think heart problems, allergies or obesity. It also serves advertising, which can be stopped by paying a subscription fee of $100 per month. Only about 10% of doctors actually want to pay for a site without ads.[24] Practice Fusion is not the only company selling valuable medical data to pharmaceutical companies. PatientsLikeMe is a web-based service with a similar business idea.

Here are some examples of the 5%/95% rule in action. Note that the retail business model is missing. There are too many real-world costs involved in retail. It is too early to list examples of companies using the emerging financial risk business model. Otherwise, the *SimplySeven* are all here.

– **Services:** PatientsLikeMe is a free web service for people affected by very serious diseases who wish to share their experiences with others with the same condition. The company makes money by selling data services to the pharmaceutical industry.

– **Subscriptions:** Skype only charges for the calls going into fixed lines, Skype to Skype calls are free. Club Penguin is a virtual world for kids in which subscribers get special benefits – but you can play for free. ReliefInsite is a free pain-monitoring service on the web; the premium service costs money.

– **Advertising:** The huge amount of content on Facebook is contributed for free. Also here, advertising is the business model which is combined with free. Craigslist charges only for a fraction of its classifieds ads such as real estate, most are free. Google makes its money with advertising; search is free.

– **Commissions:** For all consumers, Mint.com is free. The site makes money with the commissions it charges on recommending financial services to its users. Mint.com is an agent recommending and selling third-party financial services such as mortgage offers.

– **License sales:** Tencent and Zynga sell digital items in its online games. The games can be played for free.

– **Combinations of building blocks:** Heyzap helps game developers (which sell digital items) integrate into popular publisher web pages. The games can be played for free. The publishers generate advertising revenues from promoting game downloads – in turn provided by the game developers. Heyzap itself makes a commission from the advertising sales.

These types of combinations between free and paid populate the web. In fact, it is one of the essential elements driving the Internet's growth.

Competing with free

So far, this story sounded like a fairy tale, not just the part about the GNU: people contributing free data, companies respecting these donations and a cycle of business and free. How nice. But there is a dark and ugly side to free, too. At least for those companies who have to compete with free. Companies who only have to charge 5% of their customers and provide the rest of their services for free have a tendency to destroy conventional industries. The benefits go to the economy and the people at large, but employees in traditional industries are hurt. Schumpeter's "Creative Destruction" is part of economic history; traditional jobs have been destroyed while new ones have appeared. Let us look at the impact of free in two traditional segments, such as print and telecommunications.

We already described in the chapter on advertising how the newspaper industry suffered because of Craigslist and other online classifieds web sites. The traditional classifieds model is that each ad is paid for with a relatively low fixed fee by the person placing the ad. Newspapers had a clever financing approach made up of different business models. Subscriptions and newsagent sales combined with regular advertising combined with classifieds. Since the arrival of the Internet, all these revenue sources have been under attack. The most detrimental impact probably was on classifieds, however.

Craigslist only chooses to charge for a small fraction of its ads, namely jobs and real estate. All others are free. The vast majority of free listings attract visitors to the web site and make it more popular. The 5% sold – the real number probably is less than 5% – amount to a neat sum, however, about $40 million in 2006 according to Chris Anderson (the company Craigslist is private). While $40 million is nice revenue for a company with 30 employees in San Francisco and a few more elsewhere, it is nothing compared to the $326 million decline in classified ad revenues in the newspaper industry experienced in 2006. Of course, Craigslist is not alone responsible for this onslaught – but the numbers show in a convincing and also scary way the economics of free.[25]

Skype is another scary example. It is not really fair to compare Skype to a telecommunications company because a traditional telco provides networks and has a huge employee and capital base to do this. But Skype is competing against telecommunications companies and is eating into their revenues. Take a look at Table 9.1 with figures from 2007, gleaned from annual reports of eBay (when they owned Skype) and AT&T. In its first four years, Skype was able to gain 276 million registered customers. Please note especially the number of customers served by a single employee of each company. And how few employees Skype has compared to AT&T.

The most difficult challenge faced by the incumbent operators is the 5%/95% payment model of Skype. By providing most of its services for free, Skype is seriously challenging billions in telco revenues which are providing employment to tens of thousands of people. Skype cannot replace an AT&T alone, but is part of a larger ecosystem of new service providers, including Internet ISPs. "Creative Destruction" is hard on the people involved, but apart from times of severe economic distress, new jobs always tend to compensate – but this is a whole other discussion for others to carry out elsewhere.

The bottom line is that free is a powerful business strategy in competition with established industries. One of the savviest venture capitalists

Table 9.1 Comparison of AT&T and Skype in 2007

	AT&T	Skype
Age	122 years	4 years
Revenue	$119 billion	$382 million
Number of customers	14 million broadband, 70 million mobile	276 million registered users
Employees	309,000	700
Revenue/employee	$385,000	$546,000
Customers/employee	272	394,286

in this regard is Josh Kopelman of First Round Capital; we already mentioned him earlier in this chapter. Kopelman calls it "shrink the market!" He loves the stuff and invites entrepreneurs via his web site: "If you have a business that will shrink an existing market, allowing you to take $5 of revenue from a competitor for every $1 you earn, let's talk!"[26]

The Facebook dilemma

We love to use the 5%/95% rule in our discussions with entrepreneurs and executives. It is a generalization, of course, but it is a simple starting point for thinking about embedding a business model in a web site. The rule says that the web essentially is a free space, with a very small paid part. Business models need be placed onto this free foundation in a well-thought-out way. Think of the Internet as a garden landscape with many big roads and small paths – all of them full of travelers. If you need to set up your tollbooths in the landscape, make sure that you do this wisely, because there is always a way around your particular collection point.

Most Internet entrepreneurs don't need to be told to be careful; they are very hesitant to add any pay points to their web site in the fear that it will stifle the growth of their service. In this chapter, we have already described Internet services like Mint.com, Skype or Club Penguin which minimize the impact of tollbooths on the traveler, for example, by removing them altogether and letting others pay for your trip.

But to end the chapter at this point would do the Internet great injustice. While the 5%/95% rule is a very useful starting point to think about embedding business models in the web, the rule also is misleading. The 5%/95% rule suggests that 5% pays for the 95%. This is not really correct. In the real world, 95%/5% means that 95% paying customers pay for 5% freebies. The low costs of computing power, connectivity and storage have inverted this rule on the Internet. Now only 5% need to pay money – this money is used to finance the company providing the service and the technology. But while the rest 95% can enjoy the service without paying cash, they are also often paying something. They are donating their time, resource and data. We have already mentioned this, but it is worthwhile to delve into more detail here. This is because donated time, resource and data needs to be treated with great respect by companies profiting from it. Most critical is the aspect of data privacy. One company which wrestled with this challenge is Facebook.

Many web services generate their value precisely from the fact that many, many users share the platform and provide data. Take Mint.com, which we already mentioned a couple of times, which could not provide financial analysis without the tens of thousands of members who provide their personal data to the service. Or Club Penguin which would be an empty world without non-paying users. Facebook would make no sense for advertisers if hundreds of millions would not be using the social network for free. Everybody benefits from everybody else's participation. Cheap computing power, connectivity and storage explain just a small part of the free Internet, most value comes from volunteers and through donations. We have spent so much time talking about Open Source software development and Wikipedia to show the significant value that this donated data has. You can run complete Internet sites with this "free" software and you have a whole encyclopedia at your disposal with the click of a mouse. As pointed out before, Chris Anderson estimated the overall value of donated data on the web at more than €260 billion a year.

People are not naive, they know that it is their data and that it is worth something. Even though traditional media loves to depict Internet users that way, they don't see themselves as cheapskates because they use free services. People know that even a tiny speck of data is valuable and therefore are very sensitive to how it is treated and collected. Even when they click on a button to provide feedback on something, people do this with a sense that they are contributing.

Mark Zuckerberg, famed founder of Facebook, knows this, too. In his remarkable book *The Facebook Effect*, David Kirkpatrick describes in detail Zuckerberg's thinking about the value and ownership of data on the web. In 2009, the author was able to spend a lot of time with the founder and interview him several times – without having to be screened by corporate PR. This already shows that Zuckerberg embraces openness, even when it comes to himself. But Zuckerberg is a radical thinker in this respect; he thinks most people actually benefit from being as open as he himself is.

It is unsurprising that Zuckerberg cherishes even the smallest speck of personal data on Facebook. Facebook is valuable for its members precisely because it organizes data around people. The following quote by Zuckerberg: "A squirrel dying in front of your house may be more relevant to your interests right now than the people dying in Africa," may make some people cringe, but it nicely captures the billion-dollar value of Facebook and its social network competitors.[27]

What is surprising is that Zuckerberg explicitly describes the data on Facebook as "donated" by its members. Zuckerberg uses the term "potlatch," a traditional feast of native North Americans in which food is donated to the group.[28] In the mind of the Facebook founder, any individual expression of opinion on Facebook is essentially a gift to others, since it helps us understand the world around us better – even if it is only regarding the health of squirrels. By coming out with a personal expression on Facebook attached to our name, we are contributing to the common good, we are contributing to openness and transparency.

The book by Kirkpatrick appropriately starts with a description of a mass protest against the FARC guerrillas in February 2008 in Columbia – a protest that was initiated via Facebook. In January 2011, protesters in Egypt communicated in part via Facebook accounts (as well as Twitter and Youtube). This is what Mark Zuckerberg refers to when he says: "If people share more, the world will become more open and connected. And a world that's more open and connected is a better world."[29] The squirrel quote used earlier was controversial but essentially also captures the same idea of personal power over information, unfiltered and not prioritized by governments, institutions or the media.

In our view, there is no doubt that Zuckerberg is authentic when it comes to his personal mission of making the world a more open place. He sees himself and Facebook as a catalyst making openness happen. Zuckerberg also understands that the data on his web site is donated by people. And it is true that these gifts of data make the world a more open place.

At the same time, more openness also is good for Facebook's business because it helps generate data which advertisers use for targeting. This is a real dilemma. We are definitely not the types to say that what is good business cannot be good for the world; in fact, combining business and doing good probably is one of the best ways to make a sustainable impact. All we are saying here is that it is tricky. Walking the tightrope between the common good and advertising dollars requires Facebook to be much more than just a normal company with normal management. It requires extraordinary leadership and decision-making.

David Kirkpatrick mentioned in his book that Mark Zuckerberg, known for wearing Nike swimmer's sandals and a North Face fleece jacket, came into the Facebook HQ in a tie on the first working day in 2009. The explanation was that it was going to be a serious year. Facebook needs to be "leading its user base through the changes that need to continue to happen."[30] The year was going to be serious, indeed. In February 2009, Facebook changed its terms and conditions and in December 2009 it changed its default privacy settings. All this while rapidly expanding at breakneck pace from around 100 million members in early 2009 to 300 million by the end of the year.

Already before February 2009, all content posted on Facebook was deemed the property of Facebook. This had not changed. What changed was that previously, if you removed your content from Facebook, this ownership right of Facebook would expire. With the new terms and conditions, if you removed your content, Facebook still had the right to ownership. In the words of a blog, "The Consumerist," quoted by Kirkpatrick, Facebook was essentially saying that "We Can Do Anything We Want With Your Content. Forever."[31] To any legal expert it is obvious that right of removal is an important control point for users. Any businessperson will instantly argue that complete perpetual ownership naturally provides Facebook with much more flexibility regarding its data – especially for targeted advertising.

In December 2009, Facebook changed its default privacy settings to "everyone" instead of "friends" only. Facebook wanted all data to be as a default open for all. People were forced to opt out their private data from the public sphere. Some members complained and wanted it the other way around. All data is private unless opted into the public sphere. On May 31, 2010, some Facebook members planned a public "Facebook suicide" where they would all delete their entries.[32] Some pages died, but Facebook survived.

2009 was definitely not an easy year for Mark Zuckerberg. Facebook could have handled the outcry a bit better. But in the end, Facebook kept growing at breakneck speed. Regarding its terms and conditions, Facebook invited two of the original leading protesters into a joint discussion and allowed its members to vote. Zuckerberg set a prohibitively high hurdle for changing the T&Cs back, which showed that he was unsure of the outcome and nervous. But he did ask the community, and, in the end, there was no reason to worry. 660,000 votes were cast and 74% of Facebook members agreed with the new, revised T&Cs.

Facebook has made its members' involvement a permanent part of its governance now. In addition, Facebook responded to the privacy settings outcry by simplifying the way a user could manage his or her settings. And Facebook is alive and well, with half a billion users worldwide. Perhaps most importantly, management learned valuable lessons about involving its users in decisions surrounding their donated data.

It's a freemium world

"Free" is what holds the Internet together. We are not talking about free beer; we are talking about an Internet filled with volunteers who donate their time, resources and data. Companies, too, are part of the "donation economy." Most Internet companies benefit from consumer data available on the Internet in one way or another. For some businesses, data is the "fuel" that enables the web service in the first place. Especially for these companies, data privacy is an important consideration.

Weebly – adapt your customer's DNA

Weebly's office is a suite in the financial district of San Francisco. It is obvious the office is getting a little small to accommodate Weebly's growth. The room is packed with programmers and designers; it is hard to tell exactly how many there are. It is a relief when David Rusenko suggests holding our meeting at the Starbucks around the corner instead of the office.

When Rusenko speaks, it is obvious he is obsessed by one thing: providing value to his customers, relentlessly. He quickly skips the details of what seems like an amazingly interesting life growing up as an American in France and Morocco and meeting his co-founders at Pennsylvania State.

The Weebly service lets people and small- and medium-sized businesses set up personal web sites. It is not the idea of Weebly which is revolutionary but the simplicity and user friendliness of the service. Previous web site development tools were modeled after programs which were not suited to web site publishing, such as Microsoft Office products. Weebly allows straightforward WYSIWYG editing right in the web site.

The starting premise of everything that Weebly does is to be as cost conscious as possible – like its small business customers. Weebly developers are therefore not only focused on ease of use but also on developing a system which is extremely cost efficient in terms of server computing power and storage requirements.

As a result, Weebly is able to offer hosting services for free and only charges for Domain Name Registration. Professional accounts cost between $3 and 5 per month, depending on the length of the subscription. This is very low if one compares the value offered to what it would cost to combine these different services on the market, from web design to hosting and web site maintenance. Rusenko says Weebly is profitable. Given the pricing, this is a huge achievement and shows that Weebly realizes significant economies in all its cost areas.

Arriving at the right price is a challenge for most web companies because there often is no directly comparable competing service. Weebly's all-in-one approach to web site development, hosting and maintenance has no direct counterpart, so it was important to test out several different payment options to find an optimal setup. The freemium/subscription-based business model, which has emerged,

> makes Weebly very attractive for small- and medium-sized businesses. Weebly hosts 6 million web sites, about half of those are businesses. Almost 2% of all web sites worldwide are created with Weebly.
>
> Rusenko points out that many newcomers to web business think a freemium model always works automatically. This is conventional thinking: offer most services for free and something on top and 2% of all your web site users will buy it. Although many, many business plans are based on such assumptions, the expected conversions – low as they seem in terms of percentages – often do not appear. "Freemium models have to be very carefully designed," Rusenko says, "people out there are not stupid, they seek value for their money."

When it comes to setting up tollbooths in this free landscape, it is crucial that we have an acute awareness of how to combine "free" with "paid." The 5%/95% rule is a good starting point, because it provides a sense of proportion.

It is not the case, however, that simply providing some pay points on an otherwise free landscape will lead to the desired 5% conversions – or even to 2% conversions for that matter. As Weebly co-founder David Rusenko points out in his interview, freemium models are challenging to implement. A deep understanding of one's customer is a requirement. The successful companies have understood this. Elaborate, finely crafted freemium business models have emerged in the Web 2.0 era. In the next phase, sophistication will increase further because the options for carrying out a business relationship with one's customers have increased.

CHAPTER 10

The future of web business is personal

Methods and tools to guide customers

Personal business is about enabling customers to better determine how, where and at what cost they want to do business. It is about providing customers not only with increased options but also with better guidance to make the right personal choices.

While this is an exciting development, it is something that has been described and discussed for a long time now, from many different perspectives. We have mentioned some of this literature in this book, ranging from the work of John Hagel III and John Seely Brown ("pull" not "push") to the groundbreaking book *The Cluetrain Manifesto* from 1999 ("markets are conversations").[1] Timothy Ferriss' pop culture bestseller *The Four Hour Work Week* actually is a set of instructions to take financial control of one's life and sell one's value more effectively.

What is new is that these ideas can now be realized with today's methods and tools. This is what this final chapter is about, methods and tools. The most basic method is the *SimplySeven* framework. It is relevant because it shows the breadth of available business model options. Personal business has to play the whole range available on the piano keyboard, not just some single keys.

Flexible payment infrastructures, payment as web services and virtual currencies; these three solutions help businesses enable their customers to pay how they want. Then we will discuss new mobile payment systems, which provide customers the freedom to pay wherever they want. They do more than that, too; they are effectively introducing online business models into the offline world. Finally, we will show how analytical methods and systems help customers determine at what cost they want to participate in a business transaction. This is what we mean with better guidance to make the right personal choices.

Better guidance is the most interesting part of personal business models, because it goes to the heart of what we are describing: transforming consumers into business partners.

There is a darker side to personal business, too, which we will discuss in closing. This represents an opportunity, too, for businesses to flaunt their transparency and show that they deserve their trust. In a world of business partners, long-term relationships and trust matter.

Flexible payment infrastructures

The term personal business model emerged from a conversation with Mark Gorenberg, managing director of the venture capital fund Hummer Winblad. Hummer Winblad's specialty is investment in software, especially ventures that provide back-end applications and infrastructure. For some time now, there has been an increased demand for more flexible back end payment systems. A Goldman Sachs Survey on "SaaS," dated February 2010, indicated that accounting and billing was the third most important area for software cloud implementations, right after web conferencing and sales force automation.

If there is an increased need in the back end for flexible payments, this demand must be triggered from the front end. "Personalized payment is the new personalized content," Gorenberg remarked in our interview.[2]

> **Hummer Winblad – flexible payments require new billing systems**
>
> The offices of Hummer Winblad Venture Partners are located in a listed building in the old Embarcadero port of San Francisco. As spectacular as the building is today, especially because of its spaciousness and beautiful restoration, it still exudes the utilitarian spirit of its warehouse past. It was built in 1895 for the Merchants Ice and Cold Storage Company.
>
> This is fitting, because Hummer Winblad was founded in 1989 as one of the first venture capital funds to invest exclusively in software companies. As Mark Gorenberg, managing director of the fund, says, "we invest in the shovels and the pick axes of the web." As a consequence of its investment focus, Hummer Winblad deeply involved in the latest trend of cloud computing – the provision of software as a service (abbreviated SaaS).
>
> Gorenberg can switch from having a conversation about hidden cultural highlights in specific European cities to the intricacies of delivering SaaS solutions in a single sentence. Next to his day job, he supports

> his alma mater, serving as a member of the Board of Trustees for the Massachusetts Institute of Technology. He is also engaged on other boards and steering committees, as well as being politically active.
>
> At Hummer Winblad, one of Gorenberg's new focus areas is in enabling flexible and dynamic payment solutions in the cloud. Gorenberg makes a very interesting point here. Consumer companies can realize dynamic and personalized payment models only if their back ends are similarly flexible. Hummer Winblad invests in the innovation required to create flexibility in the back end.

Gorenberg sits on the Board of Aria Systems, a developer of flexible subscription solutions. One of Aria's clients, for example, is Sunnyvale-based LikeList. LikeList was founded in 2008. It helps people manage personal recommendations of local, mostly small businesses and share these tips with their friends. Local businesses subscribe to LikeList and use the system to make offers to their most valued customers. Value for these local businesses means not just loyal customers but also those who recommend actively. Effectively, a business relationship is formed between local shops and active customers. Consumers can use LikeList to generate value from their recommendations to friends.

LikeList, based on the Aria Systems back end, is just an example of personal business. Personal business means customers will increasingly request a tailored approach in order to pay how they want, how much they want and where they want.

Payment as web services

Web businesses today have further options beyond setting up their own flexible payments systems with their software partners. Apple's ecosystem has developed into a complete payments system far more sophisticated than just a shop for Apps or music tracks. For example, magazine subscriptions for the iPad can be sold over the store. Google followed as well with different payment platform initiatives. What is happening here is that business model building blocks are being offered with the modularity and simplicity of web services. This represents a challenge for the platform providers Apple, Google and the others as well. It is easy to sell an App in an Apple Store which then directs the buyer to a subscription available elsewhere, bypassing the commission to Apple. Modularity and payments within payments like Matryoshka dolls opens up existing new possibilities for new ventures, which can launch on a "micro" scale faster and with even less investment than ever before.

In recent years, people in information technology have made a big fuss about so-called Service Oriented Architectures (SOA). SOA is a world in which technical functionalities on an application level can be combined quite easily to create whole systems. Many so-called web services have developed this trend further. There are ready-for-use services out there such as SendGrid (massively scalable email service), Amazon Web Services (infrastructure web services) or Force.com (enterprise applications).

Google and Apple are leading the way to build what essentially is a business model API. In March 2011, Steve Jobs announced that Apple had more credit-card number backed accounts than any other company on the Internet – more than 200 million.[3] When this is bundled into a platform service for media companies and software developers, this is exciting news. It is a whole other level beyond what web services provided thus far.

In 2010, Apple added In-App purchases which are essentially license sales within the App (Google has followed up with Android in early 2011). It's a purchase within a purchase. Granted, many Apps which feature In-App purchases are free. All in all, this is great for Apple, because it gets its 30% cut – inside and outside of the App.

If Apple can do the Matryoshka trick, so can others. On February 1, 2011, *The New York Times* reported that Apple pulled the Sony Reader from its App Store.[4] The conflict between Apple and Sony was about which shop gets to sell which licenses. Licenses are sold by Sony for books outside of the Apple platform, but they can be read with Apple-enabled iOS Apps on Apple devices – without Apple getting a share.

In this example, the license shop of alternative providers is wrapped inside a Matryoshka available in the Apple license store. Amazon's Kindle reader for iOS works in a similar way and directs consumers away from Apple to buy books over Amazon directly.

However, the solutions provided by Google and Apple are not free and they do have strings attached. It is important to understand the offerings very closely, especially the ownership of customer data. The proprietary business building blocks offered by Apple and Google leverage these companies' Internet reach and ecosystem and generate sales from commissions. This should not be taken lightly. The ability to ask for significant commissions on sales of up to 30% (in the case of Apple) means that these companies are providing actual strong value add to their business partners to enable sales, in the form of reach, registered members, technical functionality and a device-based ecosystem. An important value-add is that Apple and Google provide a trusted environment – a big benefit for unknown brands. Executives from many other companies are watching Google and Apple closely saying: "I wish I could do that." This includes media companies, mobile phone and device manufacturers and a slew of Internet players.

Fast-track companies taking advantage of payment web services

In an interview for this book, Roland Manger, Managing Partner of the European venture capital fund Earlybird differentiated between two kinds of start-ups. Those which will attempt to independently build up their own user base and those companies, let's call them "fast track start-ups," which leverage existing platforms populated with users and built-in business model functionality. "Companies need to make a choice fairly early on in their lifetime," Manger says, "if they want to make a good living with a smart idea on the back of a proprietary platform or if they want to own their whole value chain."

But being a "fast track start-up" does not have to be a one-way street. Zynga is a powerful example of a highly successful company, which initially leveraged the Facebook platform to make its social games popular. In the past months, it went beyond Facebook with independent web- and mobile-based games. Other examples, which the serial entrepreneur and investor Dave McClure has called "mega-successful platform bitches" in a Tweet on March 6, 2011, are PayPal on the platform of eBay, YouTube on MySpace and Living Social, Groupon and Zynga on Facebook.[5]

In fact, launching "fast track start-ups" based on a unique idea, but built on preexisting business platforms, is a great way to test new concepts. Some of these will graduate to "whole value chain" status. One of the challenges is to integrate the different web services-driven technologies and building blocks into a working and scalable system.

It is this "fast track" path to success which new style seed initiatives and accelerators such as Y Combinator, 500 Startups, TechStars, The Founder Institute and others are benefiting from to launch dozens, if not hundreds of new companies. (Everybody avoids using the term "incubator" these days.)

The ecosystem of leading Internet platform players and new businesses is evolving extremely fast and resulting in significant opportunity. The power to facilitate business transactions is being added into the mix as efficiently as it is to integrate into the social web and build on other pre-developed web services.

Virtual currencies and coupons

The surest sign that virtual currencies will develop into something far more important than just a way for game developers to monetize came with Facebook's launch of Facebook Credits. Facebook Credits started in a closed beta phase in late 2009 and was fully announced at the f8 Developer Conference in San Francisco on April 21, 2010. In March 2011, one of the first nongame services accessible with Facebook Credits was the 48-hour rental of Warner Brothers movies for 30 Facebook Credits each.[6] But before we look at Facebook Credits, it is important to gain a perspective on how virtual currencies fared before the Facebook announcement.

The best-known virtual currency before Facebook Credits was the Linden Dollar (L$). Watch out for citations of L$ at conferences and in discussions. If anybody wants to discredit virtual currencies as a bag of hot air, they always point out the L$ example. Linden Dollars are an in-game currency with a fixed dollar exchange rate traded on the LindeX Exchange. You could play Second Life for free, but if you wanted to buy land or special digital items you needed to buy Linden Dollars using real money. Game developers call this type of virtual currency "Real Money Transaction" (RMT) currency to differentiate it from currency which cannot be bought by real money and can only be earned in games.

L$ were a hyped topic for a while, especially after a *Business Week* cover story on May 1, 2006. There was the oft-repeated story of Ailin Graef aka Anshe Chung, a Second Life property developer living in Frankfurt, Germany, and Wuhan, China, who somehow managed to make one million real dollars with Linden Dollars. After the hype, Second Life and L$ seemingly disappeared into nirvana. See, say critics, virtual currencies are a flop.

Far from it. Virtual currencies are huge. The virtual goods market has been estimated at $621m in 2009 for the U.S. alone.[7] The estimates for China range from eight times that to the more conservative figure of $800m.[8] Zynga, the social media gaming developer made much of its $597m 2010 revenue with in-game license sales. In 2011, Zynga revenues will reportedly grow to $1.8bn.[9]

Today, almost all online games have in-game currencies. In-game currencies motivate free users to participate actively in the game; this helps populate the game and paves the way for future paying RTM customers. Money is made on digital license sales enabled by RMT units. About 2–5% of the total user population buy RMT units; this funds the free game. Examples of RMT currencies are "FS Points" in the game

Fallen Sword, "Red Love" and "Love Chum" in the game Fish Wrangler and "Super Brie" and "Cheese" in the game Mouse Hunt. Even L$s are still alive and are far from being a zombie currency. Transaction volume in L$ was expected to rise to $500m. At least one virtual world developer, Gaia Online, employs a full-time economist to help them understand the implications of dual virtual currency economies. Virtual currencies carry the same risks as normal currencies such as inflation and deflation, asset bubbles and fraud.[10]

When we are talking about RMT and in-game currencies, we are referring to companies using the license sales business model. These companies are selling digital items. And the numbers show they have become really good at it. Virtual currencies work best when they have been designed into the complete gaming experience from the very beginning.

But evolution has continued. And gaming providers want to grow the 2–5% of the user population that actually spend real money to buy virtual currency. It is all about providing more "sources" for virtual currencies and more "sinks" to spend it on. What is happening is that flexibility and personalization are increasing regarding the options of what consumers can do with virtual currencies. New sources are not just cash but can also be advertising-funded concepts, where an Internet user agrees to watch advertising or fill out market surveys. Offerpal provides such a service. Sources can also be unused, traded-in retail coupons through services such as PlasticJungle. Or they can be used electronic items too, bought and exchanged by a service such as Gazelle or Nextworth. Sinks can be coupons from Amazon, Walmart.com or other online retailers.

Airline miles and other loyalty point systems provided by retailers or car rental companies work in the same way as virtual Internet currencies. Several loyalty point schemes are tradable, which expands the number of sources and sinks. Air miles, for example, can be traded against car rental points at a set exchange rate. Topguest is a start-up, which rewards loyalty points for being in specific locations such as hotel lobbies or airline lounges. As a consumer, I benefit from the ability to swap because it increases the potential range of things I can do with my points. As a provider of points, I make my points program more attractive.

An advantage that providers often don't speak about is that they can benefit from intransparency. A retail coupon has a certain dollar value. If it can be traded against other coupons or loyalty points, it becomes harder and harder for the consumer to track what happens to the money and which partner pockets what amount. Obviously, some deals cost providers more than others and the most powerful partners can negotiate the better terms.

Providers of either exchangeable loyalty points or virtual currencies need to be careful, therefore. There always is the potential that many more customers than expected make a certain swap and a provider has to pay out more than they planned for. Constant risk management and calibration of the system is necessary. Restricting the number of offers and a decay of points are mechanisms used to manage risk. Providing loyalty points and virtual currencies is a financial play, with many of the risks and opportunities described in Chapter 8.

As more and more sinks and sources, as well as opportunities for exchange, are introduced, smart players can take advantage of newly arising financial opportunities. Lowering transparency can be a great advantage and smart partner models can be negotiated with win-win situations for all. Risk needs to be managed. Again, creative thinking and innovation is constrained by regulation. A direct link between online games and exchanges of virtual currencies back to dollars has the potential to be regarded as gambling; providers require strong legal counsel.

So far, virtual currencies are very fragmented and agreements over sinks and sources are bilateral, agreed between single companies. The launch of Facebook Credits could change all this and create a multilateral currency system. In a thought provoking article in *Advertising Age*, Ian Schafer has likened Facebook Credits to the Gold Exchange Standard, a fixed historic exchange rate between several currencies adopted at various points in time in the 20th century. Facebook Credits provide a standardized means of micropayment in multiple countries and across multiple in-game and RMT currencies. This goes beyond what PayPal does, because its payments are always denominated in one of 19 available currencies. Just like PayPal, however, Facebook Credits has the advantage of a classic debit system, since real cash has already been spent to buy a Facebook Credit.[11] Facebook already is a leading mobile phone application being used by millions of users on their phone – below we will be how economic growth was jump started through mobile micropayments in Kenya. One of the factors still restraining adoption of Facebook Credits at the moment is the 30% exchange commission Facebook pockets from gaming companies and others using the currency.

Imagine what could happen if Facebook Credits are successful. Cash coming in from various sources including unused retail coupons, used electronic gadgets, marketing interaction is spent in a huge array of virtual sinks, such as digital items or digital media. On the Internet as well as on the mobile phone. This micropayments system will add power to the seven Internet business models – including financial management. It is only a small step to offering loans and other innovative financial services in such a system. In fact, in March 2009, an entrepreneur has been awarded a license from the Swedish government to open "Mind Bank" which will exchange real Swedish Kroners for the RMT currency "Project Entropia Dollars" (PEDs). Eventually, people will be able to receive loans in PED as well.[12] And loans, as we know, are just the first step to a huge set of potential financial innovations.

Mobile payments everywhere

While we were completing our work on the book, a friend offered some advice: "Why write a book about Internet business models, everything is Internet business these days." At first, we did not get it.

Through mobile technologies and devices, web-based business is being cast over the real world. One could call this "augmented business reality." We associate augmented reality with superimposed data over real-world, real-time images. Here, we are talking about superimposing digital business transactions over the real world, real time. The new device-based mobile payments systems by Square, Inc. are part of this development, so is Bling Nation and Kenya's exciting M-PESA mobile payments solution, but so is mobile advertising and mobile commissions.

About $2m worth of M-PESA transactions are made through Kenyan mobile phones each day. This has led to an estimated increase of rural household income by those have adopted mobile payments by about 5–30%. This is real economic growth and is an important advance indication of what may still be coming in a grand scale on the Internet and on mobile phones.[13]

In a brilliant *Vanity Fair* article about Jack Dorsey, the co-founder of Twitter, David Kirkpatrick describes what motivations Dorsey associates with his new payments start-up, Square.

> Dorsey takes his design inspiration from Apple's Steve Jobs, whom he reveres. And he sees himself, like Jobs, producing an integrated system in a business where others have assembled kludgy agglomerations. "Payment is another form of communication," he says, "but it's never been treated as such. It's never been designed. It's never felt magical … We want … to make payments feel amazing."[14]

There has, of course, always been significant interaction between the real world and the web. But it has increased continually and has now reached the next level. In the beginning, catalogues like Yahoo! or search engines such as Google provided aids to navigate the Internet world. Craigslist and Groupon are navigational aids, which help us localize deals in the real world. Facebook connects real-world people together and creates a social graph.

The next level we are talking about is the superimposition of digital business on the local, real-world environment. Some would call this mobile business, but mobile makes us think of mobile devices, which is only one part of the story. Maybe local commerce is a better term.

The observation that everything will have an IP-address and communicate with each other increasingly is nothing new. Kevin Kelly wrote about "the new biology of machines" in 1994.[15] What we are talking about here is the combination between these technical developments in wiring the world and increasingly sophisticated web-based business models.

Square Inc. is not just enabling mobile payments, it is providing offline retailers with the rich data only an online retailer so far had access to. In a video for Stanford University's Entrepreneurship Corner, Jack Dorsey describes the dearth of data real-world coffee shops live with every day.[16] They know they made $400, but have no idea with what products, at what times, sold to which clients. Data allows measurement and measurement enables experimentation and constant tweaking and evolution. There is no way to recontact customers with special offers and use these offers to build a relationship. Square is making money by realizing commissions for itself, but in the process, it is making offline retail become more like online retail.

TechCrunch and others have reported on Foursquare's 3.0 version, launched on March 8, 2011, just in time for the SXSW conference in Austin.[17] In a pilot carried out in cooperation with American Express, people can use their credit cards to unlock local merchant deals during the conference.[18] The future of local deals are real-time offers provided as bypassers move through a street. A street's business will thus be reflected in augmented reality as one walks through it. Not everyone will enjoy being bombarded with coupons. But it's not only about walking.

In automotive-obsessed Germany, a recent study found that younger clients don't seek cars for status any more, but as mobile, wired platforms communicating online for purposes of entertainment, safety (with other cars) and, yes, to point out special commercial offers on the way.[19]

Our friend Max had it right after all; real-world business is rapidly being subsumed by web-based business models. This means Internet business models are coming full circle. During the New Economy, offline business models were adapted to the online world to make web business more understandable and more intuitive to consumers, many of whom were first-time buyers on the web. Through the modularization of Web 2.0 and freemium models, web business evolved and became more sophisticated. The *SimplySeven* remained as basic building blocks. Today, web business is being applied to the offline world.

Guiding the customer

For this book, we had the opportunity to discuss personal business models with John Seely Brown, one of the smartest thinkers out there on the topic of the future of business. It is Seely Brown who pointed out the importance of learning systems in the context of personal business models. With his colleagues at the Deloitte Center for the Edge, Seely Brown has spent a lot of time analyzing new and exciting dynamic business ecosystems, which come very close to what we have analyzed related to web business. The case that is most instructive in this regard, interestingly, is not online at all, but a very traditional business – textiles and apparel.

Hagel and Seely Brown first introduce Li & Fung in their book *The Only Sustainable Edge*.[20] The company is a US$12bn global process orchestrator in the apparel industry. Its clients are private labels; Li & Fung does not have its own branded fashion. The global apparel market is traditional, but by no means backward. Year-by-year, innovative methods are developed and new textiles are sold.

What is most exciting about Li & Fung is that it sources from over 7,500 business partners. None of them are exclusive. This means that multiple participants in the network have the opportunity to apply for a specific order. The key, given the dynamic nature of the industry, is that Li & Fung has set up a system, which helps its participants learn about new trends and developments. Guidance and learning go hand in hand. Knowledge flows freely throughout the ecosystem, allowing all participants to get better and better each year. In this way, Li & Fung itself can remain highly competitive. In the words of Seely Brown, the Li & Fung network is "a learning system, which pulls all its members up to higher levels of competitiveness continuously" (author's interview).

Li & Fung's network seems at first very different from the web businesses we discuss here, but the systematic application of learning among business partners plays a very important part in both Li & Fung's and in our world.

In fact, learning from customers to offer a better service and product experience has been the credo for all successful web businesses since the days of the New Economy. Today, smart businesses are learning much more effectively than before, using analytics-based approaches. In recent years, analytics-based solutions were used very successfully to provide recommendations to consumers. This was not a trivial development; a "Long Tail" of business has emerged rivaling the mass market. They have also been used in combination with experiments to test new products and business models. Now, smart companies are using analytics in living, learning systems to provide tailored business options.

Both the online games studio Zynga and the new web-based bank BankSimple have built intelligent analytical systems that continuously learn from their customers and provide guidance to chose the right options. This is very different from knowledge as a fixed asset; it is insight gained in-flight. Both Zynga and BankSimple use this continuous insight to provide a far better customer experience than previous online versions of games and banking. Both companies are not just personalizing content but the complete business relationship between them and their customers.

More than 100 million people play Zynga games. The company, as we have seen in Chapter 1, combines art and science, especially the science of measurement and experimentation. We have also discussed in the first chapter how Zynga uses hundreds of continuous, controlled experiments in-flight to constantly test new assumptions to improve their games. The objective of Zynga is to create the most social games possible, to enable players to connect to friends all over the world through games.

What a world of connected gaming enthusiasts can accomplish was shown in January 2010 after the devastating earthquake in Haiti. Zynga players raised over $1.5m in just five days to support on-site emergency relief teams, helping victims with food and supplies. Players bought specific virtual goods, white corn in FarmVille, a Haitian drum in Mafia Wars and a Haiti fish in FishVille – the proceeds were donated.[21] Zynga players donated again when disaster struck in Japan in March 2011.[22]

Usually, Zynga sells in-game virtual goods to make money. Virtual goods are also used to improve the gaming experience; free virtual goods can be given to friends. Giving a virtual good to a friend, for example, is not a positive experience if the friend does not usually respond to virtual presents and greetings. Zynga tries to guide people away from giving items to nonresponsive users. In this case, a lack of knowledge will lower the attractiveness of the game over time. Instead, Zynga provides personalized guidance to using virtual goods.

Zynga learns from its users and provides educated choices. Companies in completely different industries, for example financial services, use learning and education in similar ways.

BankSimple is a new online bank. It has made the explicit choice to create long-term, sustainable business relationships with its customers – instead of benefiting from hidden or sudden fees. The CEO, Joschua Reich, describes the approach of BankSimple in this way:

> While there are a lot of rules that make personal financial management difficult for an individual who isn't trained in accounting or finance, computers are very good at evaluating different scenarios under different rules. The mathematics isn't complex for a computer. Unfortunately, existing financial institutions make a significant portion of their revenue from fees and charges that are levied when customers fail to understand the rules. In essence, banks make money by keeping customers confused. We've structured our business so that we do not profit from fees, so we have no incentive to make our customers lives complex.[23]

Banks make money by extending loans to people who may not have needed them if they had saved their money and planned in advance for their spending. This is where BankSimple's analytical systems come in. BankSimple evaluates a "Safe to Spend" balance across all of a customer's accounts. Clients can input big-ticket items they wish to spend money on in the future, such as a vacation. The system provides an in-flight, graphical view on the achievement of personalized savings targets.

Both Zynga and BankSimple have geared their analytics and personalization toward a long-term business relationship between their own company and their customers. This requires flexibility and tailoring of front end as well as back end systems.

Examples of personal businesses on the web

We have discussed the methods and tools available today which enable personal business on the web and off the web. Here are several examples of companies that enable their customers to pay with what they want, wherever they want and how much they want.

- Top Guest: Receiving loyalty points for showing up at hotels, restaurants, lounges.
- LikeList: Rewards for personal recommendations.
- Groupon: Discounts for people with buying intentions who pass deals on to friends.

- Sticky Bits: Scanning barcodes on products to unlock discounts.
- RelayRides: Monetizing your unused car.
- Airbnb: Monetizing the mattress in your living room.
- WePay: Allowing people to set up their own payments collection.
- Warner Brothers: Paying movies with Facebook Credits.
- Bling Nation: Pay with mobile phone or redeem loyalty points.

A personal business relationship means that consumers are transformed into business partners. What was a dialogue between businesses and customers now becomes an exchange of value. Value can mean many things, not just money: recommendations, loyalty, work or knowledge. In this context, longer-term, relationship-based aspects of a business partnership such as reputation and trust become more important than before.

Reputation and trust as an opportunity

There is a darker side to personal business models. We have seen that many of the companies mentioned in this chapter seek to reward activity, which previously has been carried out through voluntarily donated time, data or knowledge. As soon as tailored reward schemes are set up, incentives are balanced differently. A personal recommendation may be less honest if it comes with a personal reward.

Furthermore, reward schemes sometimes benefit from intransparency. In some schemes involving points or coupons, consumers actually are deluded into thinking that they are the main beneficiaries, whereas the lion's share goes elsewhere.

It is also important to point out that several of the newer ventures, on the forefront Facebook itself but also Foursquare and many others, are proprietary platforms. The data on these platforms is owned by a company that "pays" for it, not any more by the community of users itself.

All this does not mean that personal business models and innovative incentive schemes should be avoided. They can help people realize their own personal business value better. They can be very beneficial for small businesses, because they leverage something that small businesses have always been good at: local experience, personal recommendations and tips.

This is an opportunity for companies to actually benefit by being more transparent, simpler and more fair. If you are one of the good companies, flaunt it and prove it.

Back to the basics

The task of selecting the right business model for one's web business is just as important today as it always has been. People are still anxious about paying for things on the web and they want it done right. With growing sophistication, however, it has also become more complex. Back in the New Economy, when Pierre Omidyar hurriedly searched for a way to recoup his Internet traffic costs, there were seven basic options available. "Fast track" companies can now basically take business model building blocks "off the shelf" and combine them at will. And web businesses is not stopping to evolve, experiment and adapt. Now, the methods and tools are available to make people choose their preferred, personalized business building blocks.

We tried to put all our thinking in one place with the objective of helping not just Internet entrepreneurs and executives but just about anybody out there whose business life is impacted by the Internet.

In the book, we have described the seven building blocks and have discussed the advantages and disadvantages of each. It is not possible to say, however, that one module is inherently superior to another. This is the case even if we take profits as our sole evaluation criteria, in the spirit of Yuri Milner, a Russian entrepreneur and investor who invested early in some of most promising companies of the Web 2.0 era such as Facebook, Zynga and Groupon. Milner was quoted by *Business Week* as saying: "It's not about revenues: The fundamental economics in digital business is scale and margins. The top line has become the bottom line."[24]

Take, as an example, service sales, a building block, which is direct and unique and doesn't usually scale well. Skype offers direct and unique communication services, but is by its peer-to-peer nature inherently scalable and produces beautiful margins. For this reason, the whole range of module options should be considered as a basis of a web-based business model. In the right business model context, even the weakest building block of the *SimplySeven* can be perfect.

There are two ways to benefit from this book. The first is as a guidebook to help you select the perfect business model for your Internet service. It could be a service on the social web. It could be a mobile App, too. Or an online game for a console. But even if you have an existing business model that works for you, it may grow rusty over time. You may have neglected your business model in recent months and stopped trying to improve it constantly. Keep evolving. Testing. Experimenting. The second benefit of this book is about just this – awareness. And to paraphrase Andrew Grove, we want you to stay paranoid.

Some thoughts in this book will seem obvious. We cringe every day at seeing how some of the most basic lessons for Internet business are disregarded by smart and otherwise savvy people. They put a huge amount of effort into their web site – this is great – but when it comes to the business model, they approach this important step with the crudeness of a bulldozer. They pick fashionable business models that are just the hype and don't think out of the box. Then it isn't a surprise if customers flee. We believe that it is really practical things that make an Internet business really successful. The really obvious things can also – this is the flip side – ruin one's hard-won popularity in a short amount of time. This book is about making the right choices. And about helping people pay without pain.

APPENDIX

Stress-testing the *SimplySeven*

Most of this book reflects our personal experience gained by building Internet companies, investing in start-ups and consulting. However, we felt it was important to stress test the *SimplySeven* using quantitative information. It took some effort to arrive at a representative group of significant Internet companies. A combination of the Nielsen Global Top 100 with additional selection criteria finally did the trick. As shown below, we were able to generate a rich cache of data for the more popular Internet business model building blocks. The fact that there was less data on some of the others, however, indicates that the web economy has not reached maturity yet. Going for the less popular business building blocks and thinking outside of the box actually is an opportunity, which is wide open.

The so-called "universe" of 21 Internet companies is not identical to the "flagship" companies we use extensively to explain each Internet model in the book's chapters. This is because some flagship companies fail one of our stress-tests hurdles. One prominent example is Apple, which does not generate more than 50% of its sales on the Internet but still is extremely successful at digital license sales. Or Skype, which is not a public company quoted on a stock market.

Our main objective for the stress test was to understand the frequency of each building block among the most popular Internet sites. We also wanted to check how companies using the different Internet building blocks compare to each other using some basic financial indicators.

The selection criteria

To arrive at a consistent set of comparable information, we selected the companies for our so-called Internet universe according to three different parameters:

1. The company has to be present with its Internet presence on the January 2010 list of Nielsen Top 100 Global Websites.[1] We chose the

Nielsen Top 100 list to arrive at a group of significant Internet companies in a non-arbitrary way. We figured, if you are a global Internet leader, you are on that list. One problem with using this list is that it is prejudiced against B2B companies, including some prominent ones, such as Salesforce.com. B2B companies simply do not attract as many users to their web sites, compared to consumer businesses. While it is much harder for a B2B company to make the list, nevertheless, some are included. These companies have a significant base of small and medium-sized businesses as clients. Examples are both of our service sales representatives, Experian and Vistaprint. Experian provides credit information, Vistaprint a printing service.

2. The company has to be listed on a stock market. The reason for this is simple: we need reliable financial information. Specific company financial information used came from the Annual Reports of these companies. Basic financial information (Enterprise Value, CAGR, Sales, Operating Income) came courtesy of Yahoo! Finance[2] (sourced from Capital IQ and other information providers such as CSI Commodity service or Morningstar) and E*TRADE Financial.[3]

3. The company has to generate approximately 50% of its revenues through Internet business. This is tricky, but absolutely necessary. While a company that has a strong web site and generates some of its sales on the Internet is, of course, employing an Internet business model, its financial profile will reflect the whole business (unless the Internet part is separately identified in its financial reports, which is seldom the case). Comcast is on the Nielsen Top 100 list because it has a popular web presence, but it is mostly a cable TV and telecommunications company. The same applies to Time Warner. Netflix just barely made the list of Internet companies. It is included because it has successfully transformed a significant proportion of its subscription business in recent years from a postal-based DVD rental offering to a streaming-based Internet service. Netflix's Annual Report mentions that 48% of its 12m subscribers watched streaming video over the Internet in Q4 2009.[4]

Initial results: seven confirmed and unevenly distributed

We were left with 21 companies in our universe, which were on the Nielsen Top 100, and were listed on a stock exchange somewhere in the world and generated around 50% or more of their sales over the Internet. We cheered when we found out that each of our seven Internet business models was present with at least one company. We also could not identify an eighth business model. Nor was a model redundant.

There were big differences, however, to what extent the different building blocks were represented. The advertising and commissions categories were the strongest with eight and four companies represented respectively. Here, we could carry out some pretty solid analysis. Subscriptions, service sales and retail were OK, with three to two companies each. The rest are very much underrepresented with only one company each – an opportunity for thinking "out of the box."

The listing of the first pure play Internet company, the Netscape IPO, happened over 15 years ago. Since then, thousands of Internet companies have been founded and several dozens of Internet companies have been listed, each of them generating a long trail of financial information. One would expect that every business model would be represented several times on the Top 100 list and also be listed on a stock exchange. Not so.

The weakest categories each had only one representative company. They were unsurprisingly, financial risk management, and, surprisingly, digital license sales. The only financial risk management candidate, IG Group, is a strange creature, part foreign exchange spread betting service, part sports betting.

Apple is the 1,000-Pound gorilla of the digital license sales business model at the moment – but it hardly is an Internet company. We would have loved to have seen this innovative company included in the financial analysis, but Apple still makes far more than 50% of its revenues off hardware and devices. The company we were left with, Real Networks, had dismal financial results in 2009 and 2008. Just one company in the digital license sales category and that one loss-making on top of it; this does not really give us much to base our comparative analysis on.

We expect many more Internet businesses working with the models license sales or financial risk management to enter our universe of significant companies in the next months and years. We are not there yet.

A note on Dell. While Apple was grudgingly removed from our universe of Internet companies, we did include Dell. Dell is known for being the classic direct sales company – without a bricks-based retail presence (although Dell very recently has begun to enter the classic retail channel, especially in emerging economies). Unfortunately, there is no confirmed information from Dell about the proportion of direct Internet and phone sales compared to indirect retail channel sales. Also, we know that 54% of Dell's total worldwide sales in 2009 was to large enterprises and to the public sector; in these cases, the Internet is used to support the order process, but not facilitate the business model. The remaining 46%, however, is almost evenly divided between small- and medium-sized companies and consumers. In the end, it was a very close call. We decided to include Dell in our universe of Internet companies. It is a listed company, of course, and also is present on the Nielsen Top 100 List.

Table A.1 SimplySeven Internet company universe

Company	Nielsen-Rank (Jan 2010)	Unique Users	Category	Revenue 2009 (m)	Op. Income Margin 2009 (m)	CAGR (2005–09)	EV/R	Main Business
Google	#1	349,758,716	Advertising	$23,651	$8,312	40%	5,96	Search-engine optimized and information-based advertising services.
Yahoo	#3	233,479,611	Advertising	$6,460	$387	5%	2,64	Content-based advertising services.
AOL	#8	128,146,575	Advertising	$3,257	$458	−21%	0,64	Content-based advertising services and internet service provider.
eBay	#9	121,740,943	Commission	$8,727	$1,457	18%	3,01	Commission-based marketplace for businesses and consumers.
Amazon	#11	111,945,278	Retail	$24,509	$1,129	30%	2,11	Retail products for a multitude of category groups via internet.
Ask	#13	100,846,108	Advertising	$1,376	−$1,063	−28%	0,83	Advertising services based on a Q&A based search engine.
Real Networks	#16	61,513,698	License Sales	$562	−$242	15%	0,38	Internet media delivery and services.
WikiAnswers	#40	28,825,267	Advertising	$21	$5	78%	1,88	Advertising services based on a Q&A based search engine.
UOL	#43	27,726,174	Subscription	$554	−$235	14%	1,26	Internet service provider.
Expedia	#54	24,143,300	Commission	$2,995	$571	9%	1,92	Internet-based travel reservation and booking serices.

Company	Rank	(col3)	Category	(col5)	(col6)	(col7)	(col8)	Description
iG Group	#55	24,084,472	Financial Risk	$464	$258	35%	N/A	Financial derivatives and sports betting.
Dell	#57	23,324,607	Retail	$51,902	$2,172	-2%	0,33	Direct sales of computers and IT equipment.
WebMD	#62	22,642,174	Advertising	$439	$26	28%	4,67	Advertising services based on health-related information.
Netflix	#67	22,008,309	Subscription	$1,670	$192	25%	1,93	On-demand video streaming and online video rental.
Monster	#79	19,416,161	Advertising	$905	-$9	3%	2,18	Direct advertising services for employment and job adverts.
Priceline Network	#81	18,956,830	Commission	$2,338	$471	25%	3,87	Discounted travel services.
Experian	#82	18,645,754	Services	$3,873	$613	11%	2,3	Credit information services.
SuperPages	#86	18,077,680	Commission	$2,512	$741	-7%	4,11	Local business directories.
Reed Elsevier	#91	17,588,470	Subscription	$3,400	$440	-3%	2,59	Information and publishing services especially academic and legal.
Vistaprint	#94	17,426,001	Services	$516	$62	54%	4,12	Printed & promotional material and marketing services.
Geeknet	#100	16,270,479	Advertising	$66	-$13	30%	1,05	Community-based and tech-related advertising services.

Most of the 21 companies were a no-brainer to group into one of the *SimplySeven* categories. Google is a thoroughbred advertising company – at the moment, at least. The year 2010 was great for Google's mobile operating system Android and with it comes Android Marketplace, a digital license sales platform. And Google is making progress selling its office software as software-as-a-service subscriptions to companies. So far, however, a vast majority of Google sales still come from advertising.

We had to look up the revenues of some companies. As mentioned, Netflix just scraped by into our universe with its expanding online user base. Reed Elsevier actually is a long-established company – several constituent parts of which long predate the World Wide Web. But two of its main businesses, LexisNexis (42% of revenues in 2009) and Elsevier (33%) are classic subscription models.[5] LexisNexis, the legal database, is completely online and Elsevier, the academic publishing arm for scientific and health journals, almost entirely so.

AOL used to be the best-known company around for the subscription model. In 2006, AOL generated 75% of its sales from longer-term contracts as an online service provider. The degree of competition in the ISP (internet service provider) space was so tough in recent years that AOL was forced to become an advertising-based company. 56% of revenues were generated from advertising in 2009. The sad part of the story is that the switch of business models was not achieved by a strategic transformation but by sheer financial erosion of subscription sales. In 2009, AOL generated roughly the same sales from advertising as in 2006, but only a fourth of its subscription revenues.[6]

Amazon historically is one of our most active companies when it comes to testing different business models. For now, at least, Amazon stays retail. Amazon.com's initiatives with digital license sales (downloads for the Kindle reader and sale of music and video downloads) and commissions (third party marketplaces) are still developing. Amazon is moving into license sales and commissions to decrease its reliance just a little on its costly real-world warehouse and shipments business. Amazon shares the retail group with Dell, incidentally.

From a classic bricks and mortar perspective, Dell and Amazon do not have the same business model. With a few exceptions such as IT cables and accessories, Amazon sells stuff created by other companies; Dell sells its own stuff. Amazon is a retail company; Dell is IT.

For the purposes of our business model framework, both companies belong to the same group. The customers of both companies go to their respective web sites to buy physical items, which are subsequently shipped to them. Amazon and Dell face many of the same challenges; they operate an online storefront, they manage shipments and returns. Whether one company makes its own stuff or not, is not relevant for our framework since it does not change what the customer is getting for her money (a physical product). In fact, Amazon has started to introduce its own range of products, called AmazonBasics.

Indie bands selling their own music directly over the Internet and an aggregator such as Apple also share the same digital license sales business model, while in real life they are perceived as running very different businesses.

Our business model framework was created with a single perspective in mind – the customer perspective. And with a single question: what exactly is the customer buying? The customer perspective makes things very simple.

Of course, the customer will be very interested in the ease of use of the shop and the quality of the service. And she will need to find the shop in the first place and the product she seeks. Amazon or Dell may have different advantages and disadvantages in providing these services – based on the fact that they are a retailer or a direct brand owner and manufacturer.

In a way, we were very fortunate that the Internet flagship companies, such as Google, eBay or Amazon, still generate most of their sales with a single Internet business model. We are not sure how this will pan out in the future. Google may very well continue to be successful with its Android Marketplace – which is based on a digital license sales model. Amazon is moving more and more into this direction as well, with digital books and music. The most likely outcome is the following: some significant pure play companies will successfully stick to a single business model. There will be others, however, which increasingly mix the models.

At the moment, however, we can still compare basic financial information of our Internet universe companies to each other and get a good indication of the performance of particular business models.

Retail leads in sales

The inclusion of a large IT manufacturer in the category of Internet retail does mean that the total amount of revenue generated in this category is high. Retail clearly leads the pack in the amount of revenue generated by each category and the amount of monthly revenue per unique user. Dell and Amazon also lead the Top Five list of companies in our universe with the highest revenue in 2009.

It is easy for Dell to lead the list of sales generated per unique Internet user. Dell has the highest revenue of all our companies ($52bn) but has

Table A.2 Total business model revenue

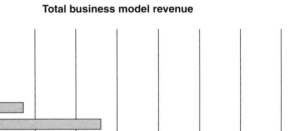

	Retail	Advertising	Commission	Subscription	Services	Licence sales	Financial
Sales (bn)	$76	$36	$17	$6	$4	$0.6	$0.5

Table A.3 Top five revenue

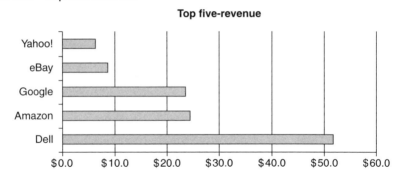

	Dell	Amazon	Google	eBay	Yahoo!
Revenue (Bn)	$51.9	$24.5	$23.7	$8.7	$6.5

relatively few unique users (23m per month). Compared to other companies in the Nielsen Global 100, it is on rank 57 for the number of unique web site users. Obviously, the users that Dell has on its web site are there to buy computers and accessories, which are pricey ticket items. Also, as discussed earlier, a 54% of Dell's revenues are generated through large enterprises and the public sector. To arrive at our statistic, we divide the average monthly sales in 2009 by the number of unique monthly users determined by Nielsen in January 2010.

Table A.4 Top five average monthly revenue/average monthly users

	Dell	Amazon	Experian	Reed Elsevier	Superpages
Revenue/User	$185.43	$18.25	$17.31	$16.11	$11.58

While advertising dominates the other lists, there are no advertising-based companies on the top five list for revenue per unique web site user. Obviously, this is because advertising has a small value contribution per unique web site user compared to all other business models. The client of the advertising business is not the web site user itself but a business; the web site user is not buying anything at all. Google leads the pack with $5.64 monthly revenue per monthly unique user; the average for all advertising Internet companies (per company) is $2.14.

Table A.5 Many users and rapid growth – the advertising business model

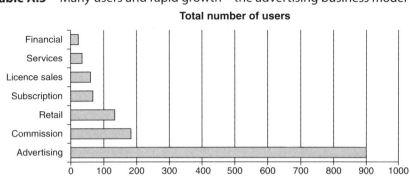

	Advertising	Commission	Retail	Subscription	Licence sales	Services	Financial
Users (m)	899	183	135	67	62	36	24

Advertising is about reaching the highest numbers of people. It also is about the quality of those people, if they are in the right target group or not. As a general rule of thumb, however, the more the better. And advertising also is the most popular business model in our Internet company universe. This explains the massive lead the advertising business model has before all others in the amount of monthly unique users. Next to the mega gorilla Google, there are some other 1,000-pound specimens in this group, such as Yahoo!, AOL and Monster.com.

The advertising business model does not just benefit the company offering advertising as a product to its business clients itself but also many other popular publisher web sites which use advertising as their revenue stream. Jointly with commissions, the advertising business model is very good at integrating different types of Internet companies in a business ecosystem.

The success story of Google in the time period we are examining is without parallel. Google generates $1.0m sales per employee – the highest of all companies in our universe. It grew a whopping 40% annually each year from 2005 to 2009, a spectacular record in itself. Google's growth is even more impressive given the fact that the global Internet, according to the web site Internet World Stats, grew a mere 15% in the same period year on year (from 1.018bn in December 2005 to 1.802bn in December 2009).[7] It is no surprise then that this is recognized by the stock market. Google also clearly leads the list of Enterprise Valuation over Sales.

Market valuations – advertising, again

We already discussed why Google is the hero of our Internet company universe. It is surprising, however, that two other advertising-based enterprises make the top EV/R list. Is this only because the stock market is deluded by advertising and Web 2.0 hype? We don't think so. WebMD and Monster are companies that do not only reach significant amounts of people, they are specialized players with a clear profile: job search and health. Both of these are huge real-world markets. As more business goes digital in these segments, these companies will benefit.

We have removed IG Group from the EV/R consideration because its EV/R ratio (500x) was distorted due to small trading volume and a significant cash pile the company has collected relative to its sales.

Table A.6 Top five enterprise value/revenue

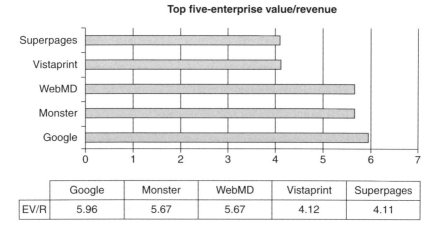

	Google	Monster	WebMD	Vistaprint	Superpages
EV/R	5.96	5.67	5.67	4.12	4.11

Margins – the beauty of aggregation

Advertising- and commission-based companies lead the list for the highest margins. This is because, as classic aggregator-type, purely digital businesses, they tend to have far lower cost bases than most others.

Other business models cannot compare to these two in terms of margins. Retail companies have to deal with shipment and warehousing costs. Amazon's operating income margin in 2009 was only 5%. Subscription-based companies usually have higher customer service costs and often need to provide a continuous stream of value to their customers to justify the subscription contract. In terms of their margins, they linger in the middle of the pack. Netflix, which runs a very tight ship, achieved a margin of 11% in 2009. Reed Elsevier generated a margin of 13%.

Service companies sell unique products or services, which also can be quite costly unless you have scalability worked out. We have two services companies in our universe. Vistaprint provides a printing service. Experian offers credit information. Both services can be automated to a high degree, resulting in margins that are not altogether bad. Vistaprint's operating income margin is 12%. Experian's is 16%.

There is an exception on the top, however. It is an indication of things to come, that our only financial risk management company, IG Group, leads the margins list. By offering foreign exchange spread betting and sports betting, IG Group is able to generate dream margins. We are sure

Table A.7 Top five operating income margin

Top five-operating income margin

	iG	Google	Superpages	WikiAnswers	Priceline
Margin	56%	35%	29%	24%	20%

that the financial model will become more attractive with growing liquidity on the Internet.

Key financial indicators

To conclude the analysis of the universe of Internet companies, we created a bubble chart showing three important financial valuation parameters: total sales, margins and growth.

Table A.8 Key financial indicators (list)

	CAGR	Margins	Sales (Bn)
IG Group	43%	35%	$0,5
Google	40%	35%	$23,7
Superpages	-7%	29%	$2,5
Priceline	25%	20%	$2,3
Experian	11%	16%	$3,9
Real Networks	-56%	15%	$0,6
Reed Elsevier	-3%	13%	$3,4
Vistaprint	54%	12%	$0,5
Netflix	25%	11%	$1,7
WebMD	28%	6%	$0,4
Amazon	30%	5%	$24,5
Dell	-2%	4%	$51,9

Appendix

We picked out the two top companies in the EV/R ranking for each business model; for financial risk management and license sales we had only one company each. These companies are regarded by investors as the best in their class.

The summary chart shows that the selected companies vary strongly regarding the growth they achieved in the last years. This was to be expected.

The summary chart also confirms yet again the heroic position of Google, which gets everything right: sales, growth and margins. IG Group, the lone representative of financial risk management is up there, too, albeit with a far smaller revenue base than Google, and therefore much less impressive in terms of sheer achievement. For the corresponding companies mapped on the chart below, please consult Table A.8 above.

What is interesting overall is that there seems to be some correlation among the business model building blocks based on margins. The highest operating income margins are achieved by financial risk management,

Table A.9 Key financial indicators (bubble chart)

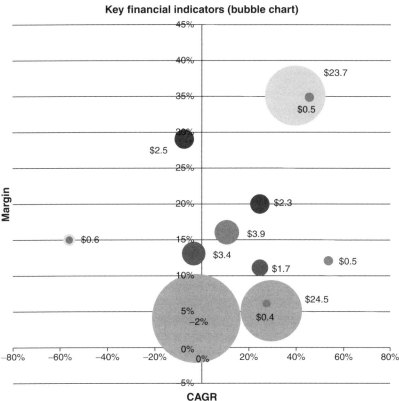

advertising and commissions, followed by services and license sales; subscriptions and retail are at the bottom. The margin of WebMD disappointed as an advertising company. We were surprised by how well the services companies did and by the lackluster performance of subscription. Obviously, with just 21 companies, we have to tread carefully. The analysis of basic financial information was carried out to complement and stress test the practical observations and experience we based *SimplySeven* on.

INTERVIEWS

- Rich Aberman, Co-Founder, WePay, Palo Alto, March 16, 2011 (Personal Interview, Palo Alto)
- Trip Adler, Co-Founder and CEO, Scribd, San Francisco, March 17, 2011 (Personal Interview, San Francisco)
- Immad Akhund and Jude Gomila, Founders, Heyzap, San Francisco, March 17, 2011 (Personal Interview, San Francisco)
- Matt Bannick, Managing Partner, Omidyar Network, March 17, 2011 (Telephone Interview)
- Roberto Bonanzinga, Partner, Balderton Capital, London, March 23, 2011 (Telephone Interview)
- John Seely Brown, Visiting Scholar at the University of Southern California and Independent Co-Chairman of the Deloitte Center for the Edge, February 24, 2011 (Telephone Interview)
- Brad Burnham, Partner, Union Square Ventures, New York, March 3, 2011 (Telephone Interview)
- Frédéric Court, General Partner, Advent Venture Partners, London, United Kingdom, March 3, 2011 (Telephone Interview)
- Esther Dyson, Principal, EDventure, New York City, March 18, 2011 (Personal Interview, Menlo Park)
- Joe Gebbia, President and Co-Founder, Airbnb, March 18, 2011 (Personal Interview, San Francisco)
- Mark Gorenberg, Managing Director, Hummer Winblad Venture Partners, San Francisco, March 16, 2011 (Personal Interview, San Francisco)
- Bill Gross, Chief Executive Officer, Idealab, Pasadena, March 15, 2011 (Personal Interview, Pasadena)
- Howard Hartenbaum, Partner, August Capital, March 16, 2011 (Personal Interview, Menlo Park)
- Roland Manger, Co-Founder and Managing Partner of Earlybird Venture Capital, Munich, Germany, February 16, 2011 (Telephone Interview)
- Joshua Reich, CEO and Co-Founder, Simple Finance Technology Corp., New York City, March 23, 2011 (Email Interview)

- Ken Rudin, General Manager of Analytics, Zynga, San Francisco, March 23, 2011 (Telephone Interview)
- David Rusenko, Founder, Weebly, San Francisco, March 16, 2011 (Personal Interview, San Francisco)
- Vivek Wadhwa, Director of Research, Center for Entrepreneurship and Research Commercialization and Executive in Residence, Pratt School of Engineering, Duke University, March 14, 2011 (Personal Interview, Menlo Park)

Notes

Chapter 1 Think outside the box, constantly experiment and evolve

1. Fred Wilson, "Airbnb," March 16, 2011, http://www.avc.com/, accessed on March 22, 2011.
2. Guy Kawaskai (2008) *Reality Check*, Penguin Group, New York, p. 460.
3. Jason Fried and David Heinemeier Hansson (2010) *Rework: Change the Way You Work Forever*, The Random House Group, New York.
4. Jessica Livingston (2008) *Founders at Work: Stories of Startups' Early Days*, Apress, Berkeley.
5. Yvon Chouinard (2005) *Let My People Go Surfing*, The Penguin Press, New York, USA.
6. TechCrunch (2011) "Ze Frank's Star.me Is Like Being In Kindergarten All Over Again," by Alexia Tsotsis, http://techcrunch.com/2011/02/04/star-me/, accessed on February 6, 2011.
7. Barbara Van Schewick (2010) *Internet Architecture and Innovation*, The MIT Press, Cambridge, MA, p. 206 (eBay mention) and p. 310 (Google mention).
8. Jessica Livingston (2008) pp. 247, 249.
9. Interview with Brad Burnham.
10. Neil J. Beaton (2010) *Valuing Early State and Venture-Backed Companies*, John Wiley & Sons, New York, p. 4.
11. Fred Wilson, "The Opportunity Fund," January 15, 2011, on the USV web site. http://www.usv.com/2011/01/the-opportunity-fund.php, accessed on March 12, 2011.
12. Wayne W. Eckerson on February 2, 2010, "Proactive Analytics That Drive the Business," http://tdwi.org/blogs/wayne-eckerson/2010/02/zynga.aspx, TDWI (The Data Warehousing Institute), accessed on March 4, 2011.
13. Ken Rudin, "Actionable Analytics at Zynga: Leveraging Big Data to Make Online Games More Fun and Social," http://tdwi.org/videos/2010/08/actionable-analytics-at-zynga-leveraging-big-data-to-make-online-games-more-fun-and-social.aspx, TDWI (The Data Warehousing Institute), accessed on March 4, 2011.
14. Ken Rudin Interview, March 23, 2011.
15. Thomas H. Davenport and Jeanne G. Harris (2007) *Competing on Analytics, The New Science of Winning*, Harvard Business School Press, Boston, pp. 4, 5.
16. Guy Kawasaki (2008) pp. 12, 13.
17. Barbara Van Schewick (2010) pp. 204–214.
18. Niko Marcel Waesche (2003) *Internet Entrepreneurship in Europe, Venture Failure and the Timing of Telecommunications Reform*, Edward Elgar, Cheltenham, p. 190, footnote 25.
19. Michael Arrington, "Start Fund: Yuri Milner, SV Angel Offer EVERY New Y Combinator Startup $150k," January 28, 2011, TechCrunch, http://techcrunch.

com/2011/01/28/yuri-milner-sv-angel-offer-every-new-y-combinator-startup-150k/, accessed on March 4, 2011.
20. *The Economist* (2010) "The Pivotal Moment: Bet on a Boss who can Twirl on his Toes," December 4, 2010, p. 74.
21. Frédéric Court Interview.
22. iXL Enterprises Inc. (1999) *S1 Securities and Exchange Commission Registration Statement*, date published April 7, 1999, p. 57.
23. Alexander Osterwalder and Yves Pigneur (2010) *Business Model Generation*, John Wiley & Sons, Inc., Hoboken.
24. Osterwalder and Pigneur (2010) p. 15.
25. Jessica Livingston (2008) p. 129.

Chapter 2   The first building block – services sales

1. Esther Dyson's Bio, on http://www.edventure.com/new-bio.html accessed March 22, 2011.
2. Esther Dyson, "Health Care's Frequent Flyers," October 20, 2010, Project Syndicate, http://www.project-syndicate.org/commentary/dyson25/English, accessed March 22, 2011.
3. Twitter @edyson, March 23, 2011.
4. *The New York Times* (2004) "Small and Smaller," by Thomas L. Friedman, http://www.nytimes.com/2004/03/04/opinion/small-and-smaller.html, accessed on February 3, 2011.
5. *The New York Times* (2006) "Academia Dissects the Service Sector, but is it a Science?" by Seteve Lohr, http://www.nytimes.com/2006/04/18/business/18services.html?_r=1&adxnnl=1&adxnnlx=1296650556-kbUdresAZPQA7kdTYZ9jAA, accessed on February 3, 2011. *Bloomberg BusinessWeek* (2005) "The Empathy Economy," by Bruce Nussbaum, http://www.businessweek.com/bwdaily/dnflash/mar2005/nf2005037_4086.htm, accessed on February 3, 2011.
6. TeleGeography Research (2010) "International Phone Traffic Growth Slows, while Skype Accelerates," http://www.telegeography.com/cu/article.php?article_id=31718, accessed on February 3, 2011.
7. Skype Technologies S.A. (2009) "Investor Group to Acquire Majority Stake in Skype," http://about.skype.com/press/2009/09/investor_group_to_acquire_majo.html, accessed on February 3, 2011.
8. A. Thomann (2006) *Skype – A Baltic Success Story* (Credit Suisse), https://emagazine.credit-suisse.com/app/article/index.cfm?fuseaction=OpenArticle&aoid=163167&coid=7805&lang=EN, accessed on February 3, 2011.
9. *Bloomberg BusinessWeek* (2006) "Searching For An Encore To Skype," http://www.businessweek.com/magazine/content/06_48/b4011067.htm, accessed on February 3, 2011.
10. *The Economist* (2005) "The Meaning of Free Speech," http://www.economist.com/node/4400704?story_id=4400704, accessed on February 3, 2011.
11. *Bloomberg BusinessWeek* (2006) "Searching For An Encore To Skype," http://www.businessweek.com/magazine/content/06_48/b4011067.htm, accessed on February 3, 2011.
12. *The Economist* (2006) "Don't Bet against the Internet," by Eric Schmidt, http://www.economist.com/node/8133511?story_id=8133511, accessed on February 3, 2011.

13. *The Economist* (2005) "The Meaning of Free Speech," http://www.economist.com/node/4400704?story_id=4400704, accessed on February 3, 2011.
14. *The Economist* (2009) "If Skype Should Fall," http://www.economist.com/node/14530209, accessed on February 3, 2011.

Chapter 3 The second building block – subscriptions

1. *The Economist* (2009) "Beyond the Ether," http://www.economist.com/node/15048791, accessed on February 3, 2011.
2. Nielsen NetRatings (2005) "Online Newspapers Enjoy Double-Digit Year-Over-Year Growth, Reaching One Out of Four Internet Users," http://www.nielsen-online.com/pr/pr_051115.pdf, accessed on February 3, 2011.
3. *The New York Times* (2007) "Times to Stop Charging for Parts of its Web Site," by Richard Perez-Peña, http://www.nytimes.com/2007/09/18/business/media/18times.html?_r=1, accessed on February 3, 2011.

Chapter 4 The third building block – retail

1. TidBITS (2001) "Where Webvan went wrong," by Adam C. Engst, http://db.tidbits.com/article/6493, accessed on February 3, 2011.
2. See Tristan Louis' web site: http://www.tnl.net/ (interim CTO of Boo.com). See also Ernst Malmsten, Erik Portanger, Charles Drazin, *Boo Hoo*, Random House, 2001, p. vii.
3. Forbes.com (2003) "Amazon.com Vs. Barnes & Noble," by Julie Watson, http://www.forbes.com/2003/09/08/cx_jw_0908mondaymatch.html, accessed on February 3, 2011.
4. *The Financial Times* (2006) "Gucci Opens Tokyo Flagship Store," November 13, 2006, p. 9.
5. Thomas H. Davenport and Jeanne G. Harris (2007) *Competing on Analytics, The New Science of Winning*, Harvard Business School Press, Boston, p. 4.
6. Chris Locke, Doc Searls, David Weinberger and Rick Levine (1999) *The Cluetrain Manifesto: The End of Business as Usual*, Perseus Books, New York.

Chapter 5 The fourth building block – commissions

1. *The Economist* (2010) "Riders on a Swarm," http://www.economist.com/node/16789226, accessed on February 3, 2011.
2. A. Cohen (2002) *The Perfect Store: Inside eBay* (Little, Brown and Company, New York), pp. 1–9, 41, 44, 64, 65, 76.
3. *The Economist* (2005) "Happy e-Birthdays: After Ten Years, what has been Learnt about Succeeding as an e-Business?" http://www.economist.com/node/4199153, accessed on February 3, 2011. *Business 2.0 Magazine* (2006) "The Big Guns' Next Target: eBay, Business" by Michael V. Copeland on CNNMoney.com (ed.), http://money.cnn.com/magazines/business2/business2_archive/2006/01/01/8368106/index.htm, accessed on February 3, 2011.

4. M. Meeker and D. Joseph (2007) *Listings * ASPs * Conversion Rates = GMV eBay US Historical Trends* (Morgan Stanley).

Chapter 6   The fifth building block – advertising

1. J. Battelle (2005) *The Search: How Google and its Rivals Rewrote the Rules of Business and Transformed Our Culture*, Portfolio, New York, pp. 2–3, 20–37, 153–188.
2. J. Battelle (2005) pp. 95–121.
3. Zenith OptiMedia (2006) *Online Advertising to Grow Seven Times Faster than Offline Advertising in 2007*, London, Press Release, date published December 4, 2006.
4. Project For Excellence in Journalism and the Pew Internet & American Life Project (2010) *The State of the News Media 2010*, http://www.stateofthemedia.org/2010/index.php (home page), accessed on February 3, 2011.
5. Zenith OptiMedia (2006) *Online Advertising to Grow Seven Times Faster than Offline Advertising in 2007*, London, Press Release, date published December 4, 2006. *The Financial Times* (2006) "Newspapers Expect to Lose Ads to Internet," http://www.ft.com/cms/s/0/b6e3452c-83c0-11db-9e95-0000779e2340.html, accessed on February 3, 2011.
6. *New York Times* (2009) "For Today's Graduate, Just One Word: Statistics" by Steve Lohr, http://www.nytimes.com/2009/08/06/technology/06stats.html, accessed on June 27, 2011.
7. N. Antosca (2007) *Facebook.com: Increasingly Overbearing and Terrible*, http://www.huffingtonpost.com/nick-antosca/facebookcom-increasingly-_b_71928.html, accessed on February 3, 2011. I. Lotinsky (2007) *Fandango and Facebook Just Violated My Privacy*, http://ianlotinsky.wordpress.com/2007/11/20/fandango-and-facebook-just-violated-my-privacy/, accessed on February 3, 2011.
8. *The Financial Times Magazine* (2009) "The Rise and Fall of MySpace," http://www.ft.com/cms/s/2/fd9ffd9c-dee5-11de-adff-00144feab49a.html, accessed on February 3, 2011.
9. *The Economist* (2010) "Clicking for Gold," http://www.economist.com/node/15557431, accessed on February 3, 2011. *The Economist* (2010) "Data, Data Everywhere (A Special Report on Managing Information)," http://www.economist.com/node/15557443, accessed on February 3, 2011.
10. John Hagel III, John Seely Brown and Lang Davison (2010) *The Power of Pull: How Small Moves, Smartly Made, Can Set Big Things in Motion*, Basic Books, New York, p. 15.

Chapter 7   The sixth building block – license sales

1. H. W. Chesbrough (2003) *Open Innovation: The New Imperative for Creating and Profiting from Technology*, Harvard Business School, Boston, pp. 93–97.
2. M. Moritz (2009) *Return to the Little Kingdom*, The Overlook Press, New York, p. 337.

Notes

3. *The New York Times* (2009) "A World of Megabeats and Megabytes," by Jon Pareles, http://www.nytimes.com/2010/01/03/arts/music/03tech.html?_r=1, accessed on July 30, 2010. Print version: *International Herald Tribune* (2010) "The Canary in the Digital Coal Mine," by Jon Pareles, p. 14, date published February 4, 2011.
4. M. Moritz (2009) *Return to the Little Kingdom*, The Overlook Press, New York, p. 15.
5. *The Financial Times* (2009) "Store Set to be the Apple of Master's Eye," http://www.ft.com/cms/s/2/8bbd4b80-ed8b-11de-ba12-00144feab49a.html#axzz1CuNf5jik, accessed on February 4, 2011.
6. M. Meeker, S. Devitt, L. Wu (2009) *Economy and Internet Trends*, Presentation at the Web 2.0 Summit, Morgan Stanley, San Francisco, http://www.morganstanley.com/institutional/techresearch/pdfs/MS_Economy_Internet_Trends_102009_FINAL.pdf, p. 38, accessed on February 4, 2011.
7. *The Financial Times* (2010) "The Vision Behind Apple's I," January 30/31, 2010.
8. J. Qiu (2004) "NTT DoCoMo: Review of a Case," paper presented at USC Annenberg School for Communication, available at http://www.ojr.org/japan/research/1097446811.php (Japan Media Review), accessed on February 4, 2011.
9. M. Moritz (2009) *Return to the Little Kingdom*, The Overlook Press, New York, p. 340. *The Financial Times* (2010) "Cash-Rich Tech Groups Avoid the M&A Path," http://www.ft.com/cms/s/2/605c69a0-508f-11df-bc86-00144feab49a.html, accessed on February 4, 2011.
10. *The Financial Times* (2010) "Spotify Hopes Major Upgrade will Wean Users off iTunes," http://www.ft.com/cms/s/0/337394a4-5193-11df-bed9-00144feab49a.html, accessed on February 4, 2011.

Chapter 8 The seventh building block – financial management

1. Peter L. Bernstein (1996) *Against the Gods: The Remarkable Story of Risk*, John Wiley & Sons, New York, pp. 1–8.
2. *USA Today* (2006) "Bush Signs Port-Security, Internet Gaming Bill," http://www.usatoday.com/news/washington/2006-10-13-bush-bill_x.htm, accessed on February 4, 2011.
3. PartyGaming Plc. (2008) *Preliminary Results FY2007*, date published March 5, 2008, p. 3.
4. PartyGaming Plc. (2008) *Preliminary Results FY2007*, date published March 5, 2008, p. 3.
5. *The Financial Times* (2010) "Online Gambling Groups Seal Link-Up," July 30, 2010.
6. *The Financial Times* (2008) "Peer to Peer Lending," December 9, 2008.
7. *The Financial Times* (2010) "Domain Name Investing," August 1, 2010.
8. John Battelle (2005) *The Search: How Google and Its Rivals Rewrote the Rules of Business and Transformed Our Culture*, New York: Portfolio, pp. 95–121.
9. *The Financial Times* (2010) "Spread Bet Groups Scout for Punters," September 17, 2010.
10. *The Economist* (2011) "China's King of E-Commerce," January 1, 2011, p. 46; Jim Erickson, "A Lending Life Raft for China's Small Businesses," Aliza.com, November 25, 2010.

11. *The Financial Times* (2010) "Wonga Pushes Web Loan Innovation," May 24, 2010.
12. *The Financial Times* (2008) "Peer-to-Peer Lending," December 9, 2008.
13. *The Economist* (2011) "Grameen Bank: Saint under Siege," January 8, 2011, p. 69.

Chapter 9   It's a freemium world

1. *Time* (2007) "Radiohead says: Pay what you want," by Josh Tyrangiel, http://www.time.com/time/arts/article/0,8599,1666973,00.html, accessed on February 7, 2011.
2. Nate Anderson (2011) "Reznor makes $750,000 even when the music is free," *Ars Technica*, March 5, 2011, accessed March 29, 2011, http://arstechnica.com/old/content/2008/03/reznor-makes-750000-even-when-the-music-is-free.ars.
3. Aemon Malone (2011) "Radiohead Abandons 'pay what you want' for upcoming album release," *Digital Trends*, February 15, 2011, accessed on March 29, 2011, http://www.digitaltrends.com/entertainment/radiohead-abandons-pay-what-you-want-for-upcoming-album-release/.
4. Internet World Stats (2009) "Usage and Population Statistics," http://www.internetworldstats.com/ (home page), global user number as on December 31, 2009, date accessed June 20, 2010.
5. Ch. Anderson (2009) *Free: The Future of a Radical Price*, Hyperion, New York, pp. 26–7.
6. Ch. Anderson (2009) p. 5.
7. S. Neiman (2009) *Moral Clarity: A Guide for Grown-Up Idealists*, Princeton University Press, Princeton. *The Economist* (2009) "Onwards and Upwards: Why is the Modern View of Progress so Impoverished?" http://www.economist.com/node/15108593, accessed on February 7, 2011.
8. L. Lessig (2001) *The Future of Ideas: The Fate of the Commons in a Connected World*, Random House, New York/Toronto.
9. GNU Project/Free Software Foundation (FSF) (2010) *The Free Software Definition*, http://www.gnu.org/philosophy/free-sw.html, accessed on February 14, 2011.
10. L. Lessig (2004) *Free Culture: The Nature and the Future of Creativity*, The Penguin Press, New York, pp. 23–8.
11. Ch. Anderson (2009) *Free: The Future of a Radical Price*, Hyperion, New York, p. 105.
12. L. Lessig (2001) *The Future of Ideas: The Fate of the Commons in a Connected World*, Random House, New York/Toronto, pp. 49–61.
13. E. S. Raymond (1999) *The Cathedral and the Bazaar*, O'Reilly Media, Sebastopol, p. 29.
14. Wikiquote (2011) "Linus Torvalds," http://en.wikiquote.org/wiki/Linus_Torvalds, date accessed February 14, 2011. Google Groups/comp.os.minix (1991) "What would you like to see most in minix?" http://groups.google.com/group/comp.os.minix/msg/b813d52cbc5a044b, date accessed February 14, 2011.
15. E. S. Raymond (1999) *The Cathedral and the Bazaar*, O'Reilly Media, Sebastopol, p. 29.
16. Josh Lerner and Jean Tirole, "The Economics of Technology Sharing: Open Source and Beyond," *Journal of Economic Perspectives*, Volume 19, Number 2, Spring 2005, p. 99.
17. *Wired Magazine* (1997) "The Greatest OS That (N)Ever Was," Issue 5.08.
18. Ch. Anderson (2009) *Free: The Future of a Radical Price*, Hyperion, New York, p. 128.
19. *Bloomberg BusinessWeek* (2005) "Wikipedia: 'A Work in Progress,'" by Burt Helm, http://www.businessweek.com/technology/content/dec2005/tc20051214_441708.htm, accessed on February 7, 2011.

20. *Bloomberg BusinessWeek* (2005) *Commentary: A Vote of Confidence in Wikipedia* by Burt Helm, http://www.businessweek.com/technology/content/dec2005/tc20051214_035216.htm, accessed on February 7, 2011.
21. Ch. Anderson (2009) *Free: The Future of a Radical Price*, Hyperion, New York, p. 168.
22. *Bloomberg BusinessWeek* (2009) "'Super Angels' Shake Up Venture Capital," by Spencer E. Ante, http://www.businessweek.com/magazine/content/09_22/b4133044585602.htm, accessed on February 7, 2011.
23. *The New York Times* (2009) "Home Economics," by Virginia Heffernan, http://www.nytimes.com/2009/05/24/magazine/24wwln-medium-t.html, accessed on February 7, 2011.
24. Ch. Anderson (2009) *Free: The Future of a Radical Price*, Hyperion, New York, p. 104.
25. Ch. Anderson (2009) p. 127.
26. Josh Kopelman (blog) (2006) "Redeye VC, Shrink a Market!" April 2, 2006, http://redeye.firstround.com/2006/04/shrink_a_market.html, accessed on March 29, 2011.
27. D. Kirkpatrick (2010) *The Facebook Effect: The Inside Story of the Company that is Connecting the World*, Simon & Schuster/Virgin Books, New York, p. 296.
28. D. Kirkpatrick (2010) p. 287.
29. *The Washington Post* (2010) *From Facebook, Answering Privacy Concerns with New Settings* by Mark Zuckerberg, http://www.washingtonpost.com/wp-dyn/content/article/2010/05/23/AR2010052303828.html, accessed on February 7, 2011. *Fast Company* (2010) "Facebook's Zuckerberg Nearly, But Not Quite, About-Faces on Privacy," by Kit Eaton, http://www.fastcompany.com/1651427/facebook-mark-zuckerberg-privacy-open-letter-security-social-networking-about-face, accessed on February 7, 2011.
30. D. Kirkpatrick (2010) *The Facebook Effect: The Inside Story of the Company that is Connecting the World*, Simon & Schuster/Virgin Books, New York, p. 302.
31. D. Kirkpatrick (2010) p. 308.
32. *The Economist* (2010) "Privacy and the Internet, Lives of Others," http://www.economist.com/node/16167766, date accessed February 7, 2011.

Chapter 10 The future of web business is personal

1. Chris Locke, Doc Searls, David Weinberger and Rick Levine (1999) *The Cluetrain Manifesto: The End of Business as Usual*, Perseus Books, New York.
2. Mark Gorenberg Interview, March 16, 2011.
3. *The Financial Times*, "Media will be Forced to Play by the Internet's Rules," March 10, 2011.
4. Claire Cain Miller and Miguel Helft (2011) "Apple Moves to Tighten Control of App Store," http://www.nytimes.com/2011/02/01/technology/01apple.html?_r=2, accessed on March 2, 2011.
5. "davemcclure @fredwilson let's count mega-successful platform bitches shall we? eBay -> PayPal. MySpace -> YouTube. Facebook -> Zynga, LivingSocial, Groupon." Dave McClure, Tweet from March 6, 2011.
6. *The Financial Times*, "Media will be Forced to Play by the Internet's Rules," March 10, 2011.

7. *EngageDigital* (2009) "Piper Jaffray: Virtual Goods Marketplace Shifting from Virtual Worlds," http://www.engagedigital.com/2009/08/14/piper-jaffray-virtual-goods-marketplace-shifting-from-virtual-worlds, accessed on February 14, 2011.
8. Chinese Market Research Group (2009) *CRM – Chinese Business Experts*, http://www.cmrconsulting.com.cn (home page), accessed on February 14, 2011.
9. Agustino Fontevecchia (2011) "Zynga Reveals Profit And Revenues As It Looks To Raise $500 Million," *Forbes*, March 2, 2011, http://blogs.forbes.com/afontevecchia/2011/03/02/zynga-reveals-profit-and-revenues-as-it-looks-to-raise-500-million/, accessed on March 29, 2011.
10. Tapjoy Inc. (2009) "Monetizing Dual Currency Economies In Online Games," Offerpal White Paper, date published October 21, 2009, pp. 3, 4, 10. *Bloomberg BusinessWeek* (2009) "Virtual Currencies Gain in Popularity," by Olga Kharif, http://www.businessweek.com/technology/content/may2009/tc2009055_070595.htm, accessed on February 4, 2011.
11. *Advertising Age* (2010) "Is this the Dawn of the Facebook Credit Economy?" by Ian Schafer, http://adage.com/digitalnext/post?article_id=143983, accessed on February 4, 2011.
12. *Bloomberg BusinessWeek* (2009) "Virtual Currencies Gain in Popularity," by Olga Kharif, http://www.businessweek.com/technology/content/may2009/tc2009055_070595.htm, accessed on February 4, 2011.
13. *The Economist* (2009) "Beyond Voice: New Uses for Mobile Phones could Launch another Wave of development," http://www.economist.com/node/14483848, accessed on February 4, 2011.
14. *Vanity Fair* (2011) "Twitter was Act One," by David Kirkpatrick, April edition.
15. Kevin Kelly (1994) *Out of Control: The New Biology of Machines, Social Systems and the Economic World*, Persius Books, Cambridge
16. "Payment is a form of communication," Video on Stanford University Entrepreneurship Corner, dated February 9, 2011, http://ecorner.stanford.edu/authorMaterialInfo.html?mid=2642, accessed on March 10, 2011.
17. *TechCrunch* (2011) "Just In Time For SXSW, Foursquare Ups The Game And Adds Recommendations," March 8, 2011, http://techcrunch.com/2011/03/08/foursquare-3-sxsw/, by M. G. Siegler, March 8, accessed on March 10, 2011.
18. *TechCrunch* (2011) "Foursquare's SXSW: Version 3.0, Party, Concert, 18 New Badges, And A Genius Amex Deal," March 4, 2011, by M. G. Siegler, March 4, accessed on March 10, 2011.
19. Nikolaus Doll (2011) "Nur voll vernetzte Autos locken junge Kunden an," *Die Welt*, March 10, 2011, p. 12.
20. John Hagel and John Seely Brown (2005) *The Only Sustainable Edge: Why Business Strategy Depends On Productive Friction And Dynamic Specialization*, Harvard Business School Press, Boston, MA p. 94.
21. Zynga, "Zynga Players Raise Over $1.5 Million for Haiti in Five Days," January 20, 2010, http://www.zynga.com/about/article.php?a=20100120, accessed on March 27, 2011.
22. "Lady Gaga Donates $1.5 Million in Total to Zynga's Japan Earthquake Relief Campaign and the American Red Cross," March 28, 2011 – Zynga Inc., http://www.zynga.com/about/article.php?a=20110328, accessed on March 29, 2011.
23. Joschua Reich, Email Interview, March 23, 2011.

24. *Business Week/GIGAOM* (2011) "Yuri Milner: Genius Investor or Gold Rush King?" by Bobbie Johnson, March 16, 2011.

Appendix Stress-testing the *SimplySeven*

1. *BBC News* (2010) "The Top 100 Sites on the Internet," http://news.bbc.co.uk/2/hi/8562801.stm, accessed on December 20, 2010.
2. *Yahoo! Finance* (2010) "Business Finance, Stock Market, Quotes, News," http://finance.yahoo.com/ (home page), accessed on December 20, 2010.
3. *E*TRADE Financial* (2010) "Stock, Options & Future Trades | Mobile & Global Trading | High-Yield Savings & Online Banking," http://us.etrade.com/ (home page), accessed on December 20, 2010.
4. Netflix Inc. (2010) *2009 Annual Report*, date published February 19, 2010, pp. 1, 27.
5. Reed Elsevier Plc. (2010) *Annual Report and Financial Statements 2009*, date published February 17, 2010, p. 11.
6. AOL Inc. (2010) *Annual Report and Form 10-K 2009*, date published March 2, 2010, p. 35.
7. *Internet World Stats* (2009) "Usage and Population Statistics," http://www.internetworldstats.com/ (home page), global user number as on December 31, 2009, accessed on June 20, 2010.

Index

37signals, 12
ABC Book Service, 50, 51
ACO, *see* Ant Colony Optimization (ACO)
Adler, Trip, 125–6
Adobe, 46, 126
Adobe Photoshop, 46
Ad pricing schemes on Internet, 85
AdSense, 76
Advent Venture Partners, 13
Advertising, 6, 8, 14, 15, 23, 62, 63, 74, 138, 165, 167, 172
   AOL, 166
   Ask, 166
   banner, 4, 75, 77–8
   catch-22 situation in, 74–5
   display, 77–8
   Facebook, 138
   Geeknet, 167
   Google, 166, 168, 175
   margins of, 173
   Monster, 167
   newspaper, death of, 82–4
   publisher and agent: as separate entities, 76; as single company, 75–6
   publishers of, 74
   search advertising, 81, 82
   search revolution, 78–80
   as a service, 87–9
   for Skype, 36
   spam and pushy banners, 77–8
   statistics, need of, 84–6
   traditional, 85
   value creation in, 74–5
   WebMD, 167
   WikiAnswers, 166
   "Wisdom of Crowds," 89
   "Wisdom of Money," 80–2
   Yahoo!, 77, 166
Advertising Age, 154
Advertising blocker, 78
AdWords, 76, 81, 87
Against the Gods, 111
Agent-based business models, 26, 62, 77

Ailin Graef aka Anshe Chung, 152
Airbnb, 1–2, 4, 22, 160
Airline miles, 29, 30, 153
Airlines, 29, 30
Air travel, 30
Akhund, Immad, 109
Aldus PageMaker, 99
Alibaba, 71, 120
AliLoan, 120, 121
Altavista, 77, 78
Amazon, 12, 14, 20, 22, 32, 49–50, 51, 53, 55–6, 57, 58, 63, 66, 71, 80, 150, 153, 166, 168, 169, 173, 174
   license sales business model, 106
   platform building, 102
   retail, 166
   success story of, 49–50
AmazonBasics, 169
Amazon Web Services, 150
American Farm Bureau, 118
Ameritrade, 114
Amit, Raffi, 66
Anderson, Chris, 55–6, 57, 129–30, 135, 137, 138, 140, 142
   5%/95% rule of, 124–7
Andreessen, Marc, 41
Android, 94, 102, 106, 168, 169
Angel's Forum, 11
Ant Colony Optimization (ACO), 61
Anti-copy protection, 92
Antosca, Nick, 87
AntRoute, 61
AOL, 14, 22, 39, 47, 130, 166, 168, 172
   advertising, 166
   rise and fall of, 40–3
Apache Web Server, 134
Apple, 13, 14, 20, 32–3, 40, 57, 91, 101, 149, 150, 163, 165
   conflict with Sony, 150
   and content owners, 91
   end-to-end user experience, 103–4
   eWorld of, 14, 40
   In-App purchases, 150

Index

license sales: revenue share model for, 104–5; platform building, 103, 105
payments systems, 149
rebirth of, 98–102
Apple App Store, 22, 32, 149
Apple Computers, 64, 99, 100, 101
Apple IIc, 11
Apple iPad, 45–6, 101, 102, 103, 105, 149
Apple iPhones, 39, 44, 101–2, 103, 104, 105
Apple iPod, 91, 100–2, 103, 105, 106
Apple iTunes, 14, 22, 56, 57, 101, 104, 105, 106, 107
Apple Macintosh, 11, 99, 100
Apple Store, 104
Apps, 101, 149, 150
App Store, 15, 102, 150
aQuantive, Inc., 32
Aria Systems, 149
Ask
  advertising, 166
ASP, *see* Average sales price (ASP)
AT&T, 41, 131, 140
August Capital, 35–6
Autotrader.com, 83
AVC blog, 125
Average sales price (ASP), 67

B2B loan service, 120
B2B trap, 68–70
B2C loans, 120
Bank
  BankSimple, 22, 158, 159
  Grameen Bank, 120
  online banking, 114, 116
  Pure Internet banks, 114
  retail bank, 113–114
BankSimple, 22, 158, 159
Banner advertising, 4, 75, 77–8, 81
Barnes and Noble, 53–4
Battelle, John, 79, 80
"Battle of platforms," in entertainment industry, 105–7
Baum, Lisa, 119
Berkeley School, 29
Berners-Lee, Tim, 41
Bernstein, Peter L., 111
Betfair, 119
Bezos, Jeff, 14, 50, 51, 54, 55, 65
Bigsize Banner (advertising format), 78
BitTorrent files, 97
Blecharczyk, Nathan, 1
Bling Nation, 155, 160

Blizzard Entertainment, 20, 31, 39, 44
Blizzard WOW, 22
Blogger, 12
Bloomberg, 39, 43, 44, 47
Bloomberg Business Week, 136
Bokus, 50, 52
Boo.com, 22, 49, 51–2, 53
Bookshops, selection of, 50–1, 53
Borland, 96
The Boston Globe, 45
"Bouncer Effect," 43–4
Breyer, Jim, 120
"Bricks" retailers, 53, 54
Brin, Sergey, 4, 78, 80
BTX, 50
Burnham, Brad, 5
Business models, 5, 16, 20, 141
  advertising, 171–172
  agent-based, 62
  of Airbnb, 2
  Business Model Generation, 20
  financial risk, 113, 118
  "freemium," 122–146
  offline, 13
  online, 15
  "perpetual beta" applied to, 10–11
  with problems (services sales) 31–34
  of Skype, 12, 36
Business Week, 152, 161
Butter and Egg Board, 69
Bwin, 116, 117

C2B loans, 120
C2C loan platforms, 120
Calculated risk taking, 111
CarsDirect.com, 10
Catch-22 situation, in advertising, 74–5
  avoidance of, 75
The Cathedral and the Bazaar, 132, 136
Celera, 22
Charles Schwab, 112
Chesbrough, Henry, 95
Chesky, Brian, 1
Chicago Butter, 69
Chicago Mercantile Exchange (CME), 69
China
  virtual currencies in, 152
Chouinard, Yvon, 3
Christensen, Clayton M., 3
Cinematch, 58–9
Citadel Investment Group, 114
CitySearch, 58–9
Classifieds, 75, 82–3, 85

Clients, 61, 62–3
    smart clients, 70
Club Penguin, 22, 141–2
Clubs, future of, 46
The Cluetrain Manifesto, 59, 147
CME, *see* Chicago Mercantile Exchange (CME)
Cohen, Adam, 66, 68
Color (the company), 22
Comcast, 164
Commission-based companies, 173
Commission Junction, 22
Commissions, 61, 139, 165, 166, 167
    B2B trap, 68–70
    clients, 61–4
    consumer-to-consumer (C2C) platforms, 64–6
    eBay, 67–8, 166
    Expedia, 166
    Gross Merchandise Volume (GMV), 66–7
    intermediary, death of, 72–3
    Mint.com, 139
    Priceline Network, 167
    smart clients, 70–2
    SuperPages, 167
Commissions Junction, 62, 63, 85
CompuServe, 14, 40, 41, 42, 47, 50, 114, 130
Computing platforms, 94–7
Consumer-to-consumer (C2C) platforms, 64–6, 108, 120
Conversion rates, 66–7
Conway, Ron, 12
Copy protection programs, 92–3, 96
CorelDraw, 95
Cost per Install (CPI) price, 109–10
Court, Frédéric, 13
CPI price, *see* Cost per Install (CPI) price
Craigslist, 4–5, 22, 26, 33, 75, 82, 83, 156
Creative class, 90, 98, 106
Currencies
    in-game, 153
    virtual, *see* virtual currencies
Customized content, 76
Cutting-edge design agencies, 29

Data Exhaust, 137
The Data Warehousing Institute (TDWI), 7
Davenport, Thomas, 10
Davison, Lang, 89
Del.icio.us, 12
Dell, 165, 167, 168, 169, 170, 174
Denver, 2, 8

Design thinking, 29
Desktop Publishing (DTP), 99, 100
Detroit, 8
Digital items, 92, 108
    sale of, 108
Digital licenses, 92, 93, 110, 152, 163, 165, 168
Digital Rights Management (DRM) technologies, 90–1, 92, 98
Digital world, 45, 90, 92
Direct customer relationships, 55
Direct services, 26
Disney, 42, 129
Display ads, 78, 82, 85
Distributed distribution, 97–8
DoCoMo, 104–5
Domain brokers, 118
Donated power for business, 137–9
"Donation economy," 144
    and innovation, 128–30
Dorsey, Jack, 155, 156
DoubleClick, 76, 85
Doujinshi comics, 129
Draper, Tim, 36
DRM technologies, *see* Digital Rights Management (DRM) technologies
D-School, 29
DTP, *see* Desktop Publishing (DTP)
Dubner, Stephen J., 67
Dyson, Esther, 27–8

Earlybird, 151
eBay, 12, 14, 20, 22, 24, 33, 36, 62, 63, 64, 65, 66, 71, 80, 98, 115, 120, 140, 151, 166, 169
    history of, 4
    investments of, 67
    pride of, 67–8
The Economist, 36, 66, 89
e-Dental.com, 69
EDventure Holdings, 27–8
E-Government, 30
eLance, 22, 26, 27, 33
Elberse, Anita, 56
EMACS, 131
The Encyclopedia Britannica, 47
End-to-end user experience, 103, 104, 105
Entertainment industry, "battle of platforms" in, 105–7
Erik, 25
E*TRADE, 113, 114, 115, 116, 164
Evian brand, 75

Index

Excel, 96
Expedia, 73, 166
Experian, 164, 167, 171, 173, 174

f8 Developer Conference, 152
Facebook, 4, 6, 12, 17, 22, 24, 53, 57–8, 65, 75, 76, 86, 87, 88, 89, 113, 118, 126, 130, 138, 141–4, 151, 154, 160, 161
   advertising as service, 87–9
   business, 143
   5%/95% rule for, 141
   in freemium world, 141–4
   recommendations for, 58
   in retailing, 53
Facebook Credits, 113, 152, 154
The Facebook Effect, 142
Fandango, 87
Feedback Driven Game Design, 7–8
Ferriss, Timothy, 147
Filo, David, 77
Financial management, 111–21
   business model, using, 117–18
   financial services online, slow growth of, 113–16
   Gibraltar, 116–17
   informal economy, substitute for, 121
   Internet-based B2B, B2C, C2C and C2B loans, 119–21
   investment in Internet real estate, 118
   investment in Internet traffic, 119
   making money with money, 111–13
   online gambling, 116
   spread-betting services, 119
   Weatherbill, 121
Financial risk, 111, 113, 167
   IG Group, 167, 175
   on Internet, 118
   management business model, 113, 118, 138
Firefox extension Adblock Plus, 78
First Round Capital, 137, 141
5%/95% rule, 124–7, 128, 137, 138, 141, 146
Fixed pricing models, 122
Flexible payment infrastructures, 147, 148–9
Flextronics, 11
Florida, Richard, 90, 133
Flu Trends, 79
Fool.com, 114
Force.com, 150
Foreign exchange spread betting, 119, 165, 173
Foursquare, 6, 22, 137, 156, 160
The Four Hour Work Week, 147
Fraud, 67–8, 86, 153
Freakonomics, 67

Free, 125, 129
Freemium world, 18, 122, 123–4, 144–6
   "as in free speech, not free beer," 129
   Chris Anderson's 5%/95% rule, 124–7
   competing with free, 139–41
   donated power, for business, 137–9
   Facebook dilemma, 141–4
   million lines of code, 132–4
   paying nothing, 122–3
   reciprocal donation economy and innovation, 128–30
   tale with GNU, 130–1
   three million articles, 134–7
   web powered by small deeds of heroism, 127–8
Free-of-charge music distribution platforms, 97
Free Software Foundation, 129
Fried, Jason, 3
Friis, Janus, 34, 35, 97, 98
Frog Design, 11

Gambling, online, 113, 116–17
Games, online, *see* Online games
Gaming ecosystem, building value in, 108–10
Gazelle, 22, 64, 153
Gebbia, Joe, 1, 2
Geeknet, 167
   advertising, 167
"General Public License" (GPL), 131, 133
Ghosts I–IV, 122
Gibraltar, 116–17
Gilt Groupe, 59
Gizmo5, 37
"Globalization 3.0," 13, 28, 29
GMV, *see* Gross Merchandise Volume (GMV)
GNU, 129, 131, 132, 133, 139
Gnutella, 97
GoDaddy, 118
Goldman Sachs, 119, 148
Gomila, Jude, 109
Google, 4, 6, 9, 13, 14, 20, 22, 36, 45, 46, 53, 57, 65, 72, 75, 78–80, 81, 82, 85, 86, 87, 93, 94, 99, 101, 102, 106, 119, 124, 137, 149, 150, 166, 168, 169, 171, 172, 174, 175
   AdSense offering, 76
   AdWords offering, 76, 81, 87
   DoubleClick AdExchange of, 85
   Google Dance, 80
   Google Mail, 87
   Google Maps/Latitude, 87, 137
Gorenberg, Mark, 148, 149
GoTo.com, 8, 22, 81, 119

GPL, *see* "General Public License" (GPL)
Grameen Bank, 120
Grammy awards, 122
Graphical User Interface (GUI), 78, 99, 100, 103
Grimm, Brothers, 129
Gross, Bill, 8–9, 80–1, 119
Gross Merchandise Volume (GMV), 67
 ASP conversion rates, 66–7
Groupon, 22, 26, 33, 65, 151, 156, 159, 161
GUI, *see* Graphical User Interface (GUI)
Guinness Book of Records, 132

"Hacker News," 21, 24
Hagel III, John, 89, 147, 157
Hansson, David Heinemeier, 3
Hartenbaum, Howard, 34, 35
Hautelook, 59
Hellohealth, 46
Heyzap, 6, 22, 108–10, 139
Horizontal platform strategy, 96
"Horizontal" era, 95–6
Howies.co.uk, 55, 59
Huffington Post, 43, 83
Hummer Winblad, 148–9

IBM, 94–5, 105, 128, 134
Idealab, 7, 8–9, 10, 80–1, 119
Ideeli, 59
Ideo, 29
IE Business School, 25
IG Group, 119, 172, 173, 174, 175
 financial risk, 167
iMode, 104–5
India, 28, 33
Informal economy, substitute for, 121
In-game currencies, 153
ING Direct, 22, 113, 114, 115, 116
Innovation, 12, 29, 95, 96, 104, 108, 112, 128–30, 154
In Rainbows, 122
INSEAD, 66
Intellectual property, 29, 90, 91–4, 96, 128, 129, 130, 132
Intermediary, death of, 72–3
Internet, 29, 36, 70, 73, 74, 79, 111, 113, 121, 130, 133, 141, 150, 161
 access, 42
 ad pricing schemes on, 85
 advertising, 85
 based B2B, B2C, C2C and C2B loans, 119–21

bookselling, 50, 52, 54
business model, 14
Chris Anderson's 5%/95% rule, 124–7
classifieds, 83–4
communication, 31, 34, 126
companies, 4, 22, 30, 112, 163–4, 165, 171, 172
 hosting costs for, 4
 investments in, 15
 loan providers, 118
 marketing, 49
 mega-colony: business models for, 62
 music distribution in, 93
 newspapers, 45
 offline companies, 3
 real estate, investment in, 118
 retail, 49, 169–70
 services on, 4, 30
 shopping, 48: steps in, 48–9
 start-ups, 46, 117, 118, 137
 traffic, investment in, 119
Internet Service Providers (ISPs), 14, 39, 41, 124, 168
Internet services, 14, 29, 30, 73, 106, 141
 advantages, 124
Intuit, 35, 115, 137
Investment
 in Internet business, 15
 in Internet real estate, 118
 in Internet traffic, 119
iOS, 150
iPad, 45, 46, 103, 105, 149
iPhone, 39, 44, 101, 102, 103, 105
iPod, 91, 100, 101, 102, 103, 105, 106
ISPs, *see* Internet Service Provider
Issey Miyake, 103
iTunes, 14, 56, 57, 101, 104, 105, 106, 107
iXL, 14, 22, 32

Jackson, Tim, 71
Japan, 56, 61, 71, 104, 129, 158
Jobs, Steve, 11, 14, 39, 40, 98, 99, 100, 101, 102–3, 150, 155

Kawasaki, Guy, 3, 11
Kazaa, 34, 35, 93, 97, 98
Kelly, Kevin, 62, 156
Kelman, Glenn, 11
King of Limbs, 123
Kirkpatrick, David, 142, 143, 155
Kiva, 120
Kleiner Perkins Caufield & Byers, 126

Index

"Knowledge Economy," 90, 133
Kohlberg, Kravis, Roberts & Co. (KKR), 11
Kopelman, Josh, 137, 141

Labor-based services, 30, 32
Lala, 107
LA Lakers, 12
LastFM, 107
Lending Club, 120
Lessig, Lawrence, 128, 129, 130
Levitt, Steven, 67
LexisNexis, 168
License, 91, 93–4, 97
License sales, 15, 21, 22, 29, 90–110, 139, 150, 152, 153, 165, 166, 169, 175
    Apple, rebirth of, 98–102
    "battle of platforms," in entertainment industry, 105–7
    business model, 106, 108
    computing platforms, indecisive history of, 94–7
    consumer-to-consumer (C2C) variation of, 108
    creative class, 90–1
    distributed distribution, 97–8
    intellectual property, 91–4
    micro license sales, 108–10
    platform building, 102–5
    Real Networks, 166
    revenue share model for, 104–5
    Tencent, 139
    Zynga, 139
LikeList, 149, 159
Linden Dollar (L$), 152
Linden Lab, 22
Linguee.com, 138
LinkedIn, 22, 89
Linux, 127, 133, 134, 136
Linux OS, 132
Living Social, 22, 151
Livingston, Jessica, 3, 4
LMAX, 119
The Long Tail, 55–6, 124
Los Angeles Times, 45
Lotus 1-2-3, 96
Lukin, Jarid, 123, 125

Mac GUI, 100
Macintosh, 11, 99, 100
Macromedia, 22
Manga cartoon characters, 129
Manger, Roland, 151
Mangrove Capital Partners, 34

Massively Multiplayer Online Role-Playing Game (MMORPG), 44
Matryoshka dolls, 149
Matryoshka trick, 150
McClure, Dave, 151
Meeker, Mary, 102, 126
"Metcalfe's Law," 44, 56
Micro license sales, 108–10
Microsoft, 35, 37, 88, 93, 94, 95, 99, 100, 101, 102, 105, 106, 125, 145
    in copy protection, 96
Middle Ages, 69, 112
Million books project (Amazon.com), 50–1
Milner, Yuri, 12, 161
Minimal Viable Product (MVP), 8, 9
Mint.com, 22, 73, 93, 112, 115, 137, 138, 139, 141
MIT Computer Science and Artificial Intelligence Laboratory (MIT AI Lab), 131
MMORPG, *see* Massively Multiplayer Online Role-Playing Game (MMORPG)
Mobile payments, 32, 155–7
Monster.com, 75, 83, 167, 172
    advertising, 167
Moral Clarity, 127
Morgan Stanley, 67, 102
Moritz, Michael, 99, 100
M-PESA, 155
MS-DOS, 99
Multiplan, 96
Murdoch, Rupert, 45, 107
Music industry, 3, 35, 93, 97, 98
    charging for licenses, 105
    content protection, 98
    experience with license sales, 105
    free-of-charge music distribution platforms, 97
    revenue erosion in, 97–8
    and sharing platforms, 97
    subscription-based music service, 107
MVP, *see* Minimal Viable Product (MVP)
MySpace, 6, 22, 86, 88, 89, 151
    mistakes of, 6, 88

Napster, 93, 97, 98
Nature, 136
Neiman, Susan, 127, 128
Netflix, 7, 10, 58, 164, 167, 173, 174
    subscription, 167
Netscape, 22, 41, 77, 133, 165
"Network Effects," 44, 56, 107
New Economy, 5, 12, 14, 15, 22, 23, 32, 33, 42, 52, 66, 123, 156, 157, 161
    failure of, 51–3

The New York Times, 45, 150
Newmark, Craig, 4, 82, 83
New Razorfish, 22
News Corp, 6, 42, 88, 107
Newspaper, 100, 139
   death of, 82–4
   subscription, in Internet, 45
New York Times, 45, 67, 150
Nielsen Top 100 Global Websites, 163–76
Nike, 143
NIN, 122
Nupedia, 135–6

Offerpal Media, 74, 153
Offshore tax return services, 28
Omidyar, Pierre, 4, 64, 65, 68, 120, 161
One-off service, 27
Online classifieds, 83–4
Online discount brokers, 114
Online gambling, 113, 116–17
Online games, 3, 8, 31, 39, 47, 75, 108, 113, 124, 152–3, 154, 158, 161
Online poker, 113
Online roulette, 113
Online self-service, by banks, 114
The Only Sustainable Edge, 157
"Open Commons," 129, 130
Open Source, 12, 127, 128, 133, 134, 136, 142
Open Source Movement, 129
Open Source operating system (OS), 127
O'Reilly (publisher), 126
O'Reilly, Tim, 123, 133
Osterwalder, Alexander, 20
Out of Control, 62
Outright.com, 138
Oversee.net, 118
Overstock, 63

Page, Larry, 4, 78
Palo Alto Research Center (PARC), 99
PARC, *see* Palo Alto Research Center (PARC)
PartyGaming, 22, 117
Patagonia, 3
Patent Trolls, 134
PatientsLikeMe, 22, 29, 138
Patricof, Alan, 12
Patzer, Aaron, 137
Payment systems, 113
   flexible payments systems, 148–9
   web services, 149–51
Paypal, 22, 113, 114–15, 151
PEDs, *see* "Project Entropia Dollars" (PEDs)
Peer-to-peer technologies, 34, 35, 97, 98

Personal business, 3, 6, 11, 13, 147
   basics, 161–2
   examples, on web, 159–60
   flexible payment infrastructures, 148–9
   methods and tools to guide customers, 147–8, 157–9
   mobile payments, 155–7
   payment, as web services, 149–51:
      fast-track companies, 151
   reputation and trust, 160
   virtual currencies and coupons, 152–5
Photoshop, 99
Picasa photo service, 8–9
Pigneur, Yves, 20
Pirate Bay, 97, 98
Pixar, 100
Plastic-Jungle, 22, 153
Platform providers, 93, 94, 149
Plattner, Hasso, 29
Power Sellers, 63, 70
Practice Fusion, 138
Priceline Network, 167, 174
"Project Entropia Dollars" (PEDs), 155
Prosper.com, 22, 120
PSINet, 14, 141
Pure Internet banks, 114
Pure play Internet services, 29, 30

Quark, 99
Quattro Pro, 96
Queen Anne, 92, 128

Radiohead, 122, 123
Rao, Jaithirth (Jerry), 28
Raymond, Eric S., 131, 132, 133, 136
RazorGator, 71
RealAge.com, 29
Reality Check, 11
Reality disorder, 53
"Real Money Transaction" (RMT), 152, 153
Real Networks, 165, 166, 174
Recommendation technology, 58–9
Redfin, 11
Reed Elsevier, 167, 168, 173, 174
Reich, Joschua, 159
RelayRides, 35, 160
Retail, 48–60, 166, 167
   Amazon, 166
   "bricks and clicks" model, 53–5
   Dell, 167
   fighting the clutter, 57–8
   "Long Tail" vs. "superstar economics," 55–6

million books project, 50–1
New Economy, failure of, 51–3
online, 48–50
personalization, 58–60
Retail banks, 113–14
Retail companies, 49, 173
Revenue share model, 104–5, 107
Reznor, Trent, 122
Rhapsody, 56
Rio, 100
The Rise of the Creative Class, 90
RMT, *see* "Real Money Transaction" (RMT)
Roller, Patricia, 11
Rotman School of Management, 29
Rudin, Ken, 7, 8
RueLaLa, 59
Rusenko, David, 145, 146

S/360, 95
SAFE Port Act, 117
Sahlman, Bill, 12
Salesforce.com, 46, 164
Salt Lake City-based SBI, 32
SBI Enteris, 32
Schafer, Ian, 154
Schiller, Vivian, 45
Schirmer, Christine, 125
Schmidt, Eric, 36
Schumpeter, 139
Scottrade, 114
Scribd, 22, 125–6
The Search, 79
Search Engine Marketing (SEM), 80
Search Engine Optimization (SEO), 80
Search revolution, 78–80
Searls, Doc, 59
SecondSpin.com, 64
Securitization, 111
Seely Brown, John, 89, 147, 157
SEM, *see* Search Engine Marketing (SEM)
SendGrid, 150
SEO, *see* Search Engine Optimization (SEO)
Service Oriented Architectures (SOA), 150
Services, 138, 167
  Experian, 167
  PatientsLikeMe, 138
  Vistaprint, 167
Services sales, 26–37
  business model with problems, 31–4
  design thinking, 29
  direct service, 26
  labor-based service, 30

one-off service, 26
pure play Internet services, 29
Skype, 30–1, 34–7
tax return services, 28
web-based services, 27, 29
Sharing platforms, 97, 98
Shifting sands, 95
Simon & Schuster, 126
Skype, 4, 12, 20, 22, 30–1, 33, 34–7, 98, 126, 138, 140, 141, 163
  comparison with AT&T, 140
Skyscraper (advertising format), 78
Smart clients, 70
Smava, 120
SOA, *see* Service Oriented Architectures (SOA)
Social networks, 75, 86, 88, 89, 142
Software as a service (SaaS), 13, 148
Spam and pushy banners, 77–8
Spamdexing, 77
Sports betting, 113, 119
Spotify, 22, 107
Spread-betting services, 119
Square Inc., 22, 32, 113, 155, 156
Stallman, Richard, 129–30, 131, 133
Statistics, need of, 84–6
"Statute of Anne," 92
Sticky Bits, 160
Stress-testing *SimplySeven*, 163
  initial results, 164–9
  key financial indicators, 174–6
  margins, 173–4
  market valuations, 172–3
  retail leads, in sales, 169–71
  selection criteria, 163–4
  users and rapid growth, 171–2
StubHub, 71
Subprime Mortgage Crisis of 2007, 111
Subscription, 38, 166, 167
  AOL, rise and fall of, 40–3
  "Bouncer Effect," 43–5
  clubs, future of, 46
  in "dog house," 45–6
  getting people, 47
  Netflix, 167
  Reed Elsevier, 167
  Skype, 138
  UOL, 166
  weapon, in arsenal, 38–9
Subscription-based music service, 107
SuperPages, 167, 174
"Superstar economics," 56, 57

Surowiecki, James, 57, 79, 136
Swan Interactive Media, 14, 22, 32
SXSW digital media conference, 1, 156

Tale with GNU, 130–1
Tax return services, 28
TDWI, *see* The Data Warehousing Institute (TDWI)
TechCrunch, 43, 156
Telecommunication services, revenue splits in, 104–5
TeleGeography, 30
Tencent, 22, 108, 139
Thomson Reuters, 39, 44, 47
TicketMaster, 9
Time Magazine, 122
Time Warner, 14, 22, 40, 42, 43, 164
Tluszcz, Mark, 34
Topguest, 153, 159
Torvalds, Linus, 132, 133
Tumblr, 5
23andMe, 22, 27, 31
2bigfeet.com, 80
Twitter, 1, 5, 6, 12, 22, 143, 155

UGC, *see* User generated content (UGC)
Union Square Ventures (USV), 2, 5–6
United Kingdom, 119
United States, 13, 29, 34, 59, 108, 152
 judiciary system, 96
 newspaper revenue, 83
 online banks in, 113, 114
 online gambling regulation in, 116, 117
 virtual currencies in, 152
UNIX, 131
UOL, 166
User generated content (UGC), 110, 137
USV, *see* Union Square Ventures (USV)
USWeb, 22, 32
Utah Jazz, 12

Vanity Fair, 155
Van Schewick, Barbara, 12
Varian, Hal, 86
Vente Priveé, 22, 59
VERT (stock ticker), 69
VerticalNet, 68, 69
"Vertical" era, 94–5
Viacom, 42
Viral Marketing, 44, 56
Virtual currencies, 15, 16, 28, 110, 113, 147, 152–5
Vistaprint, 164, 167, 173, 174

Wales, Jimmy, 136
Wallpaper (advertising format), 78
Wall Street, 67, 88, 107
Wal-Mart, 23, 153
Warner Brothers, 152, 160
Weatherbill, 22, 113, 121
Web 2.0, 3, 14, 15, 22, 123, 146, 157, 161, 172
WebMD, 167, 172, 174
WebSphere Application Server, 134
Webvan, 49
Weebly, 22, 145–6
WELL, *see* Whole Earth Lectronic Link (The WELL)
WePay, 22, 35, 112, 115, 160
Wharton, 66
Whole Earth Lectronic Link (The WELL), 41
Wide Sky (advertising format), 78
WikiAnswers, 166, 174
Wikipedia
 and Nupedia, 135–6
 freemium model of, 124–5, 127–8, 134–5
Wiley, 126
Wilson, Fred, 2, 5, 125
Windows, 95, 99, 100
"Wintel" platform, 95, 96, 100
Wired Magazine, 134
"Wisdom of Crowds," 79, 81, 82, 89
"Wisdom of Money," 80, 81, 82
Wonga, 113, 120, 121
WordPerfect, 95
The World is Flat, 28
World of Warcraft (WoW) game, 31, 39, 44
World Wide Web, 41, 62, 77, 90, 168
Wozniak, Steve, 99

Yahoo!, 12, 14, 45, 71, 77, 81, 82, 86, 155, 164, 166, 172
Yang, Jerry, 77
Y Combinator, 12, 21, 24, 151
YouTube, 75, 101, 110, 124, 125, 143, 151
Yunus, Muhammad, 121

Zanox, 62
Ze Frank, 3
Zennström, Niklas, 34, 35, 36, 97, 98
Zopa, 120
Zott, Christoph, 66
Zuckerberg, Mark, 142, 143
Zynga, 5, 6, 7, 22, 65, 108, 109, 139, 151, 152, 158, 159, 161